to Mom & Dad
from their wayward son
Rich 6/25/73

ALONG THE ROMAN ROADS
OF BRITAIN

J. H. B. Peel

ALONG THE ROMAN ROADS OF BRITAIN

CASSELL · LONDON

CASSELL & COMPANY LTD
35 Red Lion Square, London WC1R 4SJ
Sydney, Auckland
Toronto, Johannesburg

First edition April 1971
First edition, second impression March 1972

I.S.B.N. 0 304 93738 X

PRINTED IN GREAT BRITAIN BY
REDWOOD PRESS LIMITED
TROWBRIDGE, WILTSHIRE
172

To
MERVE and MEYRICK BROWNE
who came part of the way

'Tis opportune to look back upon old times, and contemplate our Forefathers.

SIR THOMAS BROWNE

Contents

1   By The Way   1

2   Watling Street: Dover to London   5

3   Watling Street: London   28

4   Watling Street: London to Wroxeter   33

5   Sarn Helen East: Llandovery to Llanfair Clydogau   53

6   Dere Street: York to Hadrian's Wall   73

7   Dere Street: Hadrian's Wall to Newstead   92

8   Peddars Way: Ixworth to Castle Acre   121

9   Peddars Way: Castle Acre to Holme-Next-The-Sea   138

10   Foss Way: Lincoln to High Cross   155

11   Foss Way: High Cross to Bath   166

12   Foss Way: Bath to Axmouth   186

Index   203

Illustrations

Appearing between pages 86 *and* 87

WATLING STREET:
Roman lighthouse and Saxon church, Dover
The old smithy at Bishopsbourne
City Gate at Canterbury
Section of the Roman Wall, St. Albans
Remains of Roman monument at High Cross
Remains of Roman Baths, Wroxeter

SARN HELEN EAST:
Llandovery Castle
1969 Award to Cilycwm
Street in Cilycwm
The Sarn Helen East road
Crossing the ford, Aber Bowlan
Part of the Roman road
The village of Llanfair Clydogau

DERE STREET:
Part of Hadrian's Wall
Near the end of Dere Street

PEDDARS WAY:
A windmill at Ixworth
Part of the Way near Swaffham
Statue of Tom Paine in Thetford
Castle Acre Priory
Blakeney on the Peddars Way

Gates on the Sandringham Estate
Holme-next-the-Sea

FOSS WAY:
Newark Castle
Windwhistle Hill
Brinklow
Upper Slaughter
Near Jackaments Bottom
Chedworth Roman villa
Ashe House, Musbury

All photographs by the Author

1 By The Way

HOW many Roman roads were built in Britain? I did once try to count them, but was forced to give up because, being neither a computer nor a mathematician, I grow weary when the sum reaches such a very round number that the phrase 'short list' ceases to seem brief. Nevertheless, a selection had to be made; and I confess that it was not easy to choose the number which best combined a need to be relatively succinct with a wish to sound reasonably comprehensive. In the end I chose five roads: three from England, one from Wales, and one that crosses the border into Scotland. Here they are:

Watling Street: the first Roman road in Britain, from Dover via Canterbury to London and thence north-west to Wroxeter.

Sarn Helen East: a mountainous road from Llandovery to Llanfair Clydogau.

Dere Street: a highway indeed, from York to County Durham and thence across the Cheviots to Newstead in Scotland.

Peddars Way: a green road from Ixworth in Suffolk to the Wash in Norfolk.

Foss Way: a kaleidoscope of England, from Lincoln to Devon via the Cotswolds.

Those five roads offer the maximum of variety. Some are rural from start to finish, and in places only a track. Others, though they carry much traffic, retain grassy sectors where the modern road goes its own way. Certainly our own ways have evolved from them. Whenever we say 'here's the bus' or 'there's the office', we speak Latin (*omnibus* and *officium*). Whenever we invoke the Courts to defend us or to redress us, we acknowledge that our law—adapted by English jurists—was nurtured in Rome. Whenever we enter a parish church, we acknowledge that Catholicism—both Roman and English—is descended from the Caesars. Despite the greed and brutality of conquest, the noblest Romans foreshadowed the British District Officer who, in return for a meagre salary, and amid some of the most excruciating climates in the world, performed dangerous and sometimes thankless duties while governing nations that were less civilized than his own.

Nevertheless, our journey is not simply a pursuit of alien ghosts and intangible heirlooms. Certainly we shall follow the Legions which inculcated the rudiments of urbane behaviour into our weird and woaded forebears; but we shall explore also the post-Roman countryside. Rome, then, shall lead; but we, who were once greater than Rome, are free to loiter, wandering off to consult the doctor (he wrote a bestseller, and died three centuries ago); to visit the home of Sir Winston Churchill (he, too, died three centuries ago); to hear a famous actor (the first ever to be knighted); to meet a young nobleman (who lost his life in order that he might retain his honour).

In his *Lettres sur les Anglais* the observant Voltaire reported: 'In England the governments of Greece and Rome are the subject of every conversation, so that each man is under the necessity of pursuing such authors as treat of them . . . and this perusal leads naturally to that of literature.' Had I been writing this book a hundred years ago—even fifty years—a considerable number of its readers would have known why Rome conquered Britain, and what she achieved elsewhere. But Latin is no longer an Esperanto among educated people. Let us therefore take it gently, bit by bit, as the occasion invites. If, at Holme-Next-The-Sea, we enquire whether the Roman ships carried a compass, no doubt someone will tell us. If, in the Welsh mountains, we remember that Rome was the Mother of Law, again someone will put the matter in its place. Call it what you please—history, topography, archaeology, sociology—our journey will explore a kingdom so diversely united that Shakespeare said: 'Britain is a world by itself.' These things being so, let us take as our motto the words with which Daniel Defoe prefaced his own exploration of Britain: 'If', he confessed, 'this work is not both pleasant and profitable to the reader, the author most freely and openly declares the fault must be in performance, and it cannot be in any deficiency in the subject.'

Watling Street

WATLING STREET

WROXETER
Viroconium

OAKENGATES
Galley

ATHERSTONE

WATLING

High Cross

STREET

Bannaventa

TOWCESTER
Lactodorum

Stoney Stratford

Fenny Stratford

HOCKLIFFE

DUNSTABLE

MARKYATE

REDBOURN

ST. ALBANS
Verulamium

R. Ouse

R. Thames

LONDON
Londinium

SPRINGHEAD
(DARTFORD)

COBHAM

ROCHESTER
Durobrivae

CHATHAM

SITTINGBOURNE

FAVERSHAM

CANTERBURY
Durovernum
Cantiorum

BISHOPSBOURNE

BARHAM DOWNS

TEMPLE EWELL

DOVER
Dubrae

LEGEND

Rivers

Roman Roads

© Cassell&Co. Ltd. 1971

2 Watling Street: Dover to London

THE Latin poet Horace wrote an essay in which he discussed the art of story-telling. 'Begin', he said, 'at the beginning, but not so close to the beginning that you reach the egg or genesis of the matter.' The Romans believed that their capital had been hatched in 753 B.C. Innumerable schoolboys have relished the legend of Romulus and Remus, twin sons of Mars, whom the Fates delivered as infants to a she-wolf, to be suckled by her and thereafter to compete for the honour of marking the site of Rome by drawing a brazen ploughshare around the Palatine Hill. Romulus and Remus, they say, were succeeded by seven kings, governing a federation of Sabines, Etruscans, Latins. The last of those kings, Tarquinius Superbus or Tarquin the Proud, may have been an historical person who did indeed lose his throne. Certainly the Romans refused to restore it, and ever after looked askance at kings, though they approved dictators, and co-opted them as part of their constitution.

For more than five centuries Rome remained a republic. Her first citizens were farmer-soldiers—clannish, hardy, frugal—whose citizenship became so highly valued that none but a freeborn Roman might receive it. Rome's neighbours remained second, third, and even fourth class citizens. And so matters stood, until, after many centuries, an Emperor devalued the citizenship by offering it to almost anyone who cared to apply. Historians date the beginning of the Empire from A.D. 14 when Octavianus, the great-nephew and heir of Julius Caesar, accepted the title of Augustus. In fact, however, the distinction between Empire and Republic is spurious because the Empire was founded and enlarged during the Republic. Augustus expressed himself content to be *Princeps* or first citizen: 'I have', he claimed, 'restored the Republic.'

The histories of the Republic and of the Empire are matters of fact; whether the one was superior to the other is a matter of opinion. I happen to prefer Rome in her patrician days; others prefer Rome in her plebeian days, when Emperors were made and unmade by a show of hands and a clash of swords. The meeting of those two ways was forged by Julius Caesar, whom De Quincey fanfared as 'Noblest of men!' The facts, however, do not confirm the fanfare. Caesar was a cunning ruffian. On his father's side, he said, he was descended from an Egyptian god, Amon; on his mother's side, from a Roman goddess, Venus herself. His own statue in Rome was inscribed 'To the Immortal God'. Genealogists prefer to state that Gaius Julius Caesar was born on 12 July 102 B.C., of the noble house of Julian. Gynaecologists believe that he came down to earth via the operation which still bears his Imperial name. Like most other patricians at that time, he was educated in the Greek fashion (by a Cisalpine slave). As a youth he composed a tragedy (which his envious successor suppressed), and showed a flair for astronomy and geography. At the age of nineteen he married the daughter of one of the most powerful men in Rome. Beyond doubt he was a brilliant soldier whose conquests endeared him to the people. Nevertheless, the great days of Roman patriotism were dead. Famous leaders, it is true, were yet to arise; soldiers and civilians would continue to serve faithfully in remote places and among thankless savages; but the tide was ebbing. Greek aesthetes had tainted the upper classes; gladiators and free food satisfied the mob. Never again would a Cincinnatus leave his farm in order to serve as a chosen dictator, and then, having fulfilled the mission, return thankfully to his plough. Power lay now with the armies and their generals. Supported by his own army—to whom he had promised higher pay and richer plunder—Caesar bided his time, watching from the Italian frontier while his rival, Pompey, ruled in Rome. When spies brought news of a rising against Pompey, Caesar struck.

Now the Romans had an ancient law whereby, as a precaution against *coups d'état*, no serving general might re-enter Italian territory without permission from the Senate. Caesar lacked that permission. On 10 January 49 B.C., being then among his troops near the frontier town of Rimini, he rode with a small party to the border itself, which was marked by a brook named Rubicon.

There, in water, lay the limit of his lawful advance. To proceed further would be to violate the constitution. According to one witness, Caesar quoted a tag from a Latin playwright—'Let the die be cast'—and then he crossed the Rubicon.

As one who was about to invade the greatest city in the world, Caesar may almost have forgotten that he had already invaded a small and unimportant island called Britain; he had invaded it twice; each time as a punitive expedition against savages who were aiding rebellious Gaul. The first of those invasions began in 55 B.C., when Caesar sailed from Portus Ithius near Calais, and landed next day on Romney Marsh. Little resistance was encountered, except by the tides which grounded his ships. As Edward Gibbon remarked: 'The wind and waves are always on the side of the ablest navigators.' Yet not even the ablest navigators can always counteract an inherent defect in their ships. Caesar's despatches revealed the basic cause of his own groundings: 'The keels of the British ships', he remarked, 'were somewhat flatter than ours, so that they could more easily encounter the shallows and ebbing tides.' Caesar, at all events, took some hostages, and after a couple of weeks returned to Gaul.

The second invasion was deeper and more lasting. Schoolboys know of it from Caesar's despatches, *Commentarii de Bello Gallico*, which reveal his amused surprise at the blue-eyed barbarians who deployed their chariots with skill and courage. The leader of those savages, King Cassivellanus, had his capital at St. Albans in Hertfordshire. Caesar therefore crossed the Thames, captured the King, took hostages, and imposed fines (most of which were never paid). That done, he returned with his army to Gaul, unwilling to winter on an island so unprofitably inclement. He had made the invasions for three reasons: to sever the British liaison with Gaul; to satisfy his geographical curiosity; and to impress the Roman mob, whom he proposed soon to govern. He never saw Britain again.

Caesar, then, invaded; but the Emperor Claudius conquered. The Roman Empire began as the defensive measure of a people who must either conquer or be conquered. But in A.D. 43 the Empire had become a bait for merchants, financiers, soldiers,

2

politicians. Claudius needed new triumphs wherewith to impress the army and the mob. Britain was an obvious victim, partly because the tribes would never unite against an invader, partly because the island was regarded as the edge of the world, and therefore a challenge to Imperial ambition. When the third invasion had been completed, Claudius himself arrived, to visit the army at Colchester or *Camulodunum*. His first need was for roads that would secure and advance the conquest. And so we come to Dover or *Dubrae*, the beginning of the most important of all our Roman roads, dominated by its Roman lighthouse alongside a Saxon church nearly 500 feet above the sea. The upper parts of the lighthouse are medieval, but the lower portion, some forty feet high, is of Roman stone and flint. By day the tower served as a landmark for shipping. At night a brazier shone from the summit. This was the hub and pivot of the Roman conquest; the lifeline with Rome. Just below the lighthouse stands Dover Castle, perhaps the most impressive castle in England, admirably conserved—though it was not always so. In 1722, for example, Daniel Defoe remarked: 'the castle is old useless, decay'd and served for little. . . .'

Dover is indeed a famous place. From its white cliffs Dorothy Wordsworth sighted France: 'the shores almost as plain as if it were an English lake'. Gazing at those cliffs, uncountable travellers, coming or going, have overhead their own inarticulate emotion in a line of verse:

> England, with all thy faults, I love thee still.

No other town in Britain has witnessed so many memorable launchings and landfalls. Here came Henry V, home from Agincourt with his band of brothers, to whom on the eve of battle he had prophesied:

> He that outlives this day and comes safe home,
> Will stand a tip-toe when this day is nam'd . . .
> And gentlemen in England, now abed,
> Shall think themselves accurs'd they were not here,
> And hold their manhoods cheap whiles any speaks
> That fought with us upon Saint Crispin's day.

Dover was one of the Cinque Ports, a Saxon confederacy (between Dover, Hastings, Romney, Hythe, Sandwich) which ultimately co-opted Rye, Winchelsea, and every port and fishing village near the Straits. The first Keeper of the King's Ships—he became Archdeacon of Taunton—was appointed by King John. About the year 1300 we find a 'Captain and Admiral of the Fleet of the Cinque Ports and of all other Ports from the Port of Dover by the sea-coast westward as far as Cornwall'. In return for certain privileges and exemptions the Portmen furnished the King with fifty-seven fully-manned ships which they maintained at sea, at their own charge, for fifteen days each year. The officers of those ships were the ancestors of the Royal Naval Volunteer Reserve and the Royal Naval Reserve. Towards the end of the Middle Ages, when the King was able to draw upon a wider circle of reserves, the Cinque Ports lost their ancient pre-eminence; but some of their traditions survive, as in the post of Lord Warden, whose official quarters are at Walmer Castle.

Dover has maintained its naval heritage. In 1914 the Dover Patrol, manned chiefly by the R.N.R. and R.N.V.R., won a renown which was explained by Joseph Conrad, himself a Master-Mariner: 'In their early days some of them had but a single rifle on board to meet the four-inch guns of German destroyers. Unable to put up a fight and without the speed to get away, they made a sacrifice of their lives every time they went out for a turn of duty. . . . It was their conception of their honour, and they carried it out of this war unblemished by a single display of weakness.' In 1940 came the survivors of a routed army. In 1944 sailed the greatest naval invasion yet recorded or ever likely to be. For the rest, impressionism must suffice: the town hall, incorporating a thirteenth-century Maison Dieu; the medieval Cloth Hall; a college in a twelfth-century priory; the smallest round church in Britain, built by the Knights Templars; a monument to Blériot, the first man to darken the Channel by flying across it; and the harbour itself, covering 600 acres.

Leaving Dover, the modern road follows the course of Watling Street through Temple Ewell; but even the latest itinerary may find itself outdated by a shifting maze of one-way streets and No

Right Turns. Like every other sizeable British town, Dover has become encrusted with fast-growing suburbs. The process is not new. Dorothy Wordsworth noticed it when she arrived in 1802: 'There was also a very old Building on the other side of the road, which had a strange effect among many new ones that are springing up everywhere. It seemed odd that it could have kept itself pure in its ancientry among so many upstarts.' Suburbs, however, soon give way to a straight road among hills. 'Sweet and rich', was Shakespeare's comment:

Sweet is the country, and full of riches.

A century later, Celia Fiennes rode this way on horseback, and she too was pleased: 'much up hill and down, it was a good Road and sort of champion country . . . you see many good woods and pretty places.' But the Roman roadmakers saw only a wilderness of woodland, interspersed with plots of cultivated land, peopled by a few families in thatched huts.

After ten miles the road reaches Barham Downs, which Defoe described as 'a pleasant champain country'. This is idyllic Kent, green as a static sea, studded with trees, sprinkled with houses whose ancient brickwork gleams in the sun. Caesar knew Barham Downs, for he fought a battle there, and might have lost it had not a British chieftain deserted with 20,000 of his men. The Downs today are peaceful, grazed by Kent or Romney Marsh sheep, massive and hornless creatures, black-nosed, pink-skinned, deep-chested. Bred on a bleak marshland, these are the hardiest sheep in southern England, yielding excellent mutton and fleece. They have gone all over the world, to Canada, New Zealand, Argentine, Australia, the Falkland Islands. Both the Romans and the Britons would have gaped at such prime flocks. More than fifteen centuries were to elapse before British farmers produced the root crops which enabled their stock to survive a long winter.

The name Barham appears a short way south of the village, at a Jacobean mansion called Tappington-Everard, ancestral home of the Reverend Richard Harris Barham, who in 1821 became a minor Canon of St. Paul's Cathedral, and spent the latter part of his life in building his own monument, *The Ingoldsby Legends*, a series of skilful verse narratives—often comic, sometimes ghoulish —several of which have passed into everyday speech; such as, for example, Lord Tomnoddy who went to watch a public hanging, but missed it because his preparatory potations caused him to fall asleep at the Magpie and Stump.

On went the road, so startlingly straight that I marvelled at the Romans' skill. By what trials and errors had they hacked a path through the wasteland? Before I could reply, a signpost pointed to Bishopsbourne, which lies a few hundred yards off Watling Street, down an avenue of oaks, in a world of its own. This was the place beside a *burna* or brook, belonging to the medieval Archbishops of Canterbury. And thither I went, for two reasons: first, because Bishopsbourne is beautiful; second, because it is the most literary village beside any Roman road in Britain. The beauty of Bishopsbourne remains unmarred. Having ended beside a church and two gracious houses, the avenue becomes the village street, which seems a wide name for a narrow lane and a few cottages alongside. Midway down that lane stands the shop, bow-windowed in the old fashion; and beside it a cul-de-sac leading to steep meadows. Nearby lies a derelict forge which in 1971 still bore the remains of the last farrier's handwrought sign.

The first great man of Bishopsbourne was Richard Hooker, a Devonian who became Master of the Temple. But it was as rector of Bishopsbourne that he completed the work by which he lives, *The Laws of Ecclesiastical Polity*, a retort to those sixteenth-century Puritans who referred every kind of problem to the Bible, and then supplied an answer that accorded with their own wishes. In the preface to his book, Hooker said of such men: 'When they and their Bibles were alone together, what strange fantastical opinion soever at any time entered into their imaginations their use was to think the spirit taught it to them.' Hooker, in short, was a reformer, not a destroyer. He sought to modify and thereafter to retain the ancient traditions. He was among the founders of the Anglo-Catholic Church party within the English Church.

The second great man of Bishopsbourne was Josef Teodor Konrad Nalecz Korzeniowski, better known as Joseph Conrad, who came of a Polish family which he described as 'land-tilling gentry'. Although Poland lacked a naval tradition, the lad wished to become a sailor. For a while he considered joining the French navy as a midshipman; in the end, however, he served before the mast of a French merchantman, *Mont Blanc*, in which he spent Christmas Day, 'running', as he put it, 'before a Gulf of Lyons gale, which made the old ship groan in every timber'. On 18 June 1878, Conrad first set foot on English soil, at the port of Lowestoft in Suffolk, among a breed of men whom he learned to admire: 'Coast men', he called them, 'with steady eyes, mighty limbs, gentle voices; men of very few words. . . . Honest, strong, steady men, sobered by domestic ties.' How was it that a Polish youth, with only a few words of broken English, became a master of its prose? Partly he learned of the sea and of the men who go down to it in ships. His first service with the Red Ensign was as an able-bodied seaman in the barquentine *Skimmer of the Seas*, plying between Lowestoft and Newcastle-upon-Tyne. In 1886 British naturalization was granted to 'Joseph Conrad Korzeniowski, subject of the Russian Empire, of the age of twenty-nine years, mariner, unmarried.' Three months later he obtained his Master's Certificate. His first command was the barque *Otago*, which he took from Bangkok to Melbourne.

Uncertain health, and the acceptance of his first novel, *Almayer's Folly*, transformed the professional seaman into a whole-time author. He married happily, begat two sons, and for many years produced famous books whose royalties scarcely enabled him to support his family. While writing *Lord Jim* he was so hard-pressed for money that he asked Cunninghame Graham to use his influence to obtain a command at sea. Only toward the end of his life did he achieve a measure of security. Fortunately, he took the deeper view: 'an artist's richest treasure', he believed, 'lies in the hearts of men and women'. The best of his own novels are based upon experiences which most other bookmen can only imagine. He was what Quiller-Couch called 'one of the great masculine objective writers'. Some people believe that in his 'desertion' of Poland lay the root of the 'loyalty' theme in many of his tales. It may be so. Whether on the high sea of narrative, or among the creeks of human motive, he was master of his craft and of its medium, prose.

Conrad retained his strong Polish accent. John Masefield, who knew him well, told me that in conversation he sometimes tangled his tenses. The pen, by contrast, never faltered. Conrad was a wizard, able to transmute a few words of broken English into a pageant of precision and elegance and power. Kent he loved above all other parts of England. For fifteen years he lived there, seldom free from physical pain, yet always sustained by what he called the best friend to his work, 'the cool green light on the fields'. He once described the writing of a novel: 'For twenty months, neglecting the common joys of life that fall to the lot of the humblest on this earth, I had, like the prophet of old, "wrestled with the Lord" for my creation. . . .' The effort of that creation caused 'a bodily fatigue such as no amount of fairly hard physical labour could account for'. Despite the pain, the poverty, and a depressive Slav temperament, cheerfulness kept breaking through. His letters are full of laughter; and when his wife wrote *A Handbook of Cookery for a Small House,* he supplied a preface which begins: 'Of all the books produced since the most remote ages by human talents and industry those only that treat of cookery are, from a moral point of view, above suspicion. The intention of every other piece of prose may be discussed and even mistrusted; but the purpose of a cookery book is one and unmistakable. Its object can conceivably be no other than to increase the happiness of mankind.'

On 3 August 1924, at half past eight in the morning, while writing some reminiscences of the sea, Joseph Conrad slipped from his chair and died. He was sixty-six years old. He lies in Canterbury cemetery, under a quotation from Edmund Spenser, which he had used on the title page of *The Rover*:

> Sleep after toyle, port after stormie seas,
> Ease after warre, death after life, does greatly please.

Now Watling Street steers among woods, through the village of Bridge, then within sight of Patrixbourne, held by William Patrick during the reign of King Stephen. But the roving eye is caught

and returned by the Street itself, so straight that again one asks
how the Romans plotted its course; and again the reply is interrupted, this time by Canterbury, the *burgh* or town of the *Cantware*
or men of Kent, which the Romans called *Durovernum Cantiorum*.
Excavation has revealed palisades and a ditch that were built a
century before the Romans landed. The city itself became an
important trading centre, linked by road to three ports at Rich-
borough, Reculver and Lympne. When Agricola, father-in-law of
Tacitus, was appointed governor of Britain, he encouraged the
natives to rebuild their houses with stone, at least for the lower
portions. *Durovernum* was rebuilt at the beginning of the second
century A.D. The main carriageway entered by the Riding Gate;
lesser roads, by the Worth and Quenin Gates. The Forum, the hub
of Roman civic and commercial life, lies beneath the present
County Hotel. The museum contains many Roman exhibits, including some exquisite glass phials in which the women kept their
cosmetics.

When Rome granted the natives their independence—when,
that is, she left them to their own resources—the natives plunged
headfirst into chaos and bloodshed. Bede's *History* paints a lurid
picture of tribes fleeing from invasion by other more virile tribes,
the Saxons, Danes, Swedes or Norwegians. Within a few years
the Roman way of life had disappeared for ever. Nevertheless, the
phrase 'Dark Ages' is misleading because it either ignores or by
implication denies the influence of Christianity. Later in our journey, when we halt beside a Roman shrine, we shall discover
something about the Roman's faith and his toleration of other
creeds. Meanwhile, at Canterbury, we confront Rome's most enduring legacy, the Church. After many tribulations, Christianity
was adopted by the Emperor Constantine as the official religion of
the Empire. When the Empire disintegrated, the people of Rome,
looking about for a leader, turned to their bishop, who in time
became the chief bishop, *primus inter pares*. Gradually he became
more than a bishop. In him and his palace Rome lived again, the
eternal city and the centre of the world. Her political prestige had
declined; the Empire itself had declined; but the Church waxed on
their waning. Today more people owe an allegiance to Rome

than at any time since the founding of the city. Such are the facts of history which raised Canterbury to the eminence of an English Rome.

Canterbury became an important religious centre at the end of the sixth century. 'In the year 596,' wrote Bede, 'Pope Gregory was inspired by God to send his servant Augustine with several other monks to preach the word of God to the English nation. Having undertaken this task at the Pope's command, they became alarmed and began to consider returning home, for they were appalled by the prospect of entering a barbarous, fierce, and pagan country whose language they could not speak.' In the end Augustine asked the Pope to excuse them from their mission. The Pope replied by letter: 'My very dear sons, to undertake any high enterprise is better than to abandon it when you have started. Therefore with God's help you must carry out this holy task. . . .' Augustine forthwith set his hand once more to the plough, and never again looked back. Under his leadership the Gospel spread and was enshrined in the Roman ritual. Kent itself became the springboard for that evangelism, with Canterbury its chief city, so that the Archbishop grew in stature, even as the Bishop of Rome had grown. Replacing others that were destroyed, the present cathedral was consecrated (1130) during Anselm's primacy, but in his absence abroad. Built in the form of a double cross, Canterbury Cathedral is an amalgam of styles from Norman to Perpendicular. During the twelfth century its chief mason or architect was a Frenchman, William of Sens, who was succeeded by William the Englishman, architect of the east crypt and Trinity chapel. The nave was rebuilt between 1376 and 1410. Cardinal Morton's central tower arose a century later. The cathedral was desecrated by the rebels during the Civil War; scarred by fire in 1871; and grazed by bombs in 1943. *Durovernum*, then, became an English Rome. That it acquired also the mystique of an English Jerusalem was due to the example of its formidable Archbishop, Thomas Becket, who transformed a provincial city into an international shrine.

Becket was born in 1118, son of a London merchant. Having taken minor orders, he served on the diplomatic staff of the

Archbishop of Canterbury, where his skill commended him to King Henry II, who was then resisting papal influence on the selecting of English bishops and on the clergy's immunity from secular law. Henry and Becket became close friends, though the servant never trimmed his own simple life to that of the Court. Soon he was appointed Chancellor or private secretary to the King; and when the See of Canterbury fell vacant, Becket was hastily consecrated priest in order that he might fill it. Henry felt that he could now defy Rome, secure in the knowledge that his friend led the English Church. Henry was mistaken. From the hour of his enthronement the new Archbishop revealed an *alter ego*. Instead of supporting the State against the Church, he defended the Church against the State, threatening to excommunicate any who crossed him. And he kept his word. The Archbishop of York was suspended; the Bishops of London and Salisbury were excommunicated. Becket's temperament, in short, confirmed a commonplace of modern psychology, that many neurotic people are attracted to religion (from which it does not follow that only neurotics are religious). His piety and courage were tainted. He slept on the bare floor of his palace, with a stone for pillow. Three times each day he was whipped by a chaplain. Lice fed on his flesh.

Bewildered and angered by an unexpected Janus, the King in an unguarded moment cried: 'Will no one rid me of this turbulent priest?' Four knights answered his question, hoping to be rewarded. Separately and secretly they travelled to England: Reginald FitzUrse, William de Tracy, Hugh de Morville, Richard Brito. When the King learned of their flight he grew alarmed, and ordered the Justiciar of Normandy to bring them back. But the Justiciar and his companions set out too late. The knights had already converged and were at Canterbury, supported by other armed men. As the winter afternoon drew to its close, the assassins accosted Becket in the cathedral, charging him with treason because he had excommunicated the Bishops who had crowned the King. Becket retorted that his actions had been ordered by the Pope. After a stormy interview the knights withdrew. The monks meanwhile implored their Archbishop to escape while he could. He refused. Presently the knights returned, and this time found

Becket standing between two altars in a chapel, a place which only desperation or disbelief would dare to violate. Again they ordered him to absolve those whom he had excommunicated. Again he refused: 'I am ready to die for my Lord,' he cried, 'and for the liberty of the Church.' And thus it was, on the evening of Friday, 29 December 1170, before the altars of his own cathedral, that Thomas Becket, Archbishop of Canterbury, was hacked to death. Our own ethos, obsessed by trade gaps and motor cars, can scarcely imagine the horror with which Christendom received news of the sacrilege. The King himself was overwhelmed by remorse. Like a common penitent he submitted to be scourged at the shrine of his erstwhile friend whose martyrdom, so far from weakening, had served rather to strengthen the papal influence.

What now remains of the old, the beautiful, city? In 1943 one third of it was destroyed by German bombers; the rest is hemmed-in and harried. To cross Watling Street by day is usually difficult and sometimes dangerous. Deafened by traffic, visitors shout at one another, trying to paraphrase their guidebook. Only in the early morning, or late at night, does Canterbury come to life. Then, in quietness, you receive the freedom of the cathedral and its medieval glass, unrivalled in Britain. You have the Roman walls which the Normans rebuilt. You have the parish churches, each with its own history, its own beauty. You have the King's School, which some say is the oldest in Britain, basing their claim on a statement by Bede: 'Sigberct ruled the kingdom of the East English . . . he founded a school in which boys might be taught grammar . . . with ushers and masters after the custom of Kentish folk.' The school was refounded by Henry VIII, with the name of King's School, for 'fifty boys, poor and destitute of the help of their friends, to be maintained out of the possessions of the church, of native genius as far as may be and apt to learn.' Among the famous Old Boys were Sir William Harvey, who in 1628 published from Frankfurt a paper describing his discovery of the circulation of the blood; Walter Horatio Pater, the Victorian and Dutch-descended Dean of Brasenose College, Oxford, a non-smoking, non-tea-drinking aesthete ('To burn always with this hard, gemlike flame, to maintain this ecstasy, is success in life');

and Somerset Maugham, a cynic's living death mask. But the most eminent Old Boy was Marlowe, one of the so-called University wits, who steeped himself in classical literature.

Christopher Marlowe, son of a shoemaker, was born (1564) in St. George's Street, Canterbury, which the Germans destroyed. From the King's School he went up to Cambridge, thence to London, and ultimately to its taverns, wherein he was killed during a brawl, at the age of thirty. As the Latin poet Ennius paved the way for Lucretius, so Marlowe made straight the path for Shakespeare. Swinburne described him as the first master of 'the highest and hardest form of verse, the only instrument since found possible for our tragic and epic poetry'. Both Marlowe and Shakespeare lived at a time when men accepted Aristotle's definition of tragedy as the downfall, through no great fault of his own, of an outstanding personality. Some of the new English dramatists prefer to depict a person of no consequence whatever, who, entirely through his own fault, becomes even more inconsequential. Marlowe, at all events, passed the torch to Shakespeare who outshone him. Yet not even Shakespeare excelled the mightiest of Marlowe's lines—the famous elegy on Helen of Troy or Ilium, for whose sake men went to war:

> Was this the face that launch'd a thousand ships,
> And burnt the topless towers of Ilium . . .

Despite the traffic, I could not help smiling as I left Canterbury, because the Street asked its question for a third time—'Whence came my straightness?'—and for a third time the answer was interrupted, for already I was at Harbledown, nowadays a suburb of the city, but in Chaucer's day a little town, set on the edge of the Downs, so that his pilgrims were asked 'Surely you know the little up-and-down town of Harbledown?'

> Wite ye nat ther stant a litel toun
> Which that y-cleped is Bob-up-and-doun,
> Under the Blee, in Caunterbury waye?

Chaucer's up-and-down etymology went wide of the mark because Harbledown was originally *Hereboldune*, the *dun* or hill where Herebeald's people lived.

On, then, to open country again, following a Street so straight that at last the question must be answered. As we have noted, the Roman invaders faced a strange terrain, a tangle of woods and waste. First, therefore, they had to fell the forest. That done, they plotted a course, rather as infantrymen used to 'dress by the right', using the next man as a marker. In clear weather and across level country they could plot short distances by means of poles; but in poor visibility, or over great distances, or when hills hid the hinterland, braziers were lit and then re-aligned until they pointed a direct course. It must have seemed a tedious task, signalling, counter-signalling, galloping to and fro. But the Romans did not adopt a policy of straight-at-any-price. If a hill was excessively steep they skirted the summit. If a swamp crossed their path they went round it rather than build massive foundations on it. Nor did they plot a new course when an old sufficed. If a Celtic track went their way they followed it, straightening and paving *en route*. But one thing they did avoid, the sweeping curve. When they were compelled to change direction they used short turns, sometimes at right angles.

Meanwhile, as though to savour the straightness, I looked back, along the way I had come: Dover, Canterbury, Barham, Bishopsbourne, and Chaucer's 'Bob-up-and-doun'. I seemed to have spent much time covering little ground. Nevertheless, I knew what lay ahead nearer London; knew also what I thought of it, which was very little and therefore scarcely worth mentioning. So, while they were still with me, I made the most of the fields and orchards which, as Faversham drew near, were enriched by the hop-fields that led Defoe to call these parts 'the Mother of Hop Grounds in England'; being the first place in England where 'hops were planted at the beginning of the Reformation, and which gave occasion to that old distich:

> Hops, Reformation, bays, and beer,
> Came into England all in a year.'

In the year of my own birth there were 35,676 acres of hops in England, more than three-fifths of which lay in Kent (to be precise, 21,944 acres). Miss Fiennes called the hop a 'fruite', but botanists classify it as *Humulus Lupulus*, a member of the stinging-nettle family (*Urticaceae*). During the season thousands of Cockneys used to combine business with pleasure by picking the hop-fields. For many it was the nearest they ever came to a summer holiday. Even today a number of East Enders maintain the old tradition. The bitterness of the hop (*lupulin*) is contained within the pistillate flowers of the female plant. Having flowered, the plants develop a head or cone, and that is what the pickers gather.

The Romans, a wine-bibbing race, would have stared in amazement at the nets and poles of a hop-field. The Saxons, too, would have stared, for hops were neglected in Britain until the Huguenot immigrants from Flanders proved that the crop could flourish on this side of the Channel. Yet the harvest continued so uncertain that Victorian members of Tattersall's gambled on the annual prices. Brewers long ago knew that hops improved the flavour of beer, but they did not know why. In 1876 Louis Pasteur's *Études sur la bière* was able to inform them that hops preserve and clarify the sugar solution. They are also valuable for their resin and oil.

Still, then, the Street went straight, but already its wooded country had fallen astern, and the land grew flat. Away to the right lay the muddy Thames estuary. But if you demand variety you must accept change, sometimes for the better, at others for the worse. Here appeared the first shape of things to come, a motorway draining much of the traffic into London and away from Faversham, anciently called *Faefersham*, the *ham* or low-lying meadow where the *faber* or farrier lived. Miss Fiennes admired Faversham: 'its a very large town,' she reported, 'and good buildings of bricke. . . .' Defoe, on the other hand, was not impressed: 'the principal business . . . was fishing for oysters, which the Dutch fetch hence. . . .' Although Defoe had joined Monmouth's rebellion against James II, he condemned Faversham's treatment of that King when—while escaping to France—the royal ship ran aground in the River Swale, and was boarded by local fishermen who behaved 'with such indignity to his person, such insolence in their behaviour, and giving him such oppro-

brious and abusive language . . . that the king himself said he
was never more apprehensive of his life than at that time'. Faversham must have been violent indeed, so to alarm a man who had
proved himself a fearless admiral. The King's grounding in the
estuary would have evoked the sympathy of Julius Caesar, who
admitted that the Roman ships excelled the British 'only in speed
and oarsmanship'. His own ships were designed for the Mediterranean; in the Channel they drew too much water. The
shallow-draught British vessels 'could heave-to securely in the
shallows, and, when left by the tide, feared nothing from the rocks
and shelves; a risk which our own ships dreaded more than
anything else'.

The best of Faversham lies along Abbey Street, a necklace of
houses of the sixteenth to the eighteenth centuries, many of which
had been allowed to decay, but were saved and restored during the
1940s by the Town Council and the Society for the Preservation
of Ancient Buildings. Rome still lingers in Faversham. The Swan
Inn (so they will tell you) stands on the site of a house that was
occupied by two Roman Christians, Crispin and Crispanus, who
had fled thither from persecution, and there set up as shoemakers.
Perhaps it is as well that Faversham's gunpowder industry no
longer prospers. Defoe himself was nearly exploded by it: 'While
I was near this town some years ago, a most surprising accident
happen'd, namely, the blowing up of a powder-mill . . . the blast
was not only frightful, but it shatter'd the whole town, broke the
windows, blew down chimneys . . .'

Two miles north of Faversham, while exercising the dog, I fell
in with a learned man, an angler and inquisitive withal, for he
capped his knowledge of trout streams by saying: 'What the hell
does Watling mean?' I replied that it meant the tract of road which
passed the Roman fort at St. Albans, the home of a tribe called
Waeclingas. Thereafter the name was used of the entire street and,
indeed, of others also, such as the road from Manchester to
Ribchester. A pause followed, while my fellow-traveller uttered
strange noises *sotto voce*. Presently he said: 'If the people were
Waeclingas, the Street ought to be Waeclinga.'

Waeclinga or Waetlinga, the *straet* or paved Roman road led

inexorably from the countryside to the perimeter of outer
London.

So I came to Sittingbourne, which the Saxons called *Sidingburn*,
the town on the side or slope of a burn or stream. The long street
is plainly uneventful. Sittingbourne may have looked better when
Celia Fiennes passed by. She certainly admired its church: 'all
built with flints headed so curiously that it looks like glass and
shines with the suns reflection.'

After Sittingbourne I began to lose contact with my mission.
Hitherto—at the Dover lighthouse, in the quiet parts of Canterbury, over Barham Downs—I had been able to imagine that I was
travelling where the Legions trod. But now I became aware of a
present which knew nothing of its past. A similar loss of contact
occurs at some point along all of our Roman roads, but nowhere
so protractedly as on Watling Street between Sittingbourne and
St. Albans, and seldom so conspicuously as on the approach to
Chatham, a place which Rome would have understood. Here
came Sir Francis Drake, Sir John Hawkins, and Stephen Borough
who in 1553 led the first English expedition to Russia. Here are
memorials to two other Empire-builders; Lord Kitchener of
Khartoum and Lieutenant Waghorn, discoverer of the overland
route to India. Here finally are the dockyard and harbour, mile
upon mile with walls forty-four feet high and twenty feet thick,
in memory of a kingdom that once ruled the waves. The rest is
noise and scurry.

Rochester, across the Medway, was a fortress, *Durobrivae*, whose
Roman wall can be seen at the Grammar School. The medieval
bridge must have been impressive. Celia Fiennes described it as
'the finest in England, nay its said to equal any in the world . . .
there are 9 large arches with the middle one which is to be opened
by drawing up to give passage to barges and little vessells . . .'
(Miss Fiennes miscounted the arches; there were eleven). The
bridge itself was demolished in 1856; the present structure (1914)
may justly claim to be the ugliest in Kent. There are some remains
of a castle that was built by William de Corbeil, Archbishop of
Canterbury during the reign of Henry I. Rochester has, too,
the oldest cathedral nave in England, seventy-five feet long

(in 1264 Simon de Montfort rode his horse through it). Those facts seem irrelevant in modern Rochester, yet you do sometimes notice a visitor admiring the few ancient buildings which remain.

In the northern suburbs of Rochester, on the road to Gravesend, stands Gad's Hill Place, the last and best-loved home of Charles Dickens, whose earliest years were spent in or near the city, his father being a clerk at Chatham Dockyard. Dickens made many childhood journeys past Gad's Hill Place, which to him seemed a palace, though it was no more than a medium-sized country house, topped by a belfry. One day, while he was staring at the house, he heard his father say to him: 'If you work hard, you may own it.' Many years later, when he had achieved fame as a novelist, and was editing *Household Words*, Dickens learned that Gad's Hill Place was for sale. After much haggling he bought it for £1,790, enlarged it, and acquired some neighbouring meadows. His first act as owner was to announce a famous affinity by means of a plaque placed above the stairway: 'This house, GAD'S HILL PLACE, Stands on the summit of Shakespeare's Gad's Hill, ever memorable for its Association with Sir John Falstaff, in his noble fancy. But my lads, my lads, tomorrow morning, by four o'clock, early at Gad's Hill! There are pilgrims going to Canterbury with rich offerings, and traders riding to London with fat purses; I have vizards for you all; you have horses for yourselves.' The quotation suggests that those words of highwaymanship were spoken by Sir John himself; but they came from one of his fellow-firebrands, Poinz.

To begin with, Dickens regarded his new house simply as the fulfilment of a child's ambition, suitable perhaps for summer holidays. Three years after he had bought it, he told his friend, John Forster: 'I have no interest in the place.' Yet the place entwined itself around his affections, which in any event were unsettled, for his marriage had disintegrated, and he had taken unto himself a young actress, Ellen Ternan. His own children were reared at Gad's Hill by his wife's sister, Georgina Hogarth: 'She is', he said, 'the active spirit of the house, and the children dote upon her.' In his will he paid another tribute, calling her 'the best and truest friend a man ever had'. Sustained by that friendship, he spent more and more of his time at Gad's Hill Place, until in the end it became his true home, a haven *pour mieux sauter*. Before they went to Eton, two of his sons were pupils at Rochester Grammar School. During their holidays they published a weekly news-sheet, *The Gad's Hill Gazette*; and when he was fifteen years old the editor went to London, to learn to work the paper's printing machine, a gift from the member of the staff of *Household Words* who had first told Dickens that Gad's Hill Place was for sale.

Dickens died at Gad's Hill, worn out by his own genius. The manner of his going would have contented him, for he was working at *Edwin Drood*. Having written the words 'Take him away', he decided that he had done enough for that day. On the next day he was himself taken, after a seizure. Georgina Hogarth summarized the role of Gad's Hill Place: 'I am glad to think that he owed the happiest . . . of the latter years of his life, to the love and interest he felt in thàt pretty home.' When the home was auctioned, his eldest (and unsatisfactory) son appeared among the bidders, so embarrassing them that they allowed him to buy the place at the next bid above its reserve price, which was £8,647— nearly five times the sum paid by his father. The new owner soon afterwards sold it to a man whom Georgina Hogarth disliked. Her comment closed the chapter sadly: 'To think it should have fallen into common and vulgar hands . . .'

Dickens once said: 'I have discovered that the seven miles between Rochester and Maidstone is one of the most beautiful walks in England.' Today it is one of the most unsightly, not simply for seven miles around, but all the way to London and beyond. Yet the Street still retains a Roman imprimatur, the straight sector, the slight change of direction, then another straight sector. Its course, however, has been either diverted or distorted by dual carriageways. Watching my fellow countrymen as they tapped their steering wheels, I wondered what impression they would have made on a Roman of the old school? Cicero believed that the genius or spirit of the Roman people was threefold: *simplicitas, pietas, gravitas.* The English language has no adequate synonyms with which to translate those words. *Simplicitas*, for example, does not mean what we now mean by simplicity; it means a down-to-earthness which declines to complicate matters by esoteric musing (the Romans had little taste for metaphysics; their philosophy stopped short at ethics). *Pietas* does not mean what we now mean by piety; it means a reasoned allegiance to the Establishment, both of gods and of men. *Gravitas* does not mean what we now mean by gravity; it means a blend of dignity, self-discipline, and a refusal to be intimidated either by the mood or by the mode of the moment. Such were the men who laid the foundations of Rome's greatness; such, when that greatness had declined, were the minority who still followed the classic ideal, behaving and believing as their forebears in the years when Roman citizenship was the stern obligation of a few, not a worthless privilege of the many.

On, then, past Brewers Wood and the lane to Cobham, where the Leather Bottle Inn brought laughter and tears to Mr. Pickwick's entourage. Cobham Hall, now a school, was the seat of Lord Darnley, who gave Dickens a key to the Park; and in that Park Dickens took his last walk, on the afternoon before he wrote his last word.

At Springhead, where the Romans built a sizeable town, I gave up battling with the traffic, and resolved to take the next turn away from it. A few hundred yards of lane led me to a farmhouse, the last outpost of a landscape which Celia Fiennes described as 'grass and flowers, gardens, orchards, with all sorts of herbage and tillage'. In her day the Kentish cherry orchards were still a novelty, having lately been planted with stock from Flanders. Kent itself was already called the Garden of England.

Refreshed by leaning over a gate, I rejoined the traffic, bracing myself against the built-up nether world of Dartford and Bexley. Only the unveering Street suggested that the land had once been fertile, its folk leisurely, the air fresh, the birds audible. For a dozen miles I took note of nothing except the traffic. I sustained myself by remembering the good things which lay ahead and by acknowledging that, of all our five roads, Watling Street was the least rural and most tedious. Suddenly I noticed a sign, Shooters

Hill. Roused from the mechanized miasma, I then remembered that I was on the Dover Road, Dickens's road. Have you read *The Tale of Two Cities* wherein a couple of pages distil the essence of a coaching era? Dickens depicts the Dover Mail on a November night, lumbering up Shooters Hill while the guard was 'beating his feet, and keeping an eye and a hand on the arm-chest before him, where a loaded blunderbuss lay on the top of six or eight loaded horse-pistols, deposited on a sub-stratum of cutlass'. It is all there, dead as now the era of steam is dead, yet living through the genius of a man who had travelled many miles by coach, and knew well the misdeeds of highwaymen, the 'Stand and deliver', the hue and the cry. Grand and gruff were the men who guarded the Mail; scarlet their coats, blazoned with a Royal device; clarion-like their horn, rousing the ostler, forewarning a turnpike, telling the time-o'-day to hamlets and sequestered farms. They were dedicated men, the guards. Several of them died defending the Mail; others died while trying to deliver it when blizzards had marooned their coach. And they were handymen too, equipped to meet the wear-and-tear of cart-track highways. It is all in the second chapter of Dickens's novel: 'The guard . . . looked to a smaller chest beneath his seat, in which there were a few smith's tools, a couple of torches, and a tinder-box.'

The modern highway more or less coincides with the course of Watling Street, but detours and dual tracks have made it im-possible to follow the Romans closely into London. Nowhere else in Britain are there so many square miles of so many mutual strangers. Again Dickens summed it up, in the same novel and in the next chapter of it, when he, too, entered the loneliness of London: 'In any of the burial-places of this city through which I pass, is there a sleeper more inscrutable than its busy inhabitants are . . . to me, or than I am to them?' By comparison, Rome was small enough to seem friendly, though Martial disliked the noisy crowds:

> Do you imagine that I can write poetry in Rome.
> Sweating with haste, a builder hustles his mules and men;
> A huge crane swings out with a beam or a block of stone;
> Brothels and steaming taverns, huge lumbering trucks . . .

Near Shooters Hill the London road forsakes Watling Street which probably entered New Cross, then followed part of what is now the course of the Old Kent Road, and passed close to the site of St. Thomas Watering (Chaucer's 'Waterynge of Seint Thomas'). We do not know at what point the Romans crossed the Thames. They may have chosen a low-water ford between Stangate and Thorney, and Aulus Plautius may have led his troops across it. One thing is certain; from Deptford the Street's alignment leads to Westminster, the seat of government, the home of Kings.

3 Watling Street: London

THE Roman name for London was *Londinium*, from a Celtic word, *londo*, meaning 'fierce' or 'bold', which may have been applied to the people who dwelt thereabouts. In its early years the Roman town was no more than a bridgehead on the Thames; the chief city being *Camulodunum* or Colchester, capital of the Belgic King Cunobelinus. In A.D. 61 Queen Boudicca, whom the Romans had injured and insulted, led a revolt of the Iceni and Trinovantes. Both Colchester and London were razed, and 80,000 of their people perished (or so the chroniclers said). When the two cities were rebuilt, precedence passed to London. First the provincial treasurer, then the civil government, moved to the new city on the Thames, the largest in Britain, covering 325 acres. Tacitus noted that *Londinium* was 'crowded with traders, a great centre of commerce'. It has remained so ever since.

During the reign of Hadrian the city was again burned, and for a second time rebuilt. About the year 200 the Emperor Severus divided Britain into two provinces, Upper Britain (with its capital at London) and Lower Britain (with its capital at York). But London suffered a set-back when Constantine named Britain as one of twelve imperial dioceses, each ruled by a *vicarius*. Upper Britain itself was divided into two provinces; so, from being the chief city of the south, London became *Flavia Caesariensis*, one of several provincial capitals. Nevertheless, it remained the largest and richest in Britain.

The best-known Roman relics in London are the names of its gates ... Ludgate, Newgate, Aldersgate, Cripplegate, Bishopsgate and Aldgate (Moorgate was a medieval postern, enlarged as a gateway in 1415). Excavation has revealed a fort, covering twelve acres in the Cripplegate area, which may have served as a supply depot or as a transit camp for troops. The hub of the city—its Basilica or town hall—stood at the summit of Cornhill. Here the city was administered. Here the natives gazed awestruck at the marble floors, the many-coloured mosaics, the cavernous arches, the vaulted ceilings with a galaxy of gods and heroes and mystical patterns. Here, like St. Paul himself, men appealed to Caesar: *Civis Romanus sum* (I am a Roman citizen).

The Temple of Mithras was discovered at Walbrook in 1954. It is an aisled rectangle, sixty feet by twenty-five, dedicated to a god whom the Roman soldiers revered. Mithraism was an offshoot from the worship of Ahura Mazda, a sky god, one of whose powers was Mithras, the spirit of light. According to the myth, Mazda's first earthly creation was a bull which Mithras slew so that its blood might fertilize the soil; whereupon Satan or Ahrima sent snakes and scorpions to lap the blood before it could enrich the crops. Although Mithraism was less a precise creed than an amalgam of eastern beliefs, it did symbolize the battle between Good and Evil, in a way which appealed to the troops, as Kipling knew:

> Many roads thou hast fashioned; all of them lead to the light,
> Mithras, also a soldier, teach us to die aright!

The site of the Governor's Palace is bounded by Suffolk Lane, Upper Thames Street, and Cannon Street. The Baths are not well represented. Only a small site has been found, under what became offices at Cheapside. Shipping is represented by portions of a flat-bottomed, keelless barge, discovered near Blackfriars Bridge in 1962. Her cargo of Kentish ragstone suggests that she came from the Medway during the rebuilding of the city *c.* A.D. 193 Little is known about the Roman roads in and around London; but the northward course of Watling Street has been traced, as well as a road from the Basilica to Bishopsgate Street, and another to Newgate. Sir Christopher Wren unearthed part of the second street while digging the foundations for his church at St. Mary-le-Bow: 'a Roman Causeway,' he reported, 'of rough stone, close and well-rammed with Roman Brick. . . .'

Looking back on his life work, the poet Horace uttered a prophecy: *Exegi monumentum aere perennius* (I have raised a monument more lasting than brass). Imperial Rome achieved a comparative longevity, for although the brass and the stones have crumbled, her legacy of commerce and law survive and is enshrined, albeit greatly Englished, in the Stock Exchange and the Law Courts. Roman Senators, who were forbidden to engage in trade, would have marvelled at the prestige which now surrounds it. Although a Senator was by no means averse to mixing with financiers who might swell his own privy purse, he despised shopkeepers and all who were employed in what we now call distribution. At most he felt a practical interest in craftsmanship and the process of manufacture. For the rest, he left the management of his estates to slaves. The medieval English word for a merchant was 'chapman', from the Latin *caupo*, meaning a tavern keeper who traded in local produce. Regarding all such men as congenital knaves, the law held them responsible for any theft or loss that occurred on their premises. Victims of modern traders will form their own estimate of the validity of the claims made by a Roman trader in London, as revealed on a die-stamp that was discovered near London Bridge: 'Gaius Silvus Tetricus's ointment for diseases and sores of the eye.'

The variety and quality of commerce in Roman Britain were conditioned by the tastes of the age and by the need of every community to be more or less self-sufficient. The chief export was tin. Pewter, too, became profitable; many of the blocks were sent downriver from Battersea. Other exports included gold, corn, jet, jewellery, dogs, quern stones, and cloth (the *birrus Britannicus* or goat's wool garment was advertised as waterproof). The principal imports reaching London were wine, olive oil, spices, silver tableware, bronzeware, marble, and (as altar fuel) pine cones. All this sounds very efficient; but the classical world scarcely came to grips with economic theories. The Romans were too greedy and too arrogant to practise good housekeeping. As the Empire expanded, so it grew corrupt; and from corruption sprang incompetence. The régime became a socialist state, a hive of bureaucrats and layabouts. And it sank beneath the weight of its own ineptitude.

Rome's second legacy, jurisprudence, became and has remained a condition of international trade. You cannot do business with brigands. Law was to the Romans as philosophy to the Greeks;

the highest expression of their intellectual achievement. Today there are 870,000,000 people living in countries whose legal system bears traces of Roman law. Confronted by that massive legacy, even Edward Gibbon confessed: 'I enter with just diffidence on the subject of civil law.'

Having begun as a privilege of the priesthood, Roman law was first codified in 450 B.C., as the Twelve Tables or statutes, each containing many clauses. According to Gibbon, the Tables evoked 'that blind and partial reverence which the lawyers of every country delight to bestow on their municipal institutions'. Cicero took a more appreciative view, praising the Tables for their moral precepts and national appeal: 'They entertain us by recalling archaic words and by reviving ancient attitudes. . . .' Several Emperors tried to compress a body of law that had come to fill thousands of volumes. By compressing 300,000,000 lines into 150,000 lines of his *Digest*, the Emperor Justinian claimed to have produced a compendium that was both moderate and lucid. Gibbon, however, thought as little of the *Digest* as of the Tables: 'a tessellated pavement', he scoffed, 'of antique and costly but not often coherent fragments.' Yet even a layman can detect the ideals and common sense of the *Digest*. Law, it says, must be interpreted humanely and also strictly.

English jurists long ago transformed the procedure of the Courts which had arbitrated in *Londinium*. Roman law knew little of the relations between our own judge, jury, and counsel. Even under the Empire a civil law suit was conducted with the formality of a Japanese tea ceremony and the precision of a medieval disputation. Describing the earliest cases under the Republic, Gibbon remarked: 'The jurisprudence of the first Romans exhibited the scenes of a pantomime.' They did indeed. The beneficiary under a will, for example, was required literally to jump for joy; plaintiffs were sometimes expected to grapple a witness. If any of the forms was omitted or mismanaged, the case could be dismissed. The great medieval jurist, Bracton, wrote a treatise *Concerning the laws and Customs of England*, in which he declared that the English must either retain Roman law or go their own way, creating new laws based on royal writs. The English went their own way. Roman law continued to offer analogies, but never again did it supply precedents.

In view of the differences between their legal systems, what does England owe to Rome? She owes, first, the Roman genius for creating and codifying laws, with a skill never before equalled nor ever after excelled. She owes also the *jus gentium* or law of the nations, which sprang from the fact that only a Roman citizen might invoke the fullest protection of Roman law. The legacy of Roman law was summarized by a phrase from the second sentence of the *Digest*: 'law is the art of the good and the just.' Two thousand years later, Lord Asquith expressed a well-founded opinion when he said: 'In the thousand years which followed the birth of Christ there was no era in which the circumstances of life were so favourable to the happiness of mankind as in the reign of the Emperor Hadrian.'

What, meanwhile, has happened to Watling Street? It has gone its own way, preceding the course of Edgware Road, where excavation revealed a layer of flints in a grouting of lime, and beneath that a layer of gravel. Thereafter the course is closely followed by Kilburn High Road and Cricklewood Broadway, neither of which is my favourite landscape. With patience therefore—and the innocence of a countryman abroad in a strange city—I looked forward to green fields, and quiet lanes, and a blackbird singing in the sun.

4 Watling Street: London to Wroxeter

THE sun and the song and the lanes and the fields were further away than I had reckoned, because Time itself had flown faster than I had reckoned, obliterating almost the whole of my slight acquaintance with suburban London. Lost in a maze of traffic signs, I gave up the pursuit of Watling Street, and was content to read what other men had written about it, which amounted to very little; as, for example, the discovery near Canon's Park of an *agger* or mound in the Frigidaire Company's sports ground (which has since been built on). To be brief and honest, I found nothing of interest to report until I entered St. Albans via a modern main road. The invisible Watling Street entered via London Gate and the massive Roman wall there, which is overlooked by the Verulam housing estate. I walked slowly along the length of that wall—more than a hundred yards of it—until a spacious green appeared, and beyond it the hill overlooking the Roman city of *Verulamium*, razed by Queen Boudicca, rebuilt by the Romans, larger than before, encircling two hundred acres with a wall. *Verulamium* had an underground water supply flowing through wooden pipes. It had a splendid archway spanning Watling Street; a Mithraic temple for the troops; a poor quarter, and a quarter of merchants' houses, half-timbered and single-storied. Tacitus classified *Verulamium* as a *municipium* or chartered town, the only one of its kind in Britain. When the Roman town disintegrated, the Saxons rebuilt the site; and there King Offa founded an abbey in honour of St. Alban, a native of the place, who is commonly accepted as the first British Christian martyr. The Saxon town soon afterwards took the martyr's name; and the Normans rebuilt the abbey.

Beside a road on the edge of the city stands the site of the only known Roman theatre in Britain, a grassy arena, criss-crossed by the remains of stone walls. Roman actors were a despised class

33

who performed interludes between chariot races and gladiatorial
fights. The curtain went up at noon and came down at 2.30 p.m.
The manager served as master of the company. Everyone in the
theatre was hired by the municipal entertainments officer. If a play
was hissed, the playwright received nothing at all; an admirable
custom. Latin drama fell far below the level of the best Latin
literature. Even the outstanding playwrights, Terence and Plautus,
took their plots from the Greek theatre; yet they did give the
characters new life. Though it is forty years since I last read a
Latin play, I still remember laughing at Colonel Blimp or *miles
gloriosus*; at the clever girl who married an old fool; at the spend-
thrift son and his pack of lies.

The Roman theatre stands on land that once belonged to Sir
Francis Bacon, first Baron Verulam and Viscount St. Albans, who
was born in 1561, the younger son (by a second marriage) of Sir
Nicholas Bacon, Lord Keeper of the Great Seal; in which high
office the son succeeded the father. Philosophy, politics, science,
literature, law; Bacon excelled in all, but chose chiefly the last.
His eloquence held men spellbound. Having heard him plead, Ben
Jonson reported: 'the fear of every man was that he should make
an end.' At the height of his career, as Lord Chancellor, Bacon was
found guilty of accepting bribes; a crime all the more heinous
because he had himself declared: 'The place of justice is a hallowed
place, and therefore . . . ought to be preserved without scandal and
corruption. . . .' He was fined a great fortune, imprisoned in the
Tower, disbarred from ever again holding either an office of State
or a seat in the Lords, and forbidden to approach the Court. The
King used his prerogative to waive the prison sentence; but
nothing more. In all English history it would be difficult to find a
sadder example of the Greek lament, 'Being great, great was his
fall'. And the irony was, having accepted the bribe, Bacon had
given judgement against the briber. Yet the fall was not a decline.
In retirement at St. Albans the ex-Chancellor wrote many books—
history, philosophy, politics—all capped by his essays. Whether he
treats of men or of affairs or of history or of religion, Bacon in his
essays writes crisply, elegantly, learnedly. Many of his aphorisms
are, or until recently were, part of an Englishman's education:

'Men fear death as little children fear to go in the dark' . . . 'Wives are young men's mistresses; companions for middle age; and old men's nurses' . . . 'Of great riches there is no real use, except it be in the distribution; the rest is but conceit.'

Bacon died in the pursuit of knowledge. One wintry morning he got out of his carriage in order to buy a chicken, which he killed and then stuffed with snow, hoping to discover that the intense cold would halt putrefaction. Having completed the experiment, he returned to his carriage, but was already shivering so violently that he could not complete the journey home. Instead, he was taken to the house of Lord Arundel, where he died a few days later. They buried him as he desired, near to his mother in the Church of St. Michael at St. Albans. 'Prosperity', he wrote, contemplating his own fall from it, 'doth best discover vice; but adversity doth best discover virtue.'

Although it is no longer possible to follow Watling Street through St. Albans, excavation has revealed that it passed north of the Forum, close to St. Michael's church, thence close to the Roman theatre and into the more or less open country of Hertfordshire. The name Hertford means 'the ford where the hart or stag crossed the stream' . . . a place not now likely to be identified. In Dean Swift's *Polite Conversation* a character remarks: 'My Lord, this moment I did myself the honour to drink to your lordship.' To which his lordship replies: 'Why then that's Hertfordshire kindness.' Fuller's *Worthies* confirmed the friendliness: 'the people in this county at entertainments drink back to them who drink to them.'

Meanwhile the Street goes straight to Markyate, where the modern road by-passes the town. Here the Romans faced a problem. Should they penetrate or should they by-pass the Dunstable escarpment of the Chiltern Hills? They compromised by making for Redbourn and by following the River Ver with a series of bends. A stiff climb followed. When the stage coaches arrived, a lower road was made, leaving nearly two miles of the Street to horsemen and pedestrians; it still exists as a minor road.

Approaching Dunstable, the Street enters Bedfordshire, formerly a galloping ground for the Mail as it followed Telford's new road to Holyhead, a work as wonderful as the Romans'. Nowadays a motorist can pass through Dunstable without noticing anything remarkable. In 1800, however, life was simultaneously more leisurely and more active. Thus, when passengers alighted from the coach at the Sugar Loaf Inn they were allowed twenty minutes in which to consume the following snack: 'A Boiled Round of Beef; a roast loin of Pork; a Roast Aitchbone of Beef; and a boiled Hand of Pork with Peas Pudding and Parsnips; a roast Goose; and a Boiled Leg of Mutton.' One wonders what they talked about.

Now comes the long descent into Hockliffe, and with it an awareness of beginning to be in the country. Small hills rise unpretentiously. Solitary elms stand like signposts to coppices. Cattle, sheep, and corn mix the farming while Watling Street steers a steady course through gentle contours that lead into Little Brickhill, an example of ethnic tautology, Saxon *hyll* and Celtic *brig*, each meaning a hill. In 1605 Little Brickhill witnessed a brief yet memorable encounter. The story begins when a group of Roman Catholics decide to assassinate the King, the Queen, the Prince of Wales, and many other notables as they assemble at the State Opening of Parliament. That done, the plotters will seize the young Duke of York, and proclaim him as a Roman Catholic King. To crown their cataclysm, they will incite a rebellion in Warwickshire. Each of the principal plotters is chosen for a specific role; Guy Fawkes, because he has served as a sapper with the Spanish army; Ambrose Rookwood, because he owns a stud of fast horses. Early in November the taverns between London and Warwickshire begin to buzz with talk of a great hunting party, for which Mr. Rookwood is supplying relays of horses at inns along Watling Street. The next part of the tale is familiar. One of the plotters (which one, we do not know) sends a message to a Roman Catholic peer, Lord Mounteagle, warning him not to attend the opening of Parliament: 'for they shall recyve a terrible blow this parleament and yet they shall not seie who hurrts them . . .' Lord Mounteagle himself is a Trimmer who has already assured the King that he wishes to turn Protestant. Fearful of being implicated, he passes the warning to Lord Salisbury, not knowing that the government is already aware of the plot. Ten days later, Guy Fawkes is arrested while standing watch over his powder barrels. News of the arrest sets London in an uproar. Under cover of the confusion, two of the plotters—Rookwood and Thomas Winter—slip away. Other conspirators, confident that all has gone according to plan, are riding ahead to assemble in Warwickshire. As they enter Brickhill they halt and look back, surprised to hear a horseman riding furiously. It is Rookwood, come to break the news. Their leisurely triumph turns into a race for life. Fenny Stratford, Stoney Stratford, Towcester . . . the fugitives gallop through every village and town, shouting that they carry despatches from the King. Rookwood himself rides thirty miles in two hours on the same horse, not daring to halt at an inn. Soon after nightfall they reach the outskirts of Daventry. Already the hue and cry is on. The King has issued a proclamation, threatening all 'who shall in any wise either receive, abette, cherish, entertaine, or adhere unto them [the plotters], or not doe their best endeavours to apprehend and take them'. Apprehended and taken they are, from holes and corners in many parts of the kingdom; and they suffer the death of traitors. Thereafter, until Queen Victoria expunged it, a form of service was included in the Book of Common Prayer, giving thanks each November the Fifth for deliverance from what Dr. Bentley, Master of Trinity College, Cambridge, described as

> . . . the Roman purgatory fire
> To make the Senate-house a pile.

After a slight change of course at Brickhill, the Street descends into Fenny Stratford, the fenlike settlement beside a ford near the *straet* or Roman road. According to Shean's *History and Topography of Buckinghamshire* (1862) the site of the settlement is 'A place now known as Dropmore, a short distance outside the town (but in the parish of Bow Brickhill) . . .' In 1857 the villagers were still unearthing Roman relics there. Fenny Stratford High Street, running at right angles from Watling Street, retains something of the character of the village which I knew fifty years ago. The Fenny Poppers or miniature cannon were presented in 1730 by the

county's historian, Dr. Browne Willis, who impoverished himself
by building the redbrick church of St. Martin in memory of his
grandfather, surgeon to King Charles II. The cannon are fired at
four-hourly intervals from 8 a.m. on what used to be called
Armistice Day, 11 November; wherefore many people suppose
that the salvos commemorate the fallen; in fact, they commemorate the birthday of Browne Willis's grandfather.

A mile beyond Fenny Stratford the Street is crossed by the
railway from Euston. A plaque on the bridge writes a footnote to
the history of British transport: 'Prior to September 1838 the
southern part of this railway terminated at this bridge where
passengers were conveyed by coach to Rugby where they
rejoined the railway for Birmingham.' On the other side of
the Street, under the shadow of that bridge, you will see a
level patch of grass, all that remains of the Denbigh Arms, a
tavern which waxed with the coaching era and then waned with
the 1930s.

The country hereabouts is placid, hilly, wooded, and served by
more footpaths per square mile than any other county possesses.
Time has not overtaken the *General View of the Agriculture of the
County of Buckingham* (1794): 'the county is principally composed
of rich loam, strong clay and chalk, and loam upon gravel. As to
the first, its ability to produce good crops without the assistance
of much manure, is evident from the uniform verdure of the
herbage . . .' Time, however, long ago overtook the report's next
sentence, citing 'the very great supply of butter which is produced
from that land. . . . The only trouble which the dairy-man has, is
to carry his butter upon a horse to the nearest point where the
carrier passes to London.'

Although parts of it were recently widened, the modern road
follows the Street closely, dipping up and down through pleasant
country. Away to the left are Buckingham and its outlying manor
of Lenborough, whose lord was Edward Gibbon, author of *A
History of the Decline and Fall of the Roman Empire*: 'It was at
Rome . . . as I sat musing amidst the ruins of the Capitol, while
the barefoot friars were singing vespers in the Temple of Jupiter,
that the idea of writing the decline and fall of the city first started

to my mind.' Such was Gibbon's account of the genesis of a work that was unrivalled in its day, and is still a set book for every student of Roman history. Edward Gibbon was born at Putney in 1737, son of a Tory Member of Parliament and kinsman to the Actons who also begat a famous historian. The boy laid the foundations of his scholarship at a school in Kingston-on-Thames, where (says his *Autobiography*), 'at the expense of many tears and some blood, I purchased the knowledge of the Latin syntax'. Two other examples of precocity soon followed. At the age of fourteen he went up to Magdalen College, Oxford; and at the age of sixteen he came down, having been received into the Roman Church. While staying at Lausanne he met a Swiss girl: 'I saw', he said, 'and loved.' His father, however, objected to a foreign match: 'I sighed as a lover, and obeyed as a son.' The sighing proved as evanescent as the conversion, for he spent the rest of his life as an anti-Christian bachelor. Porson, a shrewd old classic, put his finger on the wound when he remarked that Gibbon, a compassionate man, seemed strangely unmoved by the persecution of Christians and the suffering of women. The Swiss girl eventually married Necker, the economist.

In order to please his father, who was a major in a militia regiment, the South Hampshire Grenadiers, Gibbon served under him as captain. The experience was fruitful: 'The discipline and evolution of a modern battalion', said Captain Gibbon, 'gave me a clearer notion of the phalanx and the legion. . . .' When his father died, Gibbon inherited the lordship and manor house of Lenborough in the parish of Gawcot near Buckingham. He demolished the manor except for one wing which was converted into a farmhouse for his tenant. After the militia came the Grand Tour; after the Tour, Parliament, as Member for Liskeard; after Parliament, the *Decline and Fall*, for which he had been reading assiduously. Scholarship has discovered facts that were unknown to Gibbon, but it has not outshone his achievement. The *Decline and Fall* is not a textbook; it was addressed to an era in which every educated European possessed a considerable knowledge of classical Rome. The author himself stated: 'My book was on every table, and almost on every toilette. . . .' Unlike most

4

scholars, Gibbon was an artist. George Saintsbury, indeed, believed that large parts of the *Decline and Fall* 'are a great deal more interesting . . . than most modern novels'. Many pages of it were rewritten many times over many years. Looking back on those tentative beginnings, Gibbon confessed: 'My style degenerated into a verbose and turgid declamation.' In the end, by laborious trial and error, he forged a splendid Augustan prose. To our own ears the style sounds ornate and at times rhetorical; to Gibbon's ears our style would sound effete; and posterity will find fault with both. Many of Gibbon's contemporaries regretted the cynicism with which he mocked beliefs that were sacred to men whose intellect was as keen as his own. This mockery is especially noticeable in the famous fifteenth chapter, which sneers at the theologians who 'indulge the pleasing task of describing Religion as she descended from Heaven, arrayed in her native purity'. Like every other human activity, religion is fallible, in both its precept and its practice; but man's religious intimations continue to withstand malice and misrepresentation. In any event, Christianity was not Gibbon's basic stumbling block. A careful study of his work reveals that life itself was the offence. Gibbon wrote as a child of the first avowedly sceptical century in England. The spirit of his age aggravated the insecurity of his temperament. On his own admission, he had submitted to Rome after reading the books of a single author at a callow age; and for the rest of his life he was unnerved by a single amorous misfortune—again at a callow age. Nevertheless, the *Decline and Fall* is a monument of art and scholarship. Moreover, when disease and death did assail him, Gibbon faced them with the courageous dignity of that pagan philosophy which he admired.

Gibbon himself certainly knew Watling Street between Fenny Stratford and Stoney Stratford, the latter a handsome little town whose best parts lie away from the Street, around Horsefair Green and the Market place, which can seem as peaceful as when I first discovered them long ago, picking my way among cattle and sheep and Georgian houses. Parts of the town, and one of its two churches, were rebuilt after a fire in 1742. When Huguenot lace-makers settled in Buckinghamshire and Bedfordshire, Stoney

Stratford achieved a new importance, as a depot for packhorses trading with London. William Camden believed that Stoney Stratford was the Roman settlement of *Lactodoro* or *Lactodorum*, a Latin version of the Celtic place-name, meaning 'a river forded by stones'. Stukeley, on the other hand, maintained that the site lay beyond those stones, at Old Stratford, on the Northamptonshire side of the Ouse. Many Roman remains were found near the river, including a silver plaque (now in the British Museum) from a shrine to a Roman god.

What was the religion of Rome? To the noblest of the Romans it was self-surrender. Surrender to what? Not, certainly, to one god, but to many. As the medieval Church offered prayers for man's activities—his work, play, travel, war, marriage, sickness, death—so the Roman invoked his own multifarious deities. He had the rites of *Saturnalia* or sowing, of *Robigalia* or dispersal of mildew from crops, of *Consualia* or harvest-home, and of the household spirits that will detain us when the Foss Way passes a Roman villa at Chedworth. Were those rites based upon a specific credo? The question in that form is misleading because Roman religion changed with the times, from paganism to Christianity. Most of the pagan Romans acknowledged what the Greeks called Necessity or a Universal Will. Sometimes the Will was regarded as benevolent, sometimes as malevolent, sometimes as neutral. Like their philosophy, the Romans' pagan religion was chiefly a code of ethics and a cycle of rites. It knew nothing of the 'glad tidings of great joy' with which Christianity sought to give meaning both to life and to death. The inscriptions on pagan tombs were vague and seldom hopeful: 'To my dear wife, in the shades' . . . 'Good Tullius, farewell'. The age-old dilemma was stated on the one hand by Cicero, a reverent agnostic, who wished to believe in a divine purpose and human immortality, and on the other hand by Lucretius, who, though he acknowledged a Creator, believed that the world had been left to its fate. Therefore, said Lucretius, men must rely solely on themselves; to worship non-existent gods is to fall into superstition and thence into feuds.

The religious intimations of the early Republic were spiritual;

the eclecticism of a Greek-orientated Empire ended as Socialism or worship of the State. True, the Republic had been venerated from the beginning. Nevertheless, the old patrician ideals were so debased by alien infiltration and domestic prosperity that the State became God. The *Secular Hymn* of Horace invoked the sun, that it might ever rise more brightly on the city, 'gazing with just and kindly eyes upon those tower-topped hills of Rome, prolonging her greatness . . . into yet another cycle and thereafter into ages that shall forever grow more auspicious'. Having therefore no need to impose thirty-nine Articles, Roman paganism rarely felt itself threatened by any other religion. If a man consented to make a token sacrifice to the Emperor, and if his private credo neither threatened the State nor violated decency, then he was free to worship or not to worship. The early Christians were persecuted, not because they accepted Jesus, but because they rejected Caesar, as God.

Midway across the long bridge out of Stoney Stratford, Watling Street enters Nórthamptonshire, county of 'spires and squires', of stone houses and famous Hunts whose coverts stretch northward from Buckinghamshire; the Whaddon, Pytchley, Fernie, Cottesmore, Quorn, Atherstone, Belvoir. Like the tone of talk, the look of the land changes between North Buckinghamshire and Towcester, ancient *Tovescestre*, the *castra* or Roman camp on the River Tove which itself was named by an old Germanic word, *toven*, meaning 'to meander'. Towcester is the true site of *Lactodorum*; from it the Romans built a lesser road, linking Alchester with Dorchester-on-Thames. Many people know Towcester as a town with a race-course; a few know it as a town with comely by-ways and a church that is reached via a lane which opens on to a meadow, a cottage, and a handsome stone house.

Despite slight deviations, the modern road follows the Street closely until it reaches the site of *Bannaventa*, two miles north of Weedon, a name familiar to ageing cavalrymen. Near that point the Romans changed course in order to avoid frequent crossings of a tributary of the River Nene. For another four miles or so the Street keeps straight, flanked by a railway and a motorway. Thereafter a mix-up occurs; the M1 and M45 loop each other's loop; the railway looks in; two other roads join the mêelée. In the midst of that Babel the Street disappears and then reappears, this time as a grassy track, about a mile east of the A5, not far from Kilsby. It is a strange experience, to follow that green road while modernity thunders past within a stone's throw of rabbits basking in the sun.

After a few miles the A5 rejoins Watling Street, passing close to Dunsmore Farm in the parish of Clifton-upon-Dunsmore, where they buried Izaak Walton's friend, Christopher Harvey, who would not have approved of the motoring hordes: 'He that doth live at home, and learns God and himself, needeth no farther go.' Harvey's homely aphorism is soon submerged beneath dual carriageways racing into Warwickshire. When John Edge surveyed the neighbouring farms in 1794 he had this to say of the area 'which is in part bordered by the Watling-street-way, extending from High Cross to Withybrook . . . good strong clay and marl land . . . but much more ploughed than in the south east quarter'. It was beyond Edge's brief to add a postscript concerning the origins of county names. Warwickshire, for example, may be derived either from *Waeringas* (the home of Waer's people) or from *waering* (a weir).

> Stout Warwickshire, her ancient badge, the Bear . . .

Michael Drayton's line tallies with Shakespeare's:

> Now, by my father's badge, old Neville's crest,
> The rampant bear chained to a ragged staff.

Rampant indeed, able to make and to unmake kings.

'Approach we then this classic ground . . .' so wrote Edmund Blunden of Izaak Walton's Dovedale; and a traveller will repeat that praise when Watling Street approaches High Cross, the most famous junction in Roman Britain, where Watling Street meets Foss Way near the site of a small settlement, *Venonae*. One wishes that those two highways had converged at a point where they were green roads. As it is, meditation shrinks, conversation shouts, and pedestrians must possess the patience of Job, the speed of a hare and *in extremis* the wings of a dove. No vehicles will yield on this grim battleground. Rather, they assume that pedestrians ought not to cross their path. Celia Fiennes arrived during a less restive era: 'I came', she remembered, 'to High Cross which is esteemed the middle of England, where the two great Roads meet, that divides the kingdom in the Saxons tyme in 4 parts, the Watling Street, and the Foss Way . . .'

A few years later, in 1712, the Earl of Denbigh subscribed with other local landowners to erect a monument which they placed in the middle of Watling Street, as a 'perpetual remembrance of peace at last restored by Queen Anne'. A Latin inscription on the monument mentioned the Roman roads and a Roman officer, Claudius, who may have been buried nearby, at a place called Cloudesley Bush. In 1722 or thereabouts William Stukeley made a sketch of the monument, showing four Doric columns, each facing one of the cross roads, supported by four Tuscan pillars, each bearing a sundial. When Defoe saw the monument he composed a paean to Clio, the Muse of History: 'It is a most pleasant curiosity to observe the course of these old famous highways . . . the Watling-street, and the Foss, in which one sees so lively a representation of the ancient British, Roman and Saxon governments, that one cannot help realizing those terms to the imagination.' In 1791 this elegant monument was damaged by lightning, and the remnants were re-erected in what is now the garden of High Cross Farm, formerly an inn. In 1971 the monument was neglected and decaying.

Maps tell the truth and nothing but the truth, yet the whole truth eludes them. Thus, a modern map shows Watling Street as a straight road, stretching twelve miles from High Cross to Atherstone, without entering a village. The map shows rivers, streams, and sometimes a coppice in hunting country. Seeing it, a foreigner might say: 'Here is a road through the heart of rural England.' But when he followed that road he would encounter a two-way stream of traffic so loud that on a still night it can be heard two miles away. The Roman roadmakers, on the other hand, must have found this a relatively easy sector because it contained neither mountains nor marshes nor wide rivers. They only halted when they reached the River Anker, where they built *Manduessedum* on the outskirts of Atherstone, which is by-passed by the A5.

Beyond Atherstone the Street enters the Staffordshire coalfields, a land so long laid waste that even the weeds have lost heart. At a place named Gailey—the *gagol-leah* or meadow choked by bog myrtle—the bones of Watling Street lie buried beneath a large roundabout. In the midst of this modern England one or two curious travellers may visit Wall, which lies a little to the south of Lichfield, where the course of the Street survives as a farm track. Wall—the site of *Letocetum*, a posting station—has a first rate museum and the remains of some baths, admirably tended by the National Trust.

Watling Street from Gailey to Wroxeter was new to me. Having travelled it once, I hope never to do so again. It is among the most dangerous race-tracks in the Midlands, mocked by a 50-mile-an-hour limit which few vehicles observe. The Street itself passes a famous place, Boscobel, and enters a beautiful county, Shropshire, formerly called *Scrobbesbyrigscir* or the shire with its capital at Scrobb's burgh (Scrob being the name of the father of that Richard who *c.* 1050 built Richard's Castle in Herefordshire). The Normans' name for Shropshire was *Salopescira*, whence the abbreviation *Salop*. Mary Webb, a native of the county, described it as a land 'where the dignity and beauty of ancient things lingers long. . . .'

Boscobel village, standing just far enough from the Street to escape the din, justifies its Latin name, *boscus bellus*, the beautiful wood or Brewood Forest wherein the Giffards of Chillingham built Boscobel House, a black-and-white Tudor hunting lodge. There, in 1651, King Charles II was sheltered by the tenants, a family of Roman Catholic woodcutters named Penderel. The young King was trying to escape to France, pursued by Cromwell's rebels, who had tracked him so closely that the Penderels hid him in a hollow oak tree. Unless it has been lately razed, an oak tree near Boscobel House reminds us that it 'had the honour of sheltering from his foes His Majesty King Charles the Second' . . . a statement which, although it is untrue (the oak having disappeared long ago), may yet be not wholly false, because some say that the present tree began life as an acorn of the original oak. The King did not forget the Penderels. When he regained his throne the family received a pension and still do receive it, though nowadays so taxed and devalued that they no doubt bear it as an honourable burden. Until Queen Victoria ungraciously deleted it, a form of service was included in the Prayer Book to mark the King's deliverance from the rebels at Boscobel. At Chelsea Hospital, which Charles II founded, they are more mindful. On Oak-apple Day, 29 May, the King's birthday, the red-coated veteran soldiers parade before his statue in their main court, wearing a sprig of oak leaves. A similar ceremony is observed each year by the pensioners at the Lord Leycester Hospital in Warwick.

About eight miles beyond Boscobel the A5 sheers away, leaving Watling Street to make straight for Oakengates, a Victorian coal-town, perched on a hill whose views are refreshing though one wonders for how long because the place has been scheduled as part of a 'new town' named Telford, in memory of a roadmaker whom the Romans would have admired. If a way to the better exists, said Thomas Hardy, it entails a full look at the worst. On our own journey we have not flinched from taking a full look at the worst aspects of Watling Street. Now at last our honesty is about to be rewarded, for the worst is past, and glad tidings have appeared on the horizon:

Streamed in crimson on the wind the Wrekin's crest of light . . .

That was how Macaulay described the hilltop beacon which alerted the Marcher Country when the Spanish Armada was sighted. The Wrekin takes its name from Wroxeter, which the Saxons spelt as *Wroxcestre*, or the Roman fort of *Viroconium*. The Normans called it *La Wrekene*. This famous hill, 1,335 feet above the sea, reveals Snowdon, the Brecon Beacons, the Derbyshire peaks, the Gloucestershire Cotswolds. As the Wrekin draws nearer, so too the other summits are seen . . . Clee Hills, Welsh hills, Church Stretton hills. Nevertheless, the Street does contain an industrial town, Wellington. A few old and handsome buildings blend with the landscape, but the rest do not. If you take the road to Waters Upton and then glance back at Wellington, you will see something resembling a head at a cinema, trying to peer round a huge and disastrous hat; it is the Wrekin, which men

did not make, though at Wellington they have marred their own
vision of it.

Westward from Wellington the Street shakes itself free. The
land alongside becomes as it never has been since Dover—deep,
dramatic. After about two miles the A5 turns north in order to
skirt Overley Hill, but the Roman road goes ahead and can be
traced via a ridge in the fields. The last six miles of Watling Street
are indisputably the finest not least because they steer west toward
Wales and away from industry. Right and left the distant villages
are good to look at: Withington, for example, astride the Shropshire Union Canal. In 1954 a report by the British Transport
Commission described tracts of that canal as 'worth retaining for
transport purposes, either by reason of the tonnage of traffic
upon them or because they form part of a through route.
Every encouragement should be given to the development
of traffic.' It should indeed, if only in order that Watling Street
and all the rest of our roads may become quieter and less lethal
to travellers.

Suddenly the traffic sheers away, bearing north-west while the
Street marches straight into a narrow lane. Then Bell Brook
chimes in, flowing under the lane, to join the River Severn. The
Romans, however, were accompanied by a sterner music, the
silence of the dead, because burial was forbidden within the city,
so that the tombs stood like sentries along the approaches; evidence of Rome's vague sadness in the presence of mystery,
though not utterly without hope, for many of the departed went
well-provisioned into the shades. At *Camulodunum* the grave of a
child contained a toy pigeon, a feeding bottle, a bangle; at
Eboracum a soldier buried his infant daughter, *anima dulcissime qui
vixit menses decem* (a most sweet soul who lived for ten months).
There are no tombstones besides the Street today; only a small
cottage, which is Wroxeter Post Office, and beyond it in deep
country the site of *Viroconium*, capital of the Province of *Britannia
Secunda*, the fourth largest city in Britain, covering 180 acres. The
city was founded during the second half of the first century A.D.,
as a base from which to contain the Welsh. Basilica, Baths, and
Forum were left incomplete, no doubt because the native *Cornovii*

were too busily engaged in border warfare. Then came the
Emperor Hadrian, like a Churchill among sluggards. The whole
of Roman Britain responded to his challenge. *Viroconium* itself
was replanned and this time completed. When its Basilica and
Forum were destroyed by fire the citizens rebuilt them immediately
and more majestically. For nearly two centuries the city prospered.
In 287, however, the revolt of Carausius, a mercenary General,
severed the links between Britain and Rome; and when at last
the contact was restored, the Empire had declined steeply.
Abandoned forever by the Legions, *Viroconium* grew poor,
frightened, decrepit. Under the Anglo-Saxons it was supplanted
by a newer capital, Shrewsbury, whose townsfolk used *Viroconium*
as a quarry. Today the city is a hamlet.

In 1863 part of the site was excavated; in 1948 the site was
delegated to a government department, and is now administered
by the Ministry of Public Building and Works. Measuring 290
feet by 440, the site reveals sections of the Baths, notably an
exercise room, cold bath, warm baths, hot baths, and sweating
chamber. The museum contains, *inter alia*, pottery, glass (some of
it beautifully coloured), coins, millstones, pens, and a large
inscription, the finest of its kind yet found in Britain, which was
erected above the main entrance to the Forum in A.D. 130:
IMP. CAES DIVI TRAINI ... (To the Emperor Caesar
Trajanus Hadrianus Augustus, son of the deified Trajanus
Parthicus, grandson of the deified Nerva, Pontifex Maximus,
wielding the power of a tribune for the fourteenth year, consul for
the third time, Father of his Country, the Community of the
Cornovii erected this building). All that majesty is dominated by
the red sandstone ruins of the south-western entrance to the
Baths, a massive wall, high as a house, pierced with a gateway:
and the gateway is dominated by the Wrekin.

A few hundred yards away the River Severn flows from
Plynlimmon. The rest is silence and a ruined city. In the course of
their own conquests the Romans themselves had seen such
ruins, and the Jews before them: 'Babylon is fallen, is fallen!'
Sic transit gloria mundi. But the Romans believed that certain
places are haunted by a spirit. Insofar as the imagination does

need to be stimulated, the belief was justified because, as Mary Webb discovered, the spirit of Rome prevails at *Viroconium*, bestriding the centuries as imperiously as once it spanned the fields:

> Virocon—Virocon—
> Still the ancient name rings on
> And brings, in the untrampled wheat,
> The tumult of a thousand feet.

Sarn Helen East

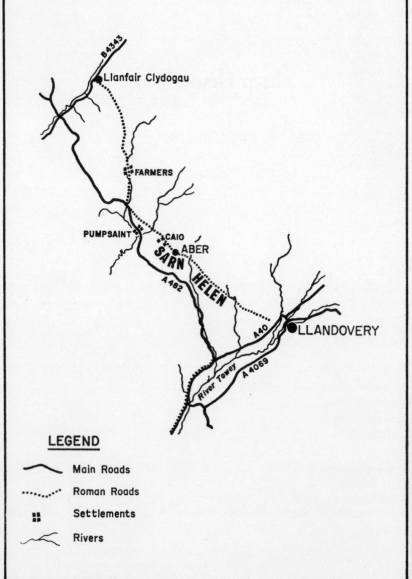

SARN HELEN EAST

LEGEND

────── Main Roads

············ Roman Roads

▪▪ Settlements

﹏ Rivers

© Cassell&Co. Ltd. 1971

5 Sarn Helen East:
Llandovery to Llanfair Clydogau

'NOWHERE', I exclaimed, 'could be more beautiful than this.' The exclamation, of course, was vague as well as refutable. Nevertheless, I repeated it: 'Nowhere could be more beautiful than this.' And with the echo still on my lips, I allowed the scene to imprint itself on my mind. Far below, steeped in a pool of the sun, I saw . . . but that is to anticipate what I did see.

The true beginning of Sarn Helen lay very close to the egg or *fons et origo* which Horace cited as an excessively remote starting-place. About 50,000 years ago the Welsh mountains were peopled by nomadic foodgatherers, a race so primitive that even our contemporary pigmies would regard them as deficient in the arts and crafts of living. Yet those nomads were already 'voyaging through strange seas of thought alone', for, in one of their caves, William Buckland, first Professor of Geology at Oxford, found proof of a ritual burial. Many millennia later—a mere 4,000 years ago—a newer race was sowing wheat, milking cows, shearing sheep. Other races followed, and gradually the Bronze and the Iron Ages wrought a more sophisticated culture. The generic name for those Continental races is Celt, though the meaning of the name has been so pared down by modern scholarship that little remains except a more or less common language. Then the Romans invaded Britain, pressing swiftly inland until, along a line between the Severn and the Trent, they met the Welsh, led by Caradog or Caractacus, who, said Tacitus, 'had in many battles, both indecisive and successful, raised himself above all other generals in Britain'. Caractacus was defeated. Having sought refuge with the Brigantes in Yorkshire, he was delivered by them to the Roman general, Ostorius Scapula. Thereafter the Romans penetrated and encircled Wales, containing it by means of several forts, of which the largest were at *Castra Legionum* (Caerleon-on-Usk) and *Deva* (Chester), Each fort was manned by 6,000 troops, and reinforced by twenty-four lesser forts, linked via hundreds of miles of Roman roads. Writing of what is now England, as it appeared in the year A.D. 80, Tacitus observed that the native aristocracy was already learning Latin, wearing togas, taking baths (just as, in the British Empire, many of the Indian Princes acquired toothpaste and a Rolls-Royce). The Welsh, by contrast, went their own ways, so that the Roman occupation remained simply an interlude except insofar as it affected the rebirth of the Welsh language and a re-alignment of the Welsh dynasties.

Who, then, was Helen? And what was Sarn? In a sense they were both Romans, or at any rate Romanized, because each was associated with a Roman general, Magnus Maximus, governor of Britain, Gaul, and Spain, who so impressed the Welsh that they co-opted him into their own legends, under the name of Macsen, King of Rome. According to *The Mabinogion*—the treasure-house of Welsh mythology—Macsen one night dreamed of a beautiful girl. When he awoke from the dream he resolved to find her, even if his search should encompass the globe. In the end he did find her, in Wales. Her name was Helen, and she exactly resembled the girl of his dreams. They married and lived happily thereafter. *The Mabinogion* contrives to leaven the poetry with engineering: 'Helen', it says, 'wished to make roads from one fort to another across the Isle of Britain. And the roads were made. And for that reason they are called the roads of Helen, and the men of the Isle of Britain would not have made those great roads for anyone save her.' Not everyone agreed with *The Mabinogion*; some held that *Sarn y Helen* was a corruption of *Sarn y Lleng* or the road of the Legions; others (led by Sir John Rhys, the Victorian scholar) thought that Helen was Elen, a pagan goddess of the gloaming: 'There is', said Rhys ,'a certain poetic propriety in associating the primitive paths and tracks of the country with this vagrant goddess of dawn and dusk.' Helen, Lleng, Elen; those are debatable; but none doubts that Sarn is the Welsh word for a road or causeway. The best-known Sarn Helen crosses the mountains of North

Wales. Our own road—sometimes called Sarn Helen East—
crosses the mountains of West Wales. It is about fifteen miles
long, and was built chiefly in order to serve a gold mine. Much of
it is a grass track, more is a steep lane.

The road begins at Llandovery, a small market town in Carmarthenshire, with a narrow high street which at its northern end
widens into a cobbled market-place with a miniature green and a
war memorial. Over all looms the husk of a twelfth-century
castle on the summit of a knoll. Llandovery College, a boys'
school, was originally a Dominican friary which Henry VIII
refounded as a collegiate church with a school. The present
buildings are not good examples of Victorian Gothic, but they
do contain parts of the medieval monastic church. As one would
expect of any Welsh town, Llandovery begat poets and proselytizers. Chief among the poets was William Williams alias Panteclyn,
greatest of all the Welsh hymn-writers, whose *Guide me, O thou
great Jehovah* still resounds bi-lingually from Bethel. Chief among
the proselytizers was the Reverend Rhys Pritchard, Chancellor
of the diocese of St. David's, whose *Cannwyll y Cymry* or *The
Welshman's Candle* is a book of sermons and a portrait of Tudor
Wales, depicting all sorts and conditions of men and women,
from the gentry and the shepherds to the spinsters and the soldiers.
The Reverend Chancellor became in his age *laudator temporis acti*,
praising times past by dispraising times present, as when he
rebuked the decline of 'plain living and high thinking' among the
gentry: 'they must', he complained, 'have their six courses with
wine and song, their sauces, vinegar, capers, samphires . . . the
sauces alone cost more than the richest dishes eaten by their
fathers. . . .' The complaint is not new.

Certainly the Romans sought new pastures when they built
Sarn Helen East. The road is first seen as a lane on the far side of
the Tywi, climbing steeply for two miles, then branching right
and left, leaving Sarn Helen as a track which in places grows
fainter than a shadow. Away to the north-east lies Cilycwm, a
National Trust village of white cottages and a sandstone Norman
church with two medieval murals. Across the street is the smallest
Post Office I ever saw; and nearby, set back a little from the road,

5

hides one of two Carmarthenshire chapels (the other is at Llansawel) which claim to be the oldest Wesleyan Meeting House in Wales. John Wesley's mother came from a Pembrokeshire family, the Whites of Henlann, of whom Griffith White served as High Sheriff in 1676.

Returning to Sarn Helen, I found that it soon became a footpath; but after a few hundred yards it rejoined the deviating lane. At Porth-y-rhyd a brook justified the place-name—'a haven beside the ford'—dominated by Careg-fawr or Great Gareg, more than a thousand feet among the larks and stonechats. At that point the lane once more deviated, and Sarn Helen became a track climbing steeply into solitude. Presently I met two farmers, speaking their native language. In Carmarthenshire alone more than 100,000 people speak Welsh; and some of the veterans speak nothing else, having no English other than 'telly' and 'Bingo' and 'hospitalization'. We got talking, leaning on a gate in May morning sunlight while the brook babbled blue, and the clouds sailed white, and hills stood green. We talked first of sheep because I had once dabbled in hill farming in those parts. Then from sheep the talk veered toward Wales, literally and metaphorically, looking the hills in the face, hearing the people voice-to-voice as they spoke with a dignity and a poetry not elsewhere to be found south of the Scottish Highlands: 'You are, Sir, an Englishman. A Sais or Saxon. And although we speak sometimes the same language, and inhabit always the same island, nevertheless you are to me as foreign as a Turk.' No offence was taken, because none was given. The man had merely recited the history of his people. Having done so, he raised his crook by way of salutation, and then disappeared over the brow of the hill, seeking his flock.

Alone once more, I considered some of the differences between the Roman and the British Empires. The former paid little attention to colour or creed, for Rome was a Babel of Europe and the East. In her sight all subject races were to be governed absolutely and without question. At no time in her history did Rome consider it possible that she would voluntarily relinquish her Empire. Britain, on the other hand, did pay attention to colour and creed. Unlike Rome, however, Britain did voluntarily relinquish her

Empire. Having trained the natives to govern themselves, she allowed the best of them to 'practise their lessons', as in India with its Indian premiers and all-Indian Cabinets. And, of course, Canada, New Zealand, and Australia had long ago weathered their Oedipus complex, and were well-content to remain self-governing members of the family.

While the two farmers went whistling among their sheep, Sarn Helen became a green track again, heading north-west, under the lee of Caio Forest and the distant Black Mountains, the remotest part of Wales. Wordsworth would have recollected those mountains in tranquillity:

> . . . the earth
> And common face of Nature spake to me
> Rememberable things . . .

Somewhere in this high solitude the Legionaries had camped while they hacked and hewed and paved Sarn Helen. First came the surveyors, seeking level ground. Having chosen their site, they marked the commander's tent, and alongside it the general headquarters, facing an open space where the standards were erected. Just as our own troops live sometimes 'under canvas', so the Legionaries lived 'under skins', their own tents being made of hide. Each tent—ten feet square with straw on the floor—held eight men. The Romans called it a *papilio* or butterfly because it could be folded like a chrysalis. An officer's tent, which stood on a box frame, was twice as big as the men's, and had a floor of fresh-cut turf. The commander's tent was bigger still. The entire camp was surrounded by a ditch, three feet wide and three feet deep, the earth forming a wall into which were driven wooden stakes, seven feet high. This barrier served to keep the soldiers in, and the natives (or their cattle) out. Who, I wondered, acted as interpreter on Sarn Helen? Was he a Roman who had learned a Celtic language? Ot was he a Celt who had learned Latin?

Now the green road began to descend. Many feet had strayed beyond its former straightness; many trees had formed an avenue so low that sometimes I needed to crouch; many autumns had set their pavement on the stones. Yet this was the undoubted course, loping down to Aber Bowlan, through a world of green and a sea of solitude. Suddenly I heard the sound of splashing, and having rounded a bend I saw the dog, fording a stream. A timber footbridge might have saved him the trouble, but it was half-hidden among bushes, and he many not have seen it. Another hundred yards brought me on to a lane that turned sharp left as though to align itself with Sarn Helen. A second hundred yards brought me uphill to Aber Bowlan, which appeared to consist of one barn and a letterbox in the hedge. Old acquaintance, however, had taught me that the hedge concealed a farm. Somewhere nearby I overheard the voice of Cymry, this time a woman's: 'It is the same at Lampeter. Always they are tuppence cheaper than Carmarthen. "How do you manage it?" I asked. And he just smiled and said nothing. They are deep, those shop-keepers. But honest, mind. I will say that for them. Years it is since I've had to haggle a bill.' Silence followed. Then: 'Are you listening, man?' A second silence; then plaintively: 'You might have told me you weren't there.'

The lane became so steep, both up and down, that I soon slackened pace. Very white was the blossom; the grass so green that it outshone the winter wheat, not that much grain was visible, for this was sheep country with a place for cattle. Despite the revolution in breeding, the ancient Welsh mountain sheep still survive, not greatly changed these past five hundred years, though their size has been increased by infusions of Lincoln, Leicester, and Down. The rams have curled horns and yellowish faces. The pure Welsh cattle are likewise an ancient breed, with local varieties. Most of them are black; a few, chocolate-coloured. Their long horns are yellow and flecked with crimson. But all I saw on the road to Caio were sheep and a few Herefords. Caio itself I saw twice; first its roofs above the brow of a hill; then, having climbed that hill, the church with shrubs sprouting from its tower.

Caio village is steep in every sense, being set on a hill among higher hills. The Post Office Store stands back from the street, rather like a small castle dominating Sarn Helen. On my last visit the church was locked, something that would have been unthinkable before the Reformation and for many years after it. Rome would have followed the history of Welsh religion with amused tolerance. Throughout the Middle Ages the Welsh had been pious sons of the Church; but during the seventeenth century they began to use dissent as a means of baiting the English, even as many of the English used it as a means of baiting not only 'the Church of England as by law established' but also the squire and his relations. The Baptists came first on the scene, with a chapel near Swansea in 1649; the Methodist Association did not appear until 1742. When Queen Victoria was born, the majority of Welsh folk went to church; when she died, the majority went to chapel. There are in Wales today thousands of people who accept Calvin's doctrine that some of us are predestined to enter Heaven, while others must descend into Hell; and nothing which we can do or say is able to alter our doom. But instead of evoking an 'eat, drink, and be merry' attitude, Calvinism frowns upon cakes and ale (and is not overfond of ballet and tobacco). That having been said, let truth show its fairer face as it has many times shone upon me in farms and cottages where the Bible was a very present comfort in the midst of sorrow, and a thankful *Te Deum* for the dawn of joy.

At the bottom of Caio hill the lane began to wriggle, and I was tempted to suppose that Sarn Helen had kept straight on, like the track which did keep straight on, into some trees and high contours. The Romans, however, knew what they were about, for the Afon Annell flows through the valley, and the wriggling lane was probably a relic of the Romans' choice of the best fording-place across it. The lane seemed to assent to this by straightening itself and advancing half a mile to the site of the gold mines at Dolaucothi, nowadays a National Trust property. These mines are unique in Britain. They had, of course, been worked before the occupation, but the Romans enlarged them and then managed them more efficiently. There were four major lodes, of varying sulphide and auriferous content, dipping south-west an an angle of thirty-five degrees, chiefly on the slopes of Allt Cumhenog and Allt Ogofau. Two aqueducts served the mines: one, the Cothi system, ran for seven miles; the other, the Annell system, ran for four miles. There were also extensive opencast workings. The mines had their own bath-house near the river at Pumpsaint. What happened to the mines when the Romans departed is uncertain, but we do know that the Normans nibbled at them. *Mirabile dictu* the mines were working until the 1930s.

A good deal is known about the Roman management of mines, chiefly from a lease, *Lex Metallae Vipascensis*, that was granted to a company at Vipasca in Spain, which states: 'The lessee of the baths, or his partner, shall entirely at his own charge and cost heat and keep open the baths . . . noon for men and women and from 1.00 p.m. to 8.00 p.m. for men subject to the Procurator in charge of Mines.' The baths were available to all who could pay the fee: 'each man half an *as* (about one farthing) and each woman an *as*.' Employees of the mines could bathe gratis: 'Freedmen and slaves of the Emperor who are in the Procurator's service shall be admitted free; so also shall miners and soldiers.' A delapidatory clause followed: 'The lessee, his partner or his agent, at the termination of the lease shall hand over in good and serviceable condition the equipment of the Baths and all things which have been assigned to him, except those that were subject to reasonable wear-and-tear.' The Romans set safety first: 'All mines shall be adequately propped and supported, and in place of old material the tenant shall substitute a new prop.' The mines were not allowed to be overworked: 'He who within the boundaries of the mining district . . . shall clean, crush, smelt, break up, separate or wash silt of copper dust, or dust from dumps, or shall undertake work of any kind whatsoever in the mines, shall declare within three days the number of slaves and freedmen whom he is sending to such work. . . .' Relations between management and men were untroubled by any kind of dispute: 'If an ore-thief be a slave the Procurator shall beat him and sell him, with the condition that he be kept perpetually in chains and shall not be allowed to live in a mining camp.'

It is no great way from the mines to the bath-house near the river at Pumpsaint. I walked there in about twenty minutes, uphill and down among woods, following a lane which, though it swerved now and then, was consciously straighter than most other lanes in the district. For the first time since Llandovery I heard a car, on the road to Lampeter. Soon Sarn Helen joined that road at Pumpsaint, so-named in memory of the *pimp* (five) who were born there: Ceitho, Celynen, Cwym, Cwyno, and Crynnoro. In 1941 part of the village, with 2,398 acres of farmland and woodland, was endowed and presented to the National Trust by Mr H. T. C. Lloyd-Johnes (his family had held the land since the reign of Henry VII), as a memorial to that family and especially to a gallant member of it, Lieutenant-General Sir James Hill-Johnes, V.C.

At the inn I recalled those faraway nights when I had driven down from Maesllan, a lonely farm, not for the sake of alcohol but in order to hear the Welsh language and the 'Welshy' English that passed to and fro above the firelight: 'Mr Peel, bach, they can never grow oats up at that old place' . . . 'There will be snow tonight, Rhys Morgan, deep as Wences, look you' . . . 'My da was a foremost shepherd of the world. Right away to Brecon they knew him' . . . 'He was a loose minister and did not last long. He smoked on the Sabbath. I was present when the Elders put him down. Go, they said, and like a lamb he went. But not to the slaughter, mind. Last I heard, he was holding his own meetings, two-bob-a-ticket, and after the Amen a silver collection in case you hadn't paid' . . . 'It's no use quoting Lloyd George, man. He's a Tory nowadays. Vote Labour, I say. They're the chaps will do away with all this money on defence. And then Hitler will see we don't mean any harm, so we'll have peace again.' At Pumpsaint in 1913 Edward Thomas wrote the dedication to his book about a pre-Roman road, *The Icknield Way*, wishing that his friend were 'with me inside the "Dolau Cothi Arms" at Pumpsaint, in Carmarthenshire'.

Beyond Pumpsaint the Lampeter road soon turned westward while Sarn Helen kept due north, soaring like a metalled arrow at 750 feet. Yet those heights were mere hillocks under the lee of Drygarn Fawr, away to the north-east, whose summit reached 2,000 feet. From every quarter the waters tumbled down: Afon

Fanafos, Afon Fanagoed, Afon Twrch, Afon Cothi, Afon Annell, Nant Clawdd, Nant Troyddyn. From his life among the open-air people of Britain, the nomadic George Borrow distilled a famous paean: 'There's night and day, brother, both sweet things; sun, moon, and stars, brother, all sweet things; there's likewise a wind on the heath, brother. Life is very sweet, brother. Who would wish to die?' Many would wish to die: those for whom life has become and must remain an agony; those who have outlived life. Nevertheless, Borrow was right; there is indeed night and day. Yet how few people now savour them neat. Without any moralizing or sentimentalizing, but stating only the facts, I marvelled at the Romans' hardihood and at our own lack of it. A man is now hailed as Spartan because, once a year, he climbs a mountain which his great-grandfather's shepherd climbed once a week, hatless with a hunk of bread and bacon. This loss of contact with the earth and elements is relatively new. When the Scottish Highlanders camped for the night they lay down in the snow, wrapped in their plaid; and one of them, who had scooped the snow into a pillow, was rebuked for his effeminacy. Writing in the year when I was born, Edward Thomas described a similar breed of men: 'where the Icknield Way through Buckinghamshire rounds the promontory Beacon of the Ivinghoe Hills I have seen men with sheep from Berkshire or Dorset journeying towards Dunstable, Royston, and the farms of Cambridgeshire and Suffolk.' Borrow himself, at the age of fifty, walked thirty miles in one day, covering the last five of them in one hour. Writing at a time when the Industrial Revolution was beginning to imprison England, old Thomas Bewick—lover of Dere Street and Northumberland—said in his *Memoir*: 'I have often thought, that not one-half of mankind knew anything of the beauty, the serenity, and the stillness of the summer mornings in the country, nor have ever witnessed the rising sun's shining forth upon a new day.' Not one-half, said Bewick: today he would need to reduce his vulgar fraction. Time alone will show whether Bewick and Borrow were mere praisers of times past, or whether mankind will once again learn to witness 'the rising sun's shining forth upon a new day', and share Bewick's belief that 'To be placed in the midst of a wood in the night, in whirlwinds of snow, while the tempest howled above my head, was sublimity itself. . . .'

At a hamlet called Farmers I passed yet another chapel, where I rested by the way, trying to decide what the Romans would have thought of Calvin. As with religion, so in philosophy, the Romans co-ordinated rather than created. The flights of Plato and the delvings of Aristotle were beyond them. Their excellence lay in administration, engineering, conquest, law. Even the names and natures of the two principal Roman philosophies, Epicureanism and Stoicism, have been so debased that the former now connotes a man who likes his spinach cooked just so; the latter, a man who faces his dentist without flinching. The Romans would have been appalled by such a caricature.

Epicureanism took its name from Epicurus (*c.* 270 B.C.) who believed that human destiny, like physical matter, is a vortex of events which men cannot control. In other words, life is a futile ordeal; and wisdom lies in escaping from as many as possible of its pains, into a quietism or freedom from anxiety. Such passiveness was alien to the average Roman. Both Vergil and Horace sampled it and then spat it out. Stoicism, on the other hand, suited the Roman temperament. Indeed, the Romans were Stoics long before news of that attitude had reached them. Less than a religion, not quite a metaphysic, Stoicism acknowledged a God or Life Force, but either kept silent or gave conflicting answers when asked to pronounce upon freewill and immortality. The wise man or *sapiens* is he who goes into action, even though his endeavours may perish and be of no avail. Epicurean and Stoic represent an ancient and universal dichotomy between hope and despair.

It is not difficult to take the wrong turning beyond Farmers. On my first of several journeys I did take it; partly because I had lost the map; partly because I was all the while gazing left and right at the mountains; and partly because, when the lane bisected itself, the right-hand fork, being the larger, seemed therefore to be the Sarn. After two hours' walking through wild loneliness, I returned to the fork, this time taking the correct or left-hand lane which forded Afon Twrch at the foot of a hill—climbed between trees so thick and banks so tall that an Exmoor man would have been only half-surprised to see a signpost saying East Buckland. How different, I thought, from the race-tracks and roundabout at Gailey on Watling Street. Not even the Romans chose to go straight up these contours. Like a wise old nag, they knew that the easiest is not always the shortest way to the summit. While I climbed, I tried to remember how many people I had passed since Llandovery. There were those two Welsh-speaking farmers, a landlord and one commercial traveller at Pumpsaint; and at Farmers a child learning to ride a bicycle. Wondering whether anyone else would appear before journey's end, I heard footsteps around the next bend, and presently an elderly man appeared who—to cut a pleasant story short—wore steel-rimmed spectacles, and had been a village schoolmaster, and was now greatly excited because a friend of his, a builder's clerk, had submitted to the Welsh National Eisteddfod a long poem about the Arthurian legend. Sometime after our brief encounter, I learned that the clerk had won the prize, being (to quote from a national newspaper) 'acclaimed with deafening applause from a huge crowd'. Is there on this planet another nation wherein a builder's clerk would be acclaimed by a huge crowd of his fellow countrymen because he had won the Bardic chair with a poem about mythology?

My Welsh friends tend to overlook the fact that it was an Englishman, King Henry II, who in 1176 convened the first truly national *eisteddfod* or festival of Welsh art, the happy issue whereof was a dead heat between the land of Gwynedd in North Wales (which won the crown for poetry) and the land of Morgan in South Wales (which won the crown for music). *The Gorsedd Beirdd Yns Prydan* or Session of the Bards of the British Isles is a relatively modern offshoot from that heritage. Its members are divided into three groups: the Ovates, whose green robes signify a rising novitiate; the Bards, whose blue robes signify an Augustan serenity; and the Druids, whose white robes signify truth. The Bards control entry into their order, reserving it for eminent scholars and artists. A second offshoot from Cymry are the Cornish and Breton *Gorseddau*; the latter sends a representative to the

Welsh sessions, bearing a half-sword of Brittany, which is joined
to the half-sword of Wales. The complete weapon was a gift
from the Bretons in 1899, as it were an olive-branch linking two
Celtic peoples. Scotland, Ireland, and the Isle of Man do not hold
their own *Gorseddau*, but they do send representatives to the Welsh
gatherings. Some people would like to abolish all such pageantry;
others still care to embalm the glories that have departed and to
infuse new life into those that remain.

By this time the road had toiled nearly a thousand feet above
the sea, having turned north and then north-west in order to
avoid a stream, Ffrwd Cynon. Steadily it climbed, ten feet every
hundred yards, passing only one cottage—a forester's—set back
from the lane. The trees grew sparse, the banks crouched down,
and suddenly the lane came into the open. Ahead stood the
mountains, and on the right lay the vista that had caused me to
exclaim: 'Nothing could be more beautiful than this.' Were I a
painter you should have that vista in all its colours; but the arts
observe each their own division of labour, and mine can do no
more than set black-and-white marks on the retina of your
imagination. Imagine, therefore, a precipice dipping into a valley
that sweeps up again to become mountains tinged by the blue
wand of distance. In that valley lay a white farmhouse, seeming
so small that it might have been a doll's house. You can judge
how deep it lay, because I set the glasses on it, and saw a tractor
starting off, yet the vehicle moved several yards before the sound
of its engine reached me; and even then the disturbance was so
slight that a westerly breeze would have whisked it away unheard.
The valley itself was long, stretching north and south, as far as
the eye could reach. Its northern end was crowned by the Black
Mountains, bald as Sibelius and no less stirring despite their
dumb immobility. Away to the east, Craigh Twrch was visibly
sheep-speckled. Bacon of *Verulamium* chose his favourite proverb
wisely: 'The vale best discovereth the hills.' Long ago, in *The
Black Book of Carmarthen*, a poet had set the scene in Welsh:

> Loud are the birds, green the groves,
> Ploughs in furrow, ox under the yoke.

The ox is a tractor nowadays, but the groves were still as green as the birds were loud; one glance at Craig Twrch would have told the poet where he stood. In such a valley, perhaps, lived Valeria, a young Roman lady whom they buried at Caerleon. When a modern Welsh poet, A. G. Prys-Jones, saw her tomb, he wished her well, both in the past and for the future:

> I like to think that long before you went
> Into the silence which knows no recall,
> You found new happiness which held you thrall
> Among these hills and vales of golden Gwent. . . .

My reluctance to leave the vista was lessened by the Sarn itself, an unfenced lane, which wheeled steeply out of sight, climbing the last yards to the summit and then disappearing over the top. Although I knew what lay beyond that top, the revelation lost none of the pleasure of its first unfolding long ago, for here was a Roman road in conventional guise, a full mile of it, straight as a breeze, through an outcrop of conifers. After the long ascent, it was good to stride at five miles an hour, with boots ringing, stick tapping, and the dog trotting to keep pace. Within ten minutes the conifers fell astern, inviting the dog to roam a bare hillside, yapping at rabbits. Far below, I sighted Nant Clywedog flowing to join Afon Teifi. Beyond them lay North Wales and the ghosts of the Druids. The English word 'Druid' was first recorded in 1563. It comes from a Celtic root, meaning a magician or soothsayer. Modern Irish and Gaelic spell it as *druidh* and *draoi*. In its earliest form the word was a plural noun, but had long since become singular when George Powell adapted Beaumont and Fletcher's *Tragedy of Boudicca*:

> Britons, strike home, revenge your country's wrongs!
> Fight and record yourselves in Druid's songs.

The Augustans, whose urbane scepticism could not conceal a relish for the romantic, believed that the Druids had built Stonehenge, hauling and ferrying the stones from Pembrokeshire. In 1702 Thomas Brown suggested that the Druids sought refuge on Anglesey because 'the Roman souldiers used the Druids but survily where ever they met them. ....' Brown was evidently drawing on the *Annals* of Tacitus and their account of the raiding of Anglesey by Suetonius Paulinus in A.D. 61, when the Druids were rounded up, and their sacred groves razed. Caesar's *Commentaries* described the priests as a highly organized body, exempt from taxation and military service. Both directly and obliquely they dominated politics, law and religion. A few years after the *Annals*, when Tacitus wrote his biography of Agricola, he made no mention of the Druids; they had ceased to exist as a body. Individually, however, they lingered on, for a fifth-century stone in the Isle of Man commemorates 'Doviado son of the Druid'. Forgetful of their own cruelties, Roman historians emphasized those of the Druids, notably the custom of offering live Britons as sacrifices. Certainly the sacrifices took place, but it seems probable that many of the victims—perhaps all—were convicted criminals. Unlike the average Roman, the Celts believed that death does not utterly erase a man for ever. Lucan, a late Latin writer, made a neat précis of the Druids' credo: 'The same spirit has a body again elsewhere, and death is but the midpoint of long life.' That is not the same as the Pythagorean immortality, on which it is sometimes said to be based; nor is it the same as Christian immortality; but it does lessen the Lucretian *angst*.

Untroubled by such problems, the dog had returned from his rovings, and now stood in the middle of Sarn Helen, having scented what I could not yet see ... another forester's cottage, just below the brow of the hill, snug as an eyrie near the roof of Carmarthenshire. The treeless tract gave way to saplings and veterans, upright despite the wind that flayed them. Had Puck been on this Pook-like hill, he might have met a centurion, full of long memories: 'I remember the place. It was just where the road begins to go down, except there was no road because we hadn't yet built one. Blazing hot, I remember, and my water-bottle empty as the quartermaster's coffers after pay day. Suddenly I heard a horse thudding the grass. There were only six of us at the time, so I shouted, "Watch out. It may be another of those bloody savages." I hoped it wasn't, though, because I'd sent a couple of scouts ahead. Well, we all relaxed when Rufus appeared.

A good man, Ruf. His grandfather was supposed to have been a prince or somesuch, sold as a slave when Caesar ... anyhow, Rufus reported he'd sighted a river. So I looked at my empty bottle and I yelled, "Come on, lads. We've struck water!" '

I turned, but the centurion had gone. Only a skylark spoke, and the song of a breeze. So I went on, loping downhill until the Sarn sent out a branch leftward to the Lampeter road at a small bridge across Nant Clywedog. The old way kept straight on, to a ford near Pont Glan-rhyd and thence into Llanfair Clydogau, a small and sleeping village astride the Afon Teifi, an outpost on the edge of the Black Mountains, the alpha and omega of Sarn Helen East. No one was about; no one at all. They were indoors, taking tea and scones and rich yellow butter and Mam's jam and, for all I knew, Da's ham and the pickles Aunt Gwyneth sent from Pontrhydfendigaid. Leaning on a venerable bridge, gazing into the water, and sometimes up at the cottages, or higher yet, to the tops of the hills ... thus engaged, wondering why the Romans had chosen to halt here ... inventing ways of joining Sarn Helen East with the nearest other Roman road ... in the midst of that busyness I heard the clip-clop of a horse coming down from the hill, turning left at the river, crossing the bridge, and at last drawing alongside. The rider was a farmer, his face rasped and rinsed by many weathers. He wore black boots, canvas gaiters, and a jacket so timelessly rained-on and lain-on and snowed-up and sun-struck that its original colour had been dyed the deepest dun. His cob was as grey as an old lag's stubble, and fatter than a mare in foal. A border collie trotted astern, her nose within six inches of the hind hooves. I would have liked to pass the time of day, to talk about sheep, to mention the Romans. But the rider decided otherwise. Raising his right forefinger, he rode on. Perhaps he was Aunt Gwyneth's brother, hastening home to her pickles. Certainly I had seen enough of him to know that he tallied with some words by a Latin poet: *Rusticus abnormis sapiens* ... (A countryman, one of Nature's philosophers ...). Those men I know, and to me they are Wales, for I have worked among them, living in many ways as they live, at a mountainous farm. Grievous are the faults of those men (grievous almost as other men's faults); ignorant men (if you set such store by books); uncultivated (until you quiz their fields); conservative (despite their politics); in a phrase, men who are much as all men were that lived by the sweat of their brow and by the inherited characteristic of good husbandry; men whom R. S. Thomas caught in a brace of lines:

> The dirt is under my cracked nails;
> The tale of my life is smirched with dung.

At *Viroconium*, you remember, Rome prevailed; and she will prevail again, elsewhere along her roads. But in the Welsh mountains she does not prevail. Unlike the men of London or of Manchester or of Birmingham, the men of Wales belong to the land of their fathers. They have the old tales by heart, and some of them are sung at the fireside, to the music of a Welsh harp. The Home Rulers who live among them are mere gnats, stinging the air of mountains whose faith and farms and language have preserved and will continue to breed the only form of national identity which can co-exist with a powerful neighbour in a commercial era. Leaning therefore on the bridge at Llanfair Clydogau, beside a road that the Romans had made, I remembered the prophecy which an old Welshman uttered to King Henry II: 'I am persuaded that no other race than this, and no other tongue than this of Wales, happen what may, shall answer in the great day of judgment for this little corner of the earth.'

Dere Street

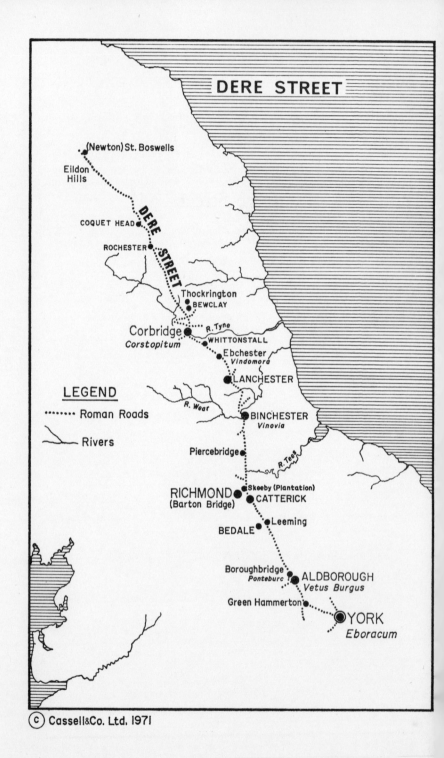

DERE STREET

(Newton) St. Boswells

Eildon
Hills

DERE STREET

COQUET HEAD

ROCHESTER

Thockrington
BEWCLAY

R. Tyne

Corbridge
Corstopitum

WHITTONSTALL

Ebchester
Vindomora

LANCHESTER

R. Wear

LEGEND

········· Roman Roads

〜〜〜 Rivers

BINCHESTER
Vinovia

Piercebridge

R. Tees

Skeeby (Plantation)

RICHMOND
(Barton Bridge)

CATTERICK

Leeming

BEDALE

Boroughbridge
Ponteburc

ALDBOROUGH
Vetus Burgus

Green Hammerton

YORK
Eboracum

© Cassell & Co. Ltd. 1971

6 Dere Street: York to Hadrian's Wall

EARLY one morning in the winter of 1829 a York choirboy went sliding on the ice beside the Minster. With a great 'Whoop' he sped, and with a loud 'Wow' he fell, flat on his back, seeing stars. There was nothing unusual in that. But behind those stars loomed something which made the boy blink. Smoke was rising from the Minster, black clouds of it, lolling on a windless air. Still rubbing the back of his head, the boy stood up, shouting, 'Auld Minster's afire!' There is a story—good, albeit unproven—that the Master of Choristers mistrusted the alarm without troubling to verify it: 'I'll give thee fire', he cried. 'Aye, and I'll give it in a place that shall make thee out-top the highest C, thou tell-tale, scaremongering rascal!'

But the lad was right. York Minster was indeed afire. York city, however, could not quench the flames unaided. So, a horseman galloped to Leeds, twenty-five miles away; and Leeds responded, cantering such engines as it possessed, which arrived in time to save the greater part of the Minster, though not before the choir stalls had been destroyed and much of the roof with them. 'An enemy', said York, 'hath done this.' He was therefore sought and arrested; by name Jonathan Martin, a crackpate with an imaginary grievance against the priesthood, who had hidden himself in the Minster overnight, making a bonfire of Bibles, Prayer Books, and cushions. Impenitent to the end, he expressed his regret that the cost of the damage amounted (in modern currency) to no more than £300,000. They found him guilty but insane. Had Archbishop de Gray not conceived York Minster, another man would have filled his place; but had Jonathan Martin destroyed York Minster, no man at all could have replaced it. To some people, therefore, the sliding choirboy and the burning Minster is the most important incident in the history of York.

The first Roman soldiers to reach York or *Eboracum* were

the right wing of the Ninth Legion, soon to be wiped out by the Brigantes, and never again to appear in the Army List. About the year 121 the Emperor Hadrian reached *Eboracum*, accompanied by the Sixth Legion. While reconnoitring for his Wall, Hadrian caused the figure of Britannia and her trident to appear on our coins, where she remained for a century and then once more arose like Venus from the water when Charles II restored her. Having ruled the waves for four hundred years, Britannia was scuttled by the British in the European Channel. The next Emperor at *Eboracum* was Severus, followed by Constantius and his son and heir, Constantine, who was proclaimed there. By that time the city had long since become the most important in Britain, chiefly because of its rôle as a spearhead against the Brigantes, the strongest tribe in the north, whose territory stretched from the Cumbrian coast to the Scottish border. And beyond Brigantia lay Caledonia, even more mysterious, even more intractable. A third threat came with the Saxon pirates, and was parried by a Roman fleet whose shallow-draught ships sailed down the Ouse from *Eboracum* to the North Sea.

Eboracum has vanished except for the lower part of the Multangular Tower and some sections of the Roman wall. Again one thinks of the poet who boasted that his songs were a monument more lasting than brass, or bronze, or stone: *Exegi monumentum aere perennius*.

At *Eboracum* the Romans did found such a monument, and it may outlive the Minster which enshrines it, because, as the Prayer Book says, the English Church is an heir of 'the Catholick and Apostolick Church' which, once persecuted, was in the end acknowledged, adopted, and organized under the Roman Empire. Throughout most of its life the Roman Church has been governed by an Italian Pope and a Curia of Italian Cardinals. Only one Englishman became Pope; a Hertfordshire peasant, Nicholas Breakspear, who in 1154 was elected as Adrian IV. The Church's most sublime contribution to secular affairs was her concept of the Two Swords, the Holy Roman Empire and the Holy Catholic Church, which should reign together, each within its own sphere. But men could not scale those heights. At Canossa the Pope humiliated the Emperor, requiring him to wait in the snow; at Canterbury the rôles were reversed when Becket was murdered in his own cathedral. Men had cause to fulminate against the medieval Church, the arrogance of some of her bishops, the lethargy of some of her monks, the knavery (as William Langland knew) of some of her friars,

> Preaching to the people for profit for themselves,
> Explaining the Gospel just as they liked,
> To get clothes for themselves. . . .

Against those shortcomings must be set the fact that, when the Empire fell, and the barbarians arose, the lamp of civilization was tended by the Church. Apart from the spiritual comfort which she brought to innumerable men and women, the Church rediscovered and studied the classics; recorded the history of her own times; sublimated some of the aggressiveness of mankind; succoured the poor, and from the same class educated the next generation of priests.

York contains many relics of its post-Roman greatness . . . the Hall of the Merchant Adventurers, slashed with splendid timbers . . . the ruins of St. Mary's Abbey and of the Archbishop's former Palace . . . St. William's raftered College . . . the King's Manor, calm as a cloister . . . Clifford's Tower, aloof on a knoll . . . Fishergate, Walmgate, Micklegate, Monkgate . . . the memory of Alcuin, founder of St. Peter's School, tutor to the sons of Charles the Great . . . and the Minster itself, nobly fronting the sunset.

The prosperity of modern York is represented by chocolate and machinery: the greatness of medieval York is represented by His Grace the Lord Archbishop of York, Primate of England. Many people suppose that the Primate of England is the Archbishop of Canterbury. They are mistaken. The Archbishop of Canterbury is the Primate of All England; a nice distinction, devised during the Middle Ages by Archbishop Islip of Canterbury and Archbishop Thoresby of York, whereby the latter yielded precedence to the former, but without losing more than a small portion of his 'face'. Today the Primate lives simply, because it is to his taste and because the expenses of his office consume most of its stipend. Medieval Primates, by contrast, were Princes of the Church, able to exert an authority greater than the sword.

Swords, however, were unsheathed when the Romans set out from *Eboracum*, building Dere Street, the great north road into Scotland. Their own scouts had forewarned them of mountains ahead, wide rivers, vast swamps, and natives who grew fiercer as the miles unfolded. The beginnings of Dere Street have been discovered near Micklegate and in Blossom Street; but the first three miles of the modern road meander among factories, offices, shunting yards, housing estates, and other signs of the industrial and technological revolutions. At a bridge across Foss Stream the Street at last identifies itself as a straight road through a county so large that it was long ago trisected into the thirdings or Ridings of North, East, West (excluding York, which stands apart).

About ten miles out of York the Street alters course from west-north-west to north-north-west, passing through Green Hammerton, whose best parts lie off the Street, notably a plum-coloured brick house with spick-and-span white paint. The landscape looks very much as it did when William Marshall described it to the Board of Agriculture in 1808: 'The surface of this extraordinary tract of country is cast in the true vale style. It is sufficiently diversified to give richness and beauty in its appearance; without any thing of steepness, to interrupt the plow and sithe; or any low flat lands that are liable to floods—unless, on the immediate banks of its brooks and rivers.' Eight years previously a land-surveyor, John Tuke, had described the climate which conditions the husbandry: 'of dryness throughout the year, and of peculiar coldness during the first half of it . . . frosts sometimes occur even in June, and greatly injure the crops . . .' It was much the same when the Romans laid the straight miles beyond Little Ouseburn and Ouse Gill Beck.

At Aldboro Moor the Street crosses a tributary of the Ure and then alters course several times, though for what reason I could not even guess, because no obstacle appeared to bar the way. On the outskirts of Aldborough I saw three farmhands playing a

game of cricket with bat and tennis ball. The sight reminded me
that in 1826 a Yorkshireman, Marsden, scored 227 against
Nottinghamshire. Yet Marsden came to the crease relatively late,
for in 1751 some of the Yorkshire towns had 'engaged professional
cricketers to amuse the populace and draw them away from cock-
fighting'. A loud 'Howzat' from the bowler led me to consider
the rôle of play in human affairs. Play helps a child to take life
seriously, and an adult to take it less seriously. There is, however,
a difference between playing games and watching them. The
Romans' mania for game-watching asserted itself during the war
against Carthage, when two patricians solemnized their father's
funeral by hiring swordsmen to fight a duel. The precedent took
root and spread like ivy. Within a few years the Roman mob was
demanding to have its own gladiators. Slaves were trained to kill
one another in public; prisoners-of-war and Christian martyrs
added their blood to the arena. In such Latin literature as I have
read I do not recall a single voice of protest. The silence was
caused partly by the spirit of the age and partly by the mob itself,
which would have started a revolution had anyone tried to deprive
it of its gladiators.

Aldborough, in the West Riding, was the *auld* or old fort, *Vetus
Burgus*, which the Romans called *Isurium*, seat of the governor of
Eboracum. To the Britons it was *Isurion*, the town on the River
Ure, capital of the Brigantes who had surrendered Caractacus to
Rome. Today Aldborough is a hillside village with a green, stocks,
and several ancient houses. The museum contains mosaics, coins,
jewellery, glassware, pottery.

At Boroughbridge the modern road zigzagged through the
town, formerly called *Ponteburc* or the bridge of the burgh of
Aldborough across the River Tut. Even the tireless Celia Fiennes
felt saddlesore when she reached Boroughbridge: 'and so I came
the 19 mile to Burrowbridge in Yorkshire, here I was most
sensible of the long Yorkshire miles, this North Rideing of that
County is much longer miles than the other parts. . . .' She may
have been correct because, although the statute mile had been
defined in 1593, many parts of the North Country were still
observing the old British mile of 2,428 yards. A similar complaint

was made in 1633, when mile posts were erected between Dover and Canterbury on Watling Street. The Mayor of Dover informed Sir Edward Dering, Lord-Lieutenant of Dover Castle, that postmen were increasing their charges because they had measured the road and found it longer than the alleged distance. Within a few months the Kentish mile was officially recognized as being longer than the statute mile. So, after all, there was some truth in the old jingle:

> Essex stiles, Kentish miles, and Norfolk wiles
> Many a man beguiles. . . .

During the eighteenth century, when the turnpike system was introduced, the mile posts achieved a new importance, each mile of road being maintained by a workman whose hat, shovel, and pickaxe were stamped with the number of his own sector. The turnpike surveyors awarded prizes for the best-kept miles of road. As for Miss Fiennes, her arrival in Boroughbridge coincided with polling day, a spectacle which did not impress the grand-daughter of the first Lord Saye and Sele: 'here I met with the clutter of the chooseing Parliament men. . . .'

Modern Boroughbridge, I found, was bedevilled by the A1 and its ceaseless thunder of traffic. The best parts of the little town lay farthest from the storm. In a battle near Boroughbridge King Edward II defeated those of the nobility who objected to his degenerate favourite, Piers Gaveston. In Marlowe's play, *Edward II*, the Duke of Lancaster warns the King:

> Your grace doth well to place him by your side,
> For nowhere else the new earl is so safe.

To the north of Boroughbridge the course of Dere Street could be traced intermittently among fields, but the task incurred trespass, and was not well-rewarded. Thereafter, the Street lay beneath a dual carriageway *en route* for the North Riding, which covers 2,218 square miles and has a population of nearly half a million, one quarter of whom live in or near to Middlesborough, a steel town on the River Tees. This Riding contains Mickle Fell, the summit of Yorkshire, 2,591 feet above the sea.

Near Leeming I escaped from the traffic in order to visit Bedale, a town of dignity and charm. The main street was flanked by cobbled pavements and venerable brick houses. They say that the church tower was built as a refuge from the marauding Scots. Defoe felt in two minds about Bedale. Having dismissed the beauty of its buildings as 'nothing that comes within the compass of my enquiry', he added that the town 'is full of jockeys, that is to say, dealers in horses, and breeders of horses, and the breeds of their horses in this and the next country [county] are so well known, that tho' they do not preserve the pedigree of their horses for a succession of ages, as they say they do in Arabia and Barbary, yet they christen their stallions here, and know them, and will advance the price of a horse according to the reputation of the horse he came of.' The men of the North Country do not waste their words. Sometimes, indeed, their silence reaps a dividend that is not always justified, as Coleridge discovered: 'Silence does not always mark wisdom. I was at dinner, some time ago, in the company of a man, who listened to me and said nothing for a long time; but he nodded his head, and I thought him intelligent. At length, towards the end of the dinner, some apple dumplings were placed on the table, and my man had no sooner seen them, than he burst forth with: "Them's the jockies for me!" '

Having returned to the traffic, I overheard Defoe again: 'This Roman way is plain to be seen, and is now called Leeming Lane, from Leeming Chapel, a village which it goes through.' Leeming took its own name from the Old English *leoma*, meaning 'brightness', a reference to the beck on which it stands. Here the Street became a minor road while the A1 raced north-westward. The Romans made two sharp bends at Leeming, probably in order to strike dry land above the beck. For nearly five miles the Street went its own way quietly until, at Thoroughway House, the A1 reappeared, and once more the Street sank under the weight of traffic. Yet it continued, with scarcely a perceptible curve, for six miles or more, through farmland as rich as any in Yorkshire.

Just beyond Holtby Grange I followed a footpath through fields. After about ten minutes I sighted a small lake where I rested, hearing the birds, smelling the hay, watching the ducks.

Not for the first time in my life I remembered Shakespeare's statement of fact: 'Britain is a world by itself.'

Until quite recent times every English county was a world by itself, having its own accent, its own patois, its own patriotism. Men belonged to Hampshire or Somerset or Norfolk. They lived there and worked there and died there. The love which they felt, and the hostility which they affected were enshrined in jingles:

> Cheshire for men,
> Berkshire for dogs,
> Bedfordshire for naked flesh,
> And Lincolnshire for hogs.

Some of those jingles contained reason as well as rhyme:

> Derbyshire for lead,
> Devonshire for tin,
> Wiltshire for hunting plains,
> And Middlesex for sin.

At Catterick I got lost; not from a lack of signposts, but because I wished to avoid the A1 and to discover the course of Dere Street. Five people assured me that Dere Street *was* the A1; six people had never heard of Dere Street; and all eleven of them were bewildered because I did not seek 'the quickest way' to wherever it was I wished to go. Finally, a clergyman directed me to the Manor House, and there I found a footpath that followed the Romans for more than a mile, skirting a race-course near the River Swale. But the path was wedged between two main roads that had crushed *Cataractonium*, the town near a cataract on the Swale. As it was 2,000 years ago, so it is today, a military camp, though now amorphous and without charm. One of the seventeenth-century lords of the manor was Richard Braithwaite, author of a verse which would have pleased Richard Hooker of Bishopsbourne:

> To Banbury came I, O profane one,
> Where I met a Puritane one
> Hanging of his cat on Monday
> For killing of a mouse on Sunday.

By this time I had become as impatient with the seventy-mile-an-hourers as they with my thirty-five-miles-an-hour. Nor was I consoled by the knowledge that the Romans were plagued by heavy traffic. When Julius became Caesar he restricted both the volume and the size of traffic passing through Rome. In 1618 the English were still trying to solve a similar problem, for in that year the King issued a proclamation that no four-wheeled wagon was to have more than five horses. In 1622 the Justices of Hertfordshire tried unsuccessfully to prohibit all heavily-laden four-wheeled wagons because they carved ruts. In 1662 an Act required certain vehicles to reduce the width of their iron tyres to four inches. In 1741 no vehicle was allowed to carry more than three tons. In 1835 a Highways Act removed all such restrictions because Macadam was building roads that withstood any wheels. I solved my own traffic problems by escaping from it along a lane which led to a little wood, called Skeeby Plantation, where once again I heard the birds, but was dismayed to see that several elm trees in the district were dying of Dutch-elm disease, a fungoid carried by beetles which breed under the bark of dying elms. Although summer was still young, the leaves of the trees were as yellow as October. Fungus being a Latin word, I asked myself what an educated Roman would have said to the question 'Why learn Latin?' Probably he would have replied: 'The fact that you have asked such a question shows that you are incapable of understanding even the simplest answer to it.' Knowledge of a foreign language sharpens the skill with which a man uses his own. At the very least it enables him to say things which his own language either cannot say at all or must paraphrase at greater length. *Ça m'est égal* is shorter and more euphonious than 'It's all the same to me'. Or there is 'So passes the glory of the world': nearly twice as long as, and without the duosyllabic finality of, *Sic transit gloria mundi*. Some people affirm that it is a waste of time to learn a language whose literature was long ago translated into English. But to translate means to carry over; and no language ever will carry over the whole of another. Even when it is wielded by a master, one language seldom offers a consistently satisfying version of another; in poetry, never. It is possible to translate the meaning, but not the music, of *flammantia moenia mundi* (the flaming ramparts of the world).

When Francis Bacon of *Verulamium* dedicated his essays to the Duke of Buckingham, he remarked: 'I thought it therefore agreeable, in my Affection, and Obligation to your Grace, to prefix your Name before them, both in English, and in Latine. For I doe conceive, that the Latine Volume of them, (being in the Universall Language) may last, as long as Bookes last.' Latin still is a 'Universall Language' throughout the worlds of medicine and law. If you say 'primrose' to a Chinese botanist it is improbable that he will understand; but if you say '*Primula vulgaris*' he will probably understand at once. So is it with the herbs that heal; their Latin names are known to every doctor and pharmacist throughout the world. So also in law, for British barristers and solicitors must be passable Latinists. For example, that most English of Latin legal phrases—*Habeas corpus*—may be translated as 'Possession of the body or person'.

I was about to return to the battle when I suddenly remembered that Skeeby Plantation was only a few minutes' drive from Richmond, so thither I went, at twenty-five miles an hour, a speed that would have appalled Celia Fiennes when she jog-trotted to Richmond three centuries ago. She was not impressed by what she saw: 'I must say it looks like a sad shatter'd town and fallen much to decay and like a disregarded place.' Things have changed since then. Richmond is a prosperous town, dominated by its Norman castle, and enlivened by a cobbled market place which caused Miss Fiennes to complain 'the streets are like rocks. . . .' While walking beside the castle walls, overlooking the River Swale far below, she watched the fishermen: 'The water falls over rocks with great force which is convenient for catching Salmon by spears when they leap over those bayes.' The church of the Holy Trinity, in the market place, is truly Erastian because part of it belongs to the Corporation, and another part to a café (why do we use the French word for coffee as our word for teashop?).

Returning to the A1, I drove stolidly to Scotch Corner, a screeching modern roundabout, most unlike the Roman crossing with its road to Penrith. The A1 meanwhile became a motorway, but Dere Street became a country road, straight as the straightest in Britain. Before following it, however, I ventured a mile or so along the motorway because I had been advised to admire the bridge at Barton, half a mile to the east. The motorway sign-boards, showing pictures of spoons and spanners and forks, recalled some words from *The Decline and Fall*: 'Among savage nations the want of letters is imperfectly supplied by visible signs.' I found Barton bridge—a pretty old piece across Five Hills Beck—and then I returned to Dere Street, spanking along at fifty miles an hour, which meant that I reached Piercebridge in about seven minutes, having crossed the River Tees on the edge of that village, and so entered County Durham, which began as a diocese and ended as a County Palatine (*palatinium*, a word used to describe a senior judicial officer of the Merovingian kings). Because the capital is almost islanded by the River Wear, it was called Durham or the island with a hill.

Piercebridge was the bridge above *persh* or osiers beside the Tees. I found it a pleasant village and unmistakably Durham, with squat houses deployed around a green that had been the centre of a Roman fort. Parts of a bath-house and of an aqueduct were discovered nearby. At the Post Office they told me that White Cross, a mile to the west, was so named because a Roman altar had been found there. The deep countryside made it difficult to believe that nearly half of County Durham's thousand square miles were exploited as a coalfield; that the rural parts of the county were as ruggedly impressive as any in England; and that the simple act of crossing a river could as it were create a new land. The last fact particularly impressed me because I had just observed it. On the Yorkshire side of the Tees I was given good-day by a man who spoke the language of *Wuthering Heights* (his exact words were: 'Reet soony weather, maister'); but having crossed the river, I overheard a different tone of voice.

For another eight miles the Street held an unerring course until it reached Brusselton, which used to be a village, but was now a colliery town. There the modern road forsook the Roman, rejoin-ing it as the main street through Bishop Auckland, where, in the year 1300, Bishop Bek converted a Norman manor house into a castle which Cromwell sold to Sir Arthur Haselrigg, who destroyed much of it in order to use the stones for a new mansion. Meanwhile, finding myself jammed in the traffic, I switched off the engine, and took a deeper view of my position. There was, I thought, an affinity between County Durham and Dere Street because each had formed part of a defensive system against the Scots; but whereas the Roman conquest built a wall, the Norman Conquest established a county whose bishop enjoyed powers which William the Conqueror withheld from all save a handful of trusted servants. Alternate bishops of Durham signed their names in Latin and in Norman-French; one bishop being *Dunelm*, his successor *Dunesm*, and the next successor *Dunelm*. Under William's successors, Durham became the greatest of all Counties Palatine. Its prince-bishops maintained their own army, their own mint, and their own courts wherein crimes were pardoned without reference to the King. The medieval jurist, Bracton, described those courts as 'regal in their power in all things'. In 1837 the Court of Pleas of Durham was annexed to the High Court of Justice in London; but the Durham Court of Chancery still sits on behalf of the Crown.

Suddenly the crocodile wagged its tail, and we proceeded on our way, following a road that had been built for carts and horses by

> Men from Asia, Germany, Spain,
> Marching along in sun and rain,
> (Forests to fell and fens to drain
> And Britons to tame and drill).

The next lap of the journey became a hide-and-seek among back streets and beside the River Wear, tracking Dere Street, sometimes as an *agger*, sometimes as the line of an alley. The course lay more or less north, passing Binchester, the site of a Roman hill camp, *Vinovia*, which, when it decayed, may have been used as a cattle shed (Old English *binn* or manger). A hypocaust was found under the bath-house, near an altar that had been erected to Jupiter by Pomponius Donatus, who probably commanded the fort. Dere Street must have headed north-west from Binchester, but no trace of it remained. At Hanwick they assured me that sixty years ago the Street could have been followed as a track; but I found only a modern road which may have covered the Street. This I followed into Willington, a colliery town. After persistent enquiry I discovered Watling Terrace, a misnomer that recalled my fellow-traveller in Kent. The Terrace seemed to mark the course of the Street. Time, however, was not the same as Eternity, so I returned to the car, following minor roads north-west.

At Ragpath Wood I struck rich when a footpath became a track into a hamlet called Quebec. That, too, I followed awhile, before driving north again, having taken a wrong turning which led to the Click 'em Inn where an old collier reported that Dere Street lay beneath the modern road to Lanchester, passing the site of *Longovisium*: 'And when my father was a bairn, yon Roman road were nobbut a track o' stanes.' Lanchester itself was the long *ceaster* or Roman fort, measuring about 180 yards by 140. A series of aqueducts watered the fort, but most of its masonry had been used to build or to repair neighbouring houses and the church tower. In 1283 Bishop Bek of Durham made the church into a collegiate church. Two recesses in the chancel accommodated the vicars choral who were required to 'read and sing aloud, distinctly, with full voice, and without skipping or cutting their words, making good pause in the middle of each verse, beginning and ending all together, not protracting or drawing the last syllable too long. . . .' Practice may have perfected the song, but some of the singers remained below par, because the statutes warned them against uttering 'any strange, variable, profane, or dishonest speeches . . . neither yet laughing, gleeing, staring, nor casting vagabond eyes toward the people remaining in the same church'. In 1804 a remarkable young man arrived at Lanchester, as master of the village school. He was John Hodgson, son of a Westmorland mason. Having taken holy orders, Hodgson served as curate of two chapelries near Lanchester. His *Poems Written at Lanchester* were published in 1807, with woodcuts by a self-taught artist, Thomas Bewick. Hodgson's poem *Longovicum, a Vision* is poor verse, but contains some useful historical notes. In 1833 Hodgson was translated to Northumberland, where he completed his lifework as the historian of that county. He had already made the first scholarly excavation of Hadrian's Wall at Housesteads. We shall meet him again, beyond that Wall.

Not for the first time since Dover I suddenly became impatient. The scene was dour, dreary. The road entered Leadgate, a town heavily scarred by slag heaps, drab houses and second-hand car marts. At Ebchester my impatience reached its zenith. There, I knew, lay the parting of the ways; the end of ugliness, the beginning of beauty. The Romans built a small fort at Ebchester, called *Vindomora*; when they left, the place was named after its chieftain, Ebbe. As at Lanchester, so at Ebchester, the Norman church was built partly with stones from the Roman fort. I made a short detour to Hamsterley Hall, a blend of medieval and eighteenth-century Gothic, rebuilt in 1769 by Henry, son of Sir John Swinburne of Capheaton Hall in Northumberland, ancestor of the poet. When Henry Swinburne died, Hamsterley Hall was bought by Anthony Surtees, a Durham landowner, whose son, Robert Smith Surtees, spent half a century there, writing of a sporting grocer, John Jorrocks, who declared: 'All time is lost wot is not spent in ' 'unting.' Surtees coined some amusing aphorisms: 'There may be said to be three sorts of lawyers, able, unable, and lamentable' . . . 'She used to say that the only thing that reconciled her to being a woman was that she could not by any possibility have to marry one' . . . 'Whoever talked o' the winter of our discontent talked like an insane man, and no sportsman. Summer is the season of our misery.' A famous pen was succeeded at Hamsterley Hall by a famous sword, in the person of Field-Marshal Viscount Gort, V.C., eldest son of the fifth Viscount Gort and of Eleanor, youngest daughter of R. S. Surtees. The Legions would have dipped their standards in salute had they met the veterans of two world wars, the Durham Light Infantry, marching to their air *The Light Barque*.

At Ebchester the Street reached a narrow bridge over the River Derwent, a sylvan crossing, marred by some unsightly shacks. Once more a river marked a county border. I was now in Northumberland, the land north of the Humber. Industry lay astern. Ahead stretched nearly a million acres of fresh air, sometimes gentle, more often wild. Of this, his native county, G. M.

Watling Street. The Roman lighthouse alongside a Saxon church in Dover.

Watling Street. The old smithy at Bishopsbourne.

Watling Street. The City Gate at Canterbury.

Watling Street. A section of the Roman wall at St. Albans.

Watling Street. Reconstructed remains of the Roman monument at High Cross.

Watling Street. Remains of the Roman Baths at Wroxeter.

Above. *Llandovery Castle (Sarn Helen East)*.

Above right. 1969 *award to Cilycwm*.

Below right. *Street in Cilycwm*.

The Sarn Helen East road.

Sarn Helen East. Crossing the ford, Aber Bowlan.

Part of the Roman road, Sarn Helen East.

Sarn Helen East. The village of Llanfair Clydogau.

Dere Street. Part of Hadrian's Wall.

Dere Street, near journey's end.

Peddars Way. A windmill at Ixworth.

Forestry Commission land near the Peddars Way, Swaffham.

Above. *Peddars Way. Statue of Tom Paine in Thetford.*

Above right. *Peddars Way. Castle Acre Priory.*

Below right. *Peddars Way. Blakeney.*

Peddars Way. Gates on the Sandringham estate.

Holme-next-the-Sea, the end of the Peddars Way.

Newark Castle on the Foss Way.

Windwhistle Hill on the Foss Way.

Above. *Near Jackaments Bottom on the Foss Way.*

Above left. *Brinklow on the Foss Way.*

Below left. *Lower Slaughter, Foss Way.*

Chedworth Roman villa on the Foss Way.

Ashe House, Musbury, on the Foss Way (home of the Churchills).

Trevelyan wrote: 'Northumberland throws over us, not a melancholy, but a meditative spell.' Under that spell the Street confirmed the vision of A. G. Prys-Jones:

> Cohorts, cohorts with breasts of flame,
> (Straight as an arrow-flight over the hill)
> This is the way the Romans came
> To build and govern, to sow and till. . . .

Through Whittonstall it went, with woods on either side, passing the site of a small Roman fort near Apperly Dene. There the road veered away while the Street held its course as a green track. Rejoining the road, Dere Street heard the voice of Northumberland at Broomhaugh, the broom-covered *haugh* or *halh*, meaning in this instance 'alluvial land beside a river'. Sure enough, the Street turned westward, following the River Tyne at Riding Mill, a *ryding* or clearing, which suggested that the Roman sawyers worked hard. Riding Mill was an attractive waterside place with some handsome old houses and a modernized inn, The Wellington, built in 1660.

Across the river lay Corbridge, the Roman fort of *Corstopitum*, in a setting which Swinburne evoked from his poem, *A Jacobite's Exile*:

> O lordly flows the Loire and Seine
> And loud the dark Durance,
> But bonnier shine the braes of Tyne
> Than a' the fields of France.

Corbridge spoke for itself so succinctly that I took the words from a signboard on its own bridge: 'Corbridge The Scene of Stormy Events in the past. In 796 A.D. Ethelred, King of Northumbria, was slain here. In 918 King Ragnal, the Dane, defeated the English and Scots Armies here. In 1138 King David I (Scotland) occupied the town. In 1201 it was searched by King John and three times burnt—in 1296 by Wallace; in 1312 by Robert Bruce; and in 1346 by David II of Scotland. The present bridge—built in 1674—was the only Tyne bridge to survive the floods in 1771. A Saxon and Roman Town. Later in medieval days

7

a town of importance, sending two burgesses to the first English Parliaments in the 13th century. *Corstopitum* (Corchester) Roman Town. About 80–400 A.D. Extensive remains. Agricola's Road. York to the North-east. Dere Street. St Andrews: Surviving church of the original four: 7th century. Saxon Tower. Pele Towers Dilston and Aydon Castles and the Roman Wall of Hadrian are nearby.' Corbridge remains unspoiled. Even its contemporary bungalows have been banished to the perimeter, leaving the gracious stone houses in as much peace as any town can expect from any main road. The principal street is high, wide, handsome; residential rather than commercial; refreshed by the sight of the river flowing past.

The site of *Corstopitum*, covering about twenty-two acres, stood half a mile to the west of Corbridge. Built as a cavalry post by Agricola in A.D. 79, enlarged seven years later to accommodate 500 horsemen and 1,000 infantrymen, the fort was abandoned when Hadrian's Wall overshadowed it. About the year 140 the Second Legion built a new and larger fort, which was reconstructed sixty years later by L. Alferius Senecio. The present site revealed the outline of the barracks, granaries, store-house, hospital, and temples. In the museum I saw Roman chisels, soldering irons, handcuffs, the mess-tin of a legionary, a child's tea-set, a baby's feeding bottle. As at *Viroconium*, Rome spoke *superbus gravisque*: 'For the Emperors and Caesars Marcus Aurelius Antonius Augustus, tribune for the seventeenth time, consul for the third time, and Lucius Aurelius Verus Augustus, conqueror of Armenia, tribune for the third time. A detachment of the XX Legion Valeria Victrix made [this building] under the direction of Sextus Calpurnia Agricola, praetorian legate of the emperors.' Overlooking the river was the site of a *mansio* or large house, 150 feet long and nearly 70 feet wide, with a terrace and a bathroom. This may have been a hostel for couriers of the Imperial post.

Corbridge folk referred to Dere Street as 'Watling Street' despite the sign on their bridge. Its course was marked by an *agger* near the school, then by a grass ridge that met a lane coming down from Sandhoe and the modern road coming up from Corbridge. Thereafter both road and ridge followed the same course

to Stagshaw Bank, with the blue Tyne astern and the grey Wall
ahead.

> This is the way the Romans came,
> Steadily steadily over the hill,
> This is the way the Romans came
> (And if you listen you'll hear them still). . . .

They were coming to Hadrian's Wall, the finest Roman building
in Britain, draped like a switchback over the hills. When William
Camden saw it, he held his breath and then broke into song:
'Verily I have seen the tract of it over the high pitches and
steep descent of the hills, wonderfully rising and falling. . . .'
One old cottager showed him a Roman altar stone; he found a
second altar in a place 'where the women beat their buck [linen] on
it'. The fort at Busy Gap he never did see, because it was occupied
by robbers (as a domestic panacea the *Pax Britannica* fell short of
Pax Romana). Defoe sampled the Wall: 'I was greatly tempted
here to trace the famous Picts Wall . . . and I did go to see several
places in the fields thro' which it passed, where I saw the remains
of it. . . .'

The story of Hadrian's Wall is part of the story of Rome's
conquest of North Britain, which began in earnest about A.D. 71
when Petilius Cerialis, Governor of Britain, moved the Ninth
Legion from Lincoln to York, made contact with the Twentieth
Legion at Chester, and from those two bases proceeded to subdue
the natives. In the year 121 Britain was visited by Hadrian, who
ordered his Imperial Legate, Aulius Plautius Nepos, to build a
wall, not simply as a barrier (Britons were allowed to pass through
the Wall northward and southward), but rather as a safeguard
against the Picts. Stretching from Wallsend-on-Tyne to Bowness-
on-Solway, the Wall was seventy-three miles long. In its heyday
the highest parts stood twenty feet above the ground. Seventeen
forts were built along the Wall, of which the largest were garrisoned either by a thousand infantrymen or by five hundred
horsemen. Each fort carried a year's supply of grain, which the
natives were required to provide as tribute. Each fort had its
shrines, baths, and quarters for families and servants. The forts

were interspersed with mile-castles, manned by fifty soldiers apiece; and between the mile-castles were two turrets or look-out posts, manned by four soldiers apiece. The northern face of the Wall was defended by a ditch, twenty-seven feet wide and nine feet deep; the southern face, by a ditch (*vallum*) set between two mounds of earth. Parallel with the *vallum* a military road linked the turrets, mile-castles, and forts. In Camden's day the road was very much a has-been: 'between the wall and the ditches', he reported, 'hath ther bene a fair way paved all along the Wall.' In 1751 the government ordered a turnpike road to be built within sight of the Wall, from Hexham to Chollerford. Local contractors thereupon quarried the Wall, and sold it as rubble to the government. The history of the Wall is as wild as its situation. In 197 the Picts breached it. In 296 they breached it again, the garrison having been withdrawn. In 396 the Wall was breached for a third time, and once more repaired. These repeated withdrawals were symptoms of decline and fall. Hitherto the command of a Legion had been confined to officers of senatorial rank, but during the third century the army was reinforced by hordes of barbarians. Ultimately the entire army became barbarized, officered by mercenaries who not only deserted their post but also took the troops with them. Despite the chaos, Hadrian's Wall continued to be manned until the end of the fourth century. We do not know when nor from what sector the last Roman soldier withdrew.

From time immemorial the local people believed that the Romans had planted herbs near the Wall, to heal their wounds. Camden noted that in summertime the Scottish physicians flocked thither, gathering simples and herbs. Even so, the Romans lagged far behind the Greeks in their understanding and practice of medicine. Cato boasted that the earliest Romans were healthy without doctors. They had need to be, for their doctors relied partly on natural recuperation and partly on superstition (victims of a dislocated limb were advised to chant a jingle, *ista pista sista*). The first Latin medical textbook—*De re medica* by Celso—did not appear until *c.* A.D. 31, and was probably a translation from the Greek; it described *inter alia* an operation to remove infected tonsils. The Romans could hardly protest that they lacked facilities for anatomical research. Their arenas alone would have delighted Burke and his body-snatchers. Every Legion had its physician or *medicus legionis*, an N.C.O. who was exempt from guard duty, combat duty and manual labour. A relief on Trajan's column shows an advance dressing station and the surgeon bandaging a soldier's leg. In medical organization, however, the Romans excelled. During the early years of the Republic a wounded soldier had to be sent home for treatment; but as the rôle of the army grew more important, so hospitals were built at major strategic posts, with wards, airy corridors, and special sanitation. When the medieval Church built hospitals for her own sick and outcast, she learned much from the *valetudinaria* or Roman military hospitals.

Dere Street crossed the line of the Wall at Portgate between the sites of a turret and a mile-castle, where an eighteenth-century antiquary, the Reverend J. Horsley, traced the remains of a gate. Northward of that gate, as the Romans discovered, the land grew wilder with every mile; the climate harsher; the natives fiercer; the comforts fewer; the Wall fainter. *Factum abiit; monumenta manent*: The deed has gone; the memorials thereof remain.

7 Dere Street: Hadrian's Wall to Newstead

'EVERY man has his own preferences.' So said the playwright Terence. My own preferences unfolded as Dere Street climbed toward Bewclay and ahead lay the Cheviots. In Northumberland you can walk for days or drive for hours, knowing that the air will be always fresh, the land fertile, the stillness deep. In Northumberland the last and best relics of feudalism still linger, for many of the villages and several of the small towns lie within a large estate. Their neatness and contentment are self-evident. In order to verify them you need only cross the border into Durham or Cumberland where relatively few great landowners reside *in loco parentis* as guardians of their people. Having crossed, you will observe how swiftly the neatness fades, and with it the awareness of belonging to a community that is cared for by one who loves it, lives in it, and understands it. Horace was just such a landowner, dedicated to his well-beloved Tivoli:

ille terrarum mihi praeter omnis
angulus ridet. . . .

(That corner of the world smiles on me more sweetly than do all the others. . . .)

At Bewclay the contours steadied themselves, and for three miles the Street steered west-north-west through country which grew wilder and lonelier. A southron might have said that the land was bare heath, yet its herbage sustained a famous breed of sheep, the Cheviot, so finely proportioned that some breeders rate them the handsomest of all. Cheviots can thrive on the scantiest fare and the bitterest climate. They used to produce the best mutton in Britain. Their fleece founded and still sustains the Lowland tweed industry. I counted hundreds of them grazing near Effing Burn as it flowed westward into the village of Chollerton, where a war memorial invited me to imagine what my life would have been like if my countrymen and countrywomen had refused to defend themselves:

> Ye that live on in English pastures green,
> Remember us, and think what might have been.

North of Chollerton the Street entered a world older than the Romans', the sites and stones of the earliest builders in North Tynedale. In the midst of those monuments the road turned east, crossed a burn, then turned west again; but the Street kept on, marked by an intermittent *agger* through the fields. After perhaps half a mile the road resumed its original alignment, passing several reservoirs: Hallington Reservoir, Sweethope Loughs, Little Swinburn Reservoir (the poet's home, Capheaton, stood seven miles to the west), and Colt Crags Reservoir, which lay alongside the Street, flashing like a kingfisher among conifers. And there an adventure befell me, beginning when I noticed a lane westward into the hills. During long sojourns in the Border country I had many times noticed the lane, always wishing to follow it, always sighing because a man's life contained more lanes than years. On this occasion I did follow it, into a realm so lonely that the sight of a bus ticket lying by the way was as startling as the sight of a corkscrew lying on the moon. Presently I reached a gate, and passed through, and skirted Colt Crags Reservoir in utter stillness except for one skylark and the perennial breeze. On and on went the lane, twisting and turning—lonelier, loftier, lovelier—until it reached a knoll which, like a telescope, scanned the four quarters of the globe. Everywhere lay green hills and over them a sky bluer than the waters. And at that moment I said aloud 'Good heavens' because I had sighted a church alone on another knoll; one church in all that solitude; and never a house within sight. Now it is part of my business to acquaint myself with the places which I explore; but that place I had not intended to explore; therefore I knew nothing of it except the name, Thockrington. I was about to walk to the church, when I noticed a clump of trees and what might have been a chimney. So I made toward it, and discovered one farmhouse and one cottage alone in unoccupied immensity. Since our forefathers did not build a church where none was needed, the mystery deepened. I went back, climbed the knoll, entered the church. Most English churches contain news of everything except themselves. Thockrington church showed a more proper pride because it contained picture postcards of itself, and on the back of them an autobiography, stating that it had been built in 1100 by a Norman family, the Umfravilles; that it was forfeit to the Archbishop of York as recompense for damage done to His Grace's property by Richard Umfraville; that after 625 years the church was restored to the diocese of Durham; and that in 1505 six men of the parish were required to 'fynd an able prest on ther proper coste and expenses . . . to celebrate divine service . . . and buyld a sufficient stone hus . . . for the defence of the preste and ye fermer and their guddes . . . agenst the Scottes . . .' The last sentence of the autobiography explained why Thockrington church lacked a village: 'The old village lay to the north of the church. In 1847 a returning sailor brought cholera and the population was wiped out. It was never rebuilt.'

Among the six Thockrington men who had provided 'a sufficient stone hus' were three named Shafto, a family first mentioned *c.* 1240. Five centuries later the family were living at Bavington Hall, a few miles north-east of Thockrington. In 1715, when they joined the Jacobites, their estates were forfeit to the Crown. The Shaftos owned land in Durham also, and still do own it, at Whitworth Hall beside the River Wear. An eighteenth-century member of the family, assisted by his daughter, Miss Camilla Shafto, excavated Benwell fort on Hadrian's Wall. The most celebrated Shafto was Robert, Member of Parliament for County Durham, a handsome flaxen-haired man, whose portrait by Reynolds still hangs at Whitworth Hall. Robert Shafto died in 1797, yet lives in the ballad of the unrequited love of a daughter of his neighbour, Sir Henry Belasyse of Brancepeth Castle:

> Bobby Shafto's gone to sea,
> Silver buckles on his knee;
> He'll come back and marry me,
> Bonnie Bobby Shafto.

That lovely air, originally called *Brave Willy Forster*, is still played on the Northumbrian bagpipes. But the fame of the Shafto family rests upon something more substantial than a ballad, for in 1683 the Reverend John Shafto founded the Grammar School at Haydon Bridge, which still flourishes. In 1953 a later Bobby—Mr. Robert D. Shafto—returned to Bavington Hall.

I was as reluctant to leave Thockrington as I had been to leave the high vista on Sarn Helen. I thought how admirably the situation would have suited the French poet, Maurice de Guérin, who said: 'The older I grow, and the clearer I discern between true society and false, the more strongly am I inclined to live, not as a savage or misanthrope, but as a solitary man on the frontiers of society, on the outskirts of the world.' Even the gregarious Romans understood Wordsworth's 'all-sufficing power of solitude'.

Back once more on Dere Street, I determined to make the most of it, having long ago discovered that it would soon become elusive and ultimately invisible. So, for another straight mile, I continued my journey. But there was one more call to be made, this time at a place where the Street curved gently from west-north-west to north-north-west through a land of blue water— Prestwick Burn, Holywell Burn, Curtis Burn, Blackbog Burn, Broomhog Burn—all baptizing a farm named Waterfalls. I had often noticed the track beside the Street; now I was about to follow it, led thither by a guidebook which mentioned a Roman milestone that had been erected as a memorial to an English nobleman. On a haugh it stood (said the guide), immediately visible and only a short distance from Dere Street. I walked up the track, and at the first bend saw Waterfalls, a derelict farmhouse, typical of its North Country kind, stone-built and made-to-measure for a man whose wife and children snuggled unhygienically in four rooms without anything that a Roman soldier would have accepted as any kind of convenience, either modern or ancient. Yet they survived; not indeed all, but enough to maintain the hardiest sheep in England, to follow the North Northumberland Foxhounds, and to make the Northumberland Fusiliers feared wherever they fought. From an earlier and even more unhygienic Waterfalls, fierce farmers rode northward with a song:

> Over the Borderland, wha' will gang wi' us,
> Saddle your horses an' buckle your blades,
> We will bring back wi' us fat Scottish cattle,
> Good Scottish horses and fair Scottish maids.

I peered inside the house, saddened by the relics of good husbandry, domestic happiness, inevitable sorrow, the whole cycle of human life, and a large segment of English history. The man who might have lived at Waterfalls was at Newcastle, in a factory.

The farmstead itself lay under a spur of high land. This I climbed, and at once sighted a stone on the skyline, three hundred yards to the nor'ard. But appearance deceived; the stone was a shrub. After a while I gave up the search, and had already put about *re infecta* when I saw a shepherd.

'Naw,' he said, in answer to my question, 'auld gurt stane fell doon.' He pointed to the way I had come. 'Thou'lt see it yon, away in't grass.'

I climbed the knoll again, and found the stone, as the shepherd had said, lying like a log in the grass. *Sic transit gloria mundi*. Yet the story is worth telling. In 1685 King Charles II was succeeded by his brother, James, a convert to Roman Catholicism. For more than a century the English people had been Protestants, and were resolved to remain so. If the new King had behaved with tact toward what his brother had called 'tender consciences' he might have retained both his creed and his crown; but he did not behave with tact. Against the advice of the Pope he went out of his way to alarm and affront the majority of his subjects. The Whigs, eager for power, were prompt to practise politics under the guise of religion. The Tories, on the other hand, faced a painful dilemma, because they were Anglicans as well as Jacobites. Inept to the last, James himself eased the pressure by fleeing to France, deserted even by his daughter, Mary, who succeeded him, ruling jointly with her husband, who, on her death, ruled alone as the Dutch William III, and he was succeeded by his wife's sister, Queen Anne. So far the dynasty had remained more or less Stuart; but when Anne died, pre-deceased by her children, the

throne passed to the great-grandson of James II, a German prince-
ling who disliked England and could not speak its language. All
this was good for trade, and better still for the Whig oligarchs
who, since the King could not speak, were pleased to do so for
him. But even some of the Protestant English began to feel that a
Roman Catholic native might be preferable to a Lutheran
foreigner. A number of the nobility and gentry looked across the
water to James Francis Edward Stuart, whom they acknowledged
as their King *de jure*. James, indeed, had long since been proclaimed at St. Germain as King James III and VIII of England,
Scotland, Ireland (in deference to his host, however, the style 'and
of France' was omitted, though the *fleur-de-lys* continued to be
blazoned on the royal arms). James himself was a brave man. At
Malplaquet, facing the might of Marlborough, he had twelve
times charged with the *Maison du Roi*. But he possessed neither the
wit of his uncle, Charles II, nor the charm of his son, Bonnie
Prince Charlie. 'For me', he once said, 'it is no new thing to be
unfortunate.' He even managed to be absent when his supporters
declared war against the German usurper, led by some twenty
peers, both English and Scottish.

On 6 October 1715, a party of Jacobites assembled on the high
ground above Waterfalls, where they were joined by the young
Earl Derwentwater. On 2 November the small army reached
Penrith, opposed only by the Westmorland Militia, of whom an
eye-witness wrote: 'They appeared with their pitchforks on the
very ground through which the rebels were to march, and most of
their parsons with them, applauding their zeal and courage.' But
the flesh proved hungrier than the spirit: 'about one o'clock,
when no enemy appeared abroad, and great gnawing began to be
felt within, and no opportunity of refreshment in view, the
infantry began to drop off.' When at last the Jacobites did appear,
the rest of the Militia 'wisely retreated'.

From Penrith the invaders proceeded via Kendal to Preston,
where they enlisted 1,600 ill-armed recruits. That was as far as
they got. Hanoverian troops under General Willis attacked the
town. Stripped to the waist, Earl Derwentwater urged the defen-
ders to cut their way out; but Thomas Forster, Member of

Parliament for Northumberland, was sent secretly to surrender. The chief prisoners were taken to London. Although the young Countess of Derwentwater was expecting a second child, she hurried to Court, begging for her husband's life. The King turned away, refusing to listen. Nineteen Scottish peerages were attainted, together with the English earldom of Derwentwater and the English barony of Widdrington. The final verdict was inevitable: 'It is adjudged by this Court that you James, Earl of Derwentwater; William, Lord Widdrington; William, Earl of Nithsdale; Robert, Earl of Carnwath; William, Viscount Kenmure; and William, Lord Nairne; and every one of you, return to the prison whence you came, from thence you must be drawn to the place of execution; when you come there, you must be hanged by the neck, but not until you be dead; for you must be cut down alive, then your bowels must be taken out, and burnt before your faces; then your heads must be severed from your bodies, and your bodies afterward divided each into four quarters; and these must be at the King's disposal. And God Almighty have mercy on your souls.' At the last moment the sentence was changed to beheading.

Earl Derwentwater went to the block at Tower Hill. On the previous night he had composed his own epitaph:

> Albeit that here in London town
> It is my fate to die,
> O carry me to Northumberland
> In my father's grave to lie.
> There chant my solemn requiem
> In Hexham's holy towers,
> And let six maids of fair Tynedale
> Scatter my grave with flowers.

On the scaffold the Earl revealed that he had been offered a reprieve if he would disown his King and his Faith: 'Some means', he said, 'have been proposed to me for saving my life, which I look upon as inconsistent with honour and conscience, and therefore reject them, for, with God's assistance, I shall prefer any death to the doing a base action.' In the few remaining moments of his life, the young man justified himself, saying that he had hoped to 'contribute to the re-establishment of the ancient and fundamental

Constitution of these kingdoms, without which no lasting peace or true happiness can attend them. As it is, I can only pray that those blessings may be bestowed upon my dear country; and since I can do no more, I beseech God to accept my life as a small sacrifice towards it.'

Ignoring the Earl's last wish, George I refused to allow his body to be buried in Northumberland. Nevertheless, some friends contrived to smuggle the coffin from the Tower. Accompanied by the widowed Countess, the party set out on their journey north, travelling by night, hiding by day; and with them went Frank Stokoe, the only man to escape after the battle of Preston. Despite the gallantry of individuals, the Jacobite risings were ill-led, bedevilled by rivalry, betrayed by cowardice, doomed to fail. Yet the words and deeds of the young Earl shine like stars on the waters of dissension. His monument, however, the Roman milestone, lies neglected in the grass.

Hitherto for several miles the Street had switchbacked over the summit of the hills, so that motorists, racing at sixty miles an hour, were sign-warned against the blind dip beyond each skyline. At Broomhope Burn the road sheered away, near the site of a Roman fortlet, leaving the Street as a track which did at last deviate from some of the steepest contours. After three miles it crossed the River Rede, at the site of a large fort, *Habitancum*, once manned by the First Cohort of *Vangiones*. Amid such scenes Defoe remarked: 'Here is abundant business for an antiquary; every place shews you ruin'd castles, Roman altars, inscriptions, monuments of battles, or heroes killed, and armies routed. . . .' A contemporary of Defoe—the Reverend John Hodgson, whom we met at Lanchester—did much field work in and around *Habitancum*. He served as vicar of Kirkwhelpington, six miles north-east of Thockrington, where he wrote the greater part of his *History of Northumberland*, finding therein some solace after the death of his wife and two children, whom he buried on the same day.

The landscape was becoming even wilder now. This was Redesdale, the dale of the Rede or reddish river; an apt name for No Man's Land. As late as the reign of Henry VIII the Commissioners reported that the Redesdale robbers were at least as troublesome as the marauding Scots. They built their houses behind 'banks and cheughs of wood wherein of old time for the more strength great trees have been felled and laid athwart the ways and passages . . . it will be hard for strangers having no knowledge thereof to pass by. . . .' And yet, after all, it was the Border feuds that most beset Northumberland. Sometimes the feud was formal, as when the Scots were routed at Flodden Field:

> We'll hear nae mair lilting at our ewe milking,
> Women and bairns are heartless and wae,
> Sighing and moaning on ilka green loaning
> The flowers of the forest are a' wede away.

More often the feud was private, as in W. H. Ogilvie's ballad:

> Last night a wind from Lammermoor
> Came roaring down the glen
> With the tramp of trooping horses
> And the laugh of reckless men,
> And struck a mailed hand on the gate,
> And cried in rebel glee,
> Come forth! Come forth! my Borderer,
> And ride the March with me!

It is idle to judge an era by standards which it did not possess. Although chivalry held personal honour in high esteem, life itself was cheap. During the Border feuds thousands of people lived under the shadow of a stealthy arrow, a creeping dagger, a firebrand from the darkness.

Dere Street passed within a mile or so of the scene of a famous Border feud, the Battle of Chevy Chase, which was commemorated by a plinth in a grove near the village of Otterburn. When Defoe travelled that way he was astounded by the people's knowledge of the battle: 'We could not but enquire of the good old women every where, whether they had heard of the fight at Chevy Chace: They not only told us they had heard of it, but had all the account of it at their fingers end. . . .' The battle began by moonlight on 19 August 1388, when the Scottish Earl of Douglas, having ravaged Durham and Newcastle, was overtaken near Otterburn by the English under Sir Henry Percy. The Earl was killed, Sir Henry was captured.

Two famous ballads, each composed by an unknown poet, give their own stirring and inaccurate account of the battle. The Scottish ballad is called *The Battle of Otterbourne*:

> It fell about the Lammas tide,
> When the muir-men make their hay,
> The doughty Earl of Douglas rode
> Into England, to catch a prey.

The English ballad is called *Chevy Chase*:

> 'O heavy news' King James can say,
> 'Scotland may wittenesse bee
> I have not any captaine more
> Of such account as hee!'
> Like tydings to King Henery came
> Within as short a space,
> That Pearcy of Northumberland
> Was slaine in Chevy Chase.

If the British people ever do turn from the alien folklore of Tin Pan Alley, those ballads may again be sung in taverns, as a requiem for old wounds long since healed. Certainly they deserve to be sung, for they are the voice of the people and therefore 'to be understanded of the people'. G. M. Trevelyan stated a fact when he said: 'The Border people wrote the Border Ballads.'

> God save our King, and blesse this land
> With plentye, joy, and peace!
> And grant hencforth that foul debate
> Twixt noble men may ceaze!

At Dargues Burn, in a wood, I found the site of a prehistoric settlement. On the far side of the Burn I found the site of a Roman camp, less than a mile from the site of a Roman fort. Keen-eyed those sentries must have been; thankful for their splendid equipment. Many a legionary was saved by his bronze helmet. The earliest type resembled a modern fireman's helmet, curving over the nape. Claudius devised a simpler and safer model, rather like a crash helmet, fitted with an iron skullcap. Every soldier wore a linen slip under a woollen tunic, short-sleeved and ending above the knee. His armour defended the chest, ribs, shoulders. His sandals, which had several layers of studded leather sole, were fastened about the shin by thongs. A centurion wore lighter sandals. The curved and rectangular shields were made of strips of wood bound with bronze or with iron, and covered by decorated leather. Each soldier carried a sword and a dagger; the former was two feet long and two inches wide; the latter was leaf-shaped and about a foot long. The soldier carried also two wooden javelins, seven feet long, with an iron barb.

From those martial musings I looked westward and presently walked thither, three miles or more, to greet an old friend, the Pennine Way, Britain's longest footpath, stretching 250 miles from Edale in Derbyshire to Kirk Yetholm in Roxburghshire. Gazing down the Street, I imagined a Legion encamped there for the night. Scouts were posted beyond the four gates. Each gate was defended by guards and the palisades were patrolled by *excubiae*. Every four hours the nightwatch were changed. The watchword was written on wooden tablets, and entrusted to four picked men whose task was to pass them on.

It was proof of Northumberland's spacious sanity that, on returning from the heights to the Street, I found almost as much quietude as I had left. Kipling caught the very timbre of the Roman road through Redesdale: 'The hard road goes on and on, and the wind sings in your helmet-plume, past altars to legions and generals forgotten, and broken statues of gods and heroes, and thousands of graves where the mountain foxes and hares peep at you.' Many times on Dere Street the paving stones rang to the marching Legions; sometimes forced marching to fill the breach or to rescue a cohort. Twenty-five miles a day they could march, armed and armoured; never less than fifteen miles if the journey were long. Rome rightly held that her army was most vulnerable when it marched through hostile country. In his military textbook, written during the first century A.D., Frontinus urged every commander to make a map of the area through which he proposed to march. The map would require native guides, and they must be treated with suspicion. Scouts, said Frontinus, must precede the main body, searching for traps and ambushes. The order of marching seldom varied. First came the cavalry, jingling a lordly way before the infantry; after them, the baggage, the senior officers, the Legion itself, flanked by auxiliaries and more horsemen. Last came the least experienced auxiliaries.

And so I reached Rochester village, which may have been either *hrof ceaster* (the camp on the roof) or *hroc ceaster* (the camp on a rock). Each hypothesis suited the situation. The porch of the village school was made of Roman stones; the porch of the church (a modern building) contained part of a Roman altar; and above them stood *Bremenium*, overlooking the place at which Dere Street once forded Sills Burn (whence the name *Bremenium*, from *Brimo* or the roaring one). But the Burn flowed less loudly than in A.D. 142 when the Governor of Britain, Lollius Urbicus, lodged at the fort, on his way north to build a Scottish wall for Antonius Pius. Nearly a century later, when that Wall had been abandoned, *Bremenium* became more than ever an important strategic outpost, marooned in enemy territory, miles from the shelter of Hadrian's Wall. Indeed, the fort was enlarged and strengthened at the end of the second century; and Roman coins proved that it had been manned from the reign of Otho to the reign of Carausius, a span of nearly 170 years.

A modern lane entered the site via what used to be the south gate, marked by a guard-house, eight feet square and massively walled. The interior of the fort resembled a village green, dotted with one or two cottages. During the middle of the nineteenth century a Duke of Northumberland excavated *Bremenium*, revealing its drains, heating chambers, and a treasury or 'safe', sealed by a huge stone on iron wheels. Because it lay so far from adequate cornland, the fort contained an extra granary. In 1850 a certain William Coulson, an Inland Revenue Officer, was sent to live at the fort, with special reference (as the examiners say) to Scottish whisky smugglers. During his leisure moments he uncovered the base of a monument which may have been erected to a Roman officer after cremation.

Bremenium was the only fort which had yielded evidence of Roman artillery. The light artillery was represented by catapults on wheels, designed to protect the flanks of a Legion, unleashing

8

four-foot arrows with iron warheads. The medium artillery worked on the same cross-bow principle as the catapults, unleashing javelins with a range of 300 yards. The siege artillery was represented by the *onager*, a truly formidable weapon, dragged by oxen, and worked on a torsion principle whereby a skein of twisted rope pulled back a timber arm, to which was attached a huge boulder. Five gunners manned the *onager*; four to twist the rope, one to release the trigger. Every Legion carried ten of those weapons, one to each cohort.

When Lord Lytton saw the majesty of Ffestiniog he exclaimed: 'One may pass an age here, and think it a day.' Whenever I visit *Bremenium* I share a similar experience. Hadrian's Wall was incomparably larger than *Bremenium*, yet for that reason alone it seemed less vivid as an example of the long arm of Rome and the short life of her soldiers. The Wall was (so to say) a grapevine whose tendrils were tough as well as talkative, strengthening the whole by transmitting news from its parts. Moreover, it traversed tracts of relatively sheltered country, whereas *Bremenium* stood alone, an islet in an ocean of ferocity:

> Over the frosty moorland
> The moon is riding high,
> And out of the wintry silence
> The wraiths of Rome come by.

Again Prys-Jones caught the *numen* or spirit of the place; and if you wander the heights beyond it, you will stumble on the shadows of smaller Roman posts—outposts of outposts—themselves overshadowed by the hovels and caves of prehistory. Yet even those remote areas were answerable to Roman law. At their regional capitals four of the leading natives served annually as elected magistrates. The junior pair supervised the maintenance of roads and buildings. The senior pair tried lesser criminal and civil cases. Serious cases went either to the Governor's Courts or to his juridical deputy, at assize centres. Even the remotest region was visited by a *beneficarius* who controlled road traffic and also collected taxes. Sometimes a remount officer appeared. Everywhere the Romans maintained a hierarchy of Celtic tribesmen. This is a land of forests and hills and brooks . . . Sills Burn, Black Burn, Bellshiel Burn, Runners Burn, Southope Burn, Ridlees Burn, Deerbush Burn, Tarn Burn, Smaithope Burn, Grindstone Burn, Wind Burn. The exiled Jacobite told the truth:

> On Keilder side, the wind blows wide,
> There sounds nae hunting horn
> That ring saw sweet as the winds that beat
> Round banks where Tyne is born.

A southron will protest that the Tyne is not in Scotland; and he will be correct; his error is to suppose that 'nae' and 'sae' are Scottish. What we call Lowland Scots began life as Highland English, for the wind of change blew from the south, and you may hear it still, sometimes without understanding, like Defoe: 'I must not quit Northumberland', he wrote, 'without taking notice, that the natives of this country . . . are distinguished by a shibboleth upon their tongues, namely, a difficulty in pronouncing the letter *r*, which they cannot deliver from their tongues without a hollow jarring in the throat, by which they are plainly known, as a foreigner is, in pronouncing the *th*. This they call the Northumbrian *r*, and the natives value themselves upon that imperfection, because, forsooth, it shews the antiquity of their blood.' And so it does. The medieval Earls of Northumberland were full of 'sae' and 'nae', yet they ruled like kings, as many a king discovered despite his West End accent. Wherefore the ayes have it, and the saes and the naes as well; and in Northumberland long may it be so:

> Tweed says to Twill,
> 'What gars ye rin sae still?'
> Says Twill to Tweed,
> 'Though ye rin wi' speed
> An' I rin slaw,
> Where ye droon yin man, I droon twa.'

Bremenium marked a parting of the ways. The road turned northwest to Carter Bar while the Street kept more or less straight, watered by burns, flanked by forests, until at Feather Wood it approached an artillery range, and became out of bounds to civilians. At that point the Romans had confronted a network of small becks, so they turned east for a few hundred yards and then recovered the former alignment, and built a camp there; but soon changed course again, no doubt because the land was too steep and damp. At 1,400 feet the Street became a track, turning from due north to west-north-west. Soon the track assumed a new name, Gamel's Path. I could not discover who Gamel was, but every Borderer knew that his path led to a place where the Scottish and English once met to settle disputes; sometimes peaceably, sometimes by single combat, sometimes *en masse*. At Carter Bar, they say, occurred the last of those affrays, when Sir John Forster, Henry VIII's Warden of the English Border, rode with his men to confer with the Scottish Warden, Sir John Carmichael. As the ballad tells, things began well:

> Yet was our meeting meek enough
> Begun wi' merriment and mowes [grins],
> And at the brae above the heugh
> The clerk sat down to call the rowes [rolls].

Alas, words ended in misdeeds. Lives were lost, prisoners were taken, and much blood shed.

At Coquet Head, where the River Coquet arose in a *cocwudu* or forest of wild birds, I met the Pennine Way again, though the Pennines themselves lay so far astern that the Way was now a Cheviot Way. There I revisited four camps which the Romans built near Chew Green, a region so wild and lonely that I hoped no Spanish nor Provençal Legionary had been posted there, to shiver in the mist. Excavation unearthed the bones of a Roman soldier who died at Chew Green, more likely of the climate than by a Pictish spear. Nearby stood the site of a medieval chapel where two or three had gathered together, away from the wind, finding peace in the midst of themselves. I could not discover when that chapel was last used. Perhaps it had lived long enough to chant William Kethe's sixteenth-century Psalter:

> Al people yt on earth do dwel,
> sing to ye lord, with chereful voice

> Him serve wt fear, his praise forth tel,
> come ye before him and reioyce.

Despite the political and economic importance of southern England, it was the North Country that dominated the cultural life of the so-called Dark Ages. King Alfred—himself a beacon of the English *Kulturkampf*—mourned because few men south of Lincoln could translate a Latin sentence into English. Dere Street, in fact, crossed the country of three great writers: Cynewulf, Caedmon, Bede. Cynewulf, a Northumbrian, wrote *Elene*, a poem in fifteen cantos, describing Helena's search for the true Cross (a topical search because the Church had lately warned Christendom against the worship of pagan symbols). The poem's last canto, translated into modern English, strikes a note beyond the range of pagan Rome: 'I am old and ready to depart, having woven wordcraft, and pondered deeply in the world's darkness. I was once gay in society, receiving gifts of gold and treasure, yet was I carked with care, fettered by sins, surrounded with sorrow, until at last the Lord of all Might and Power granted me his grace, and revealed to me the mystery of the Holy Cross.'

Caedmon came late in life as a novice to the monastery of *Streonshalh* or Whitby, which was ruled by the Abbess Hilda according to the Celtic usage. Bede summarized his genius: 'In the monastery of the abbess, there was a certain brother especially distinguished and exalted by divine grace because he was wont to make songs that tended to religion and piety.' Caedmon was an example of *paeta nascitur non fit*: 'He had lived in the secular world until an advanced age, and had never learned poetry.' His finest poems paraphrase the books of Genesis, Exodus and Daniel. One line, translated from Daniel, describes the Angel of the Lord appearing above the fiery furnace, as welcome as the

> Dropping down of dew-rain at the dawn of day.

Bede, a proser writer, lacked the poetic genius of his peers, but outshone them in scholarship and versatility. He wrote metrical lives of the saints, commentaries on the Bible, studies of eminent churchmen, textbooks of metre and spelling, and the invaluable *History of the English Church and People*.

Partway up Brownhart Law, at about 1,500 feet, the Romans built a signal station which symbolized the length and breadth of their rule, for just such a station stood not a great way from my home on Exmoor, overlooking the Severn Sea. All this while I had been hugging the English side of the border, sometimes within a few yards of the demarcation, which at no point was more than a wire fence. At Scraesburgh Fell the Pennine Way changed course, zigzagging north-east toward Auchope Cairn and the slow curve westward that would bring it to rest at Kirk Yetholm. The Street, however, was chiefly a line of shadows and ridges until it crossed a lane from Morebattle, revealing several young hikers in the bi-sexual uniform of nonconformity. Well-bred Romans, by contrast, wore a toga or long linen robe. A boy's toga had a purple border but when he passed from puberty to early manhood he wore a plain white robe. Under the Empire the toga was whittled down, first to a short *pallium*, then to a mere band of cloth. Dandies favoured an embroidered garment, *tunica palmata*. The earliest Romans had been bearded, but razors came into fashion under the Empire, and continued so until the reign of Hadrian, when beards resumed the vogue. For centuries the Roman women wore much the same costume as the men, to which they added a bust bodice. Their favourite colours were red, yellow, blue, gold. Imperial hair styles became so ornate that every Roman lady employed a hairdresser. Blondes were preferred; brunettes were bleached. When the Empire was divided between Rome and Byzantium the fashions grew more than ever oriental. Emperors chose their Empress at a beauty competition, girls being procured from all parts (the Empress Theodora was the daughter of a man who worked in a bear-baiting establishment). No such wantonness was to be seen when the Romans paved their road around Scraesburgh Fell, where my own wanderings led at last into Scotland and thence back to that remote past which Horace called the egg or first beginning of the story.

Nearly 7,000 years before the birth of Christ, people were living in the County of Nairn. We know it because a layer of peat was found there, containing chips of quartz that had been struck by human agency during the Boreal period. That is the earliest evidence of mankind in Scotland. When the Romans arrived they named the country Caledonia. At the battle of Mons Graupius the Caledonians were defeated by Agricola. The site of that battle is uncertain. A careless scribe wrote 'Grampius' instead of 'Graupius', whence the name of the Grampian Mountains. In 1970 the search for the site was narrowed by an announcement from the Ordnance Surveyors that a newly-discovered earthwork in a wood near Dunning in Perthshire may have been the base from which Agricola advanced the last few miles to his victory at Mons Graupius in A.D. 84. Certainly the earthwork revealed a camp which conformed with a type that was used only during Agricola's Scottish campaign of A.D. 79–84. Certainly, too, Agricola's son-in-law, Tacitus, reported that the battle itself had been fought by auxiliaries while the Legion waited in reserve somewhere between its base and the enemy.

According to Ammarius Marcelinus, the resistance to Rome was led by the Scots and the Picts. The former came from Ireland; the latter consisted of two tribes, the *Verturiones* and the *Dicalydonae* whom Ptolemy called *Kaledonioi*. They must have been a hardy race because Procopius described the climate north of Hadrian's Wall as so vile that only serpents could thrive there (a rumour which he picked up from Englishmen at Byzantium). In 685, the Romans having departed, a Pictish leader, Brude mac Bili, led his people to victory over Northumbria, the most powerful among the English kingdoms; thereafter for nearly a thousand years the Scots remained under their own rival leaders. While England was ruled by Danes, Scotland adopted its present name, and fixed a border at the River Tweed. The process sounds simpler than it was, because Caledonia contained kingdoms other than the Pictish. There was Dalriada, a community of Gaelic-speaking Celts from Ireland; Strathclyde, a Welsh-speaking settlement; and Bernicia, the Lothians, Berwickshire, and part of Northumberland. Both Scotland and Wales would in any event have been conquered by weight of English numbers, but each nation hastened its defeat by fulfilling the hopes of Tacitus when he said: 'Seldom will two or three nations join to repel an invader. Each resisting singly, all are conquered.' Some Caledonians submitted

to Rome, like the *Damnonii* who founded the kingdom of Strathclyde; others waged a 'cold' war and at times a warm one, like the
Picts who breached Hadrian's Wall; a few retreated to the Isles
and the Highland Glens. Rome did not try, and probably did not
wish, to occupy Caledonia as she had occupied England and
Wales. Her effective influence or *imperium* ended in Perthshire.
She may, however, have traded northward of Perth, even with the
Hebrides, where a Roman plough of the second century A.D. was
discovered. In 1296 Edward I of England launched the campaign
that resulted in the conquest of Scotland after valiant resistance.
The Scots in assembly at Arbroath despatched to the Pope a
challenge and a plea: 'It is not for glory, riches or honours that we
fight, but only for freedom, which no good man will abandon but
with his life.' In 1603, when James VI of Scotland became James I
of England, the two kingdoms merged.

Soon after entering Roxburghshire the Street identified itself
more clearly. From Shibden Hill it ran straight for six miles,
sometimes as a lane, more often as a track, and for half a mile as
a path beside a wood. The contours grew gentle again, sloping
to 300 feet. The high solitudes of Northumberland lay astern.
But when I reached the River Teviot I felt like the men of the Old
Testament: 'We ask the way to Zion, looking thitherward.' There
was no way. Time had obliterated all traces. I wondered how
many other Roman roads lay hidden, from Perthshire south to
Cornwall. In 1968, for example, a workman unearthed a Roman
fire-dog near Baldock in Hertfordshire. Two years later some
archaeologists from the Ministry of Public Building and Works
discovered on the same site a Roman road, rammed with gravel
and cobbles, and flanked on either side by a ditch.

After consulting maps, books, and Scots, I trespassed inten-
tionally along a path to Monteviot House, and there I found the
Street again, tracking its way uphill through a copse and thence
running parallel with the road to Newtown St. Boswells, which it
joined at Forest Lodge, in a land of green hills, gold corn, shaggy
sheep, and one shepherd so surely astride his horse that he verified
Kipling's saying: 'A man who rides much knows exactly what his
horse is going to do before he does it.'

At the village of Newtown St. Boswells I renewed an 'auld acquaintance' with typical Lowland dwellings—squat, spruce, stony, much given to red paint. The pavement was so spick and span that I would have dined off it; every garden gay, trim, fruitful. In the village itself I once more lost the way, but was rewarded by the ruins of a sandstone Abbey, lawn-laced and tree-trellised, within sight of a river. St. Boswells Abbey symbolized the ruin of *Ecclesia Scotanica* or the medieval Scottish Church, which was co-founded by Irish monks from St. Columba's Ionian settlement. In 1560 the Scottish Parliament disowned the Pope and denounced the Mass. Thereafter for more than a century Scotland was torn between Calvinism and Catholicism. Having lain fallow many decades, the Roman Church re-established a Scottish hierarchy in 1867. Today its two archbishops and six bishops feed 700,000 of their faithful. Methodists, Baptists, Congregationalists, and other brethren number about 140,000. The English Church, which never did take deep root there, is represented by the Episcopal Church of Scotland with 55,000 members. To most Englishmen those facts will seem tediously archaic; not so to the Scots, who are still a religious people, followers of Calvinism, a creed known sometimes as Presbyterianism. Each congregation is governed by a kirk of presbyters or elders, chosen by the laity; its clergyman is merely a president or moderator. The multitudinous kirks are represented at sixty-six presbyteries or regional sessions. Over all is the General Assembly of the Church of Scotland, which meets annually in May, under a Moderator who holds office for one year. The Sovereign is represented at the Assembly by a High Commissioner who, unless he happens to have been sent there as an elder, is not a member of that Assembly. Those conventions suit a nation so steeped in theology that it out-votes its own clergy on their own ground and in what an English priest would call their own vestry.

There was a paradox in all this because Calvinism reached a nation which one of its sons, Thomas Carlyle, described as 'a poor barren country, full of continued broils, dissensions, massacrings, a people in the last state of rudeness and destitution'. Yet Calvinism raised that nation to fame in many fields. Yet (again) Calvin himself had said: 'God has predestined certain souls to salvation, others to damnation, and these decrees are unalterable.' . . . to which Coleridge replied: 'Calvinism, or the belief in election, is not simply blasphemy, but superfetation of blasphemy.' Since damnation never was a spur to lifelong endeavour, one must assume that the Almighty had assured the Scottish Presbyterians that He was on their side. Yet (finally) that same Calvinism, speaking through a Moderator of the General Assembly, the Very Reverend Dr. John Baillie, defined man's dilemma briefly and beautifully: 'The ultimate sadness', wrote Dr. Baillie, 'is that nothing lasts; that the bloom so soon disappears from all things that are young, that the vigour of maturity is so short-lived, while age brings weariness and forgetfulness and decay . . . To call to mind the carefree days of our youth, to see the friends of youth disappear one by one from our earthly company with hopes only half fulfilled and work only half done, and to know that no task of our own can ever be completed nor any joy held in possession for more than a few fleeting years—this is our great heaviness of heart. And for it I know no healing, nor for the problems of suffering any final prospect of solution, save as we are able to share St. Paul's faith when he cried: "For I reckon that the sufferings of this present time are not worthy to be compared with the glory which shall be revealed to us." ' For the Romans, as for the Greeks, that evangelism or good news would have seemed a stumbling block to the *hubris* of their intellect. Despite his charge of blasphemy, Coleridge shared Sir Thomas Browne's belief that men of goodwill may differ among themselves charitably. Wherefore Coleridge put into the mouth of his Ancient Mariner an invitation—

> To walk together to the kirk
> And all together pray,
> While each to his great Father bends,
> Old men, and babes, and loving friends,
> And youths and maidens gay!

Every traveller in Scotland must feel impressed by its village schools, not least because they *are* village schools, some of them as old as the year 1633 when the Scottish Parliament first decreed that local ratepayers should build and maintain a well-appointed school in every parish. From those schools went clever and industrious pilgrims, travelling the rich road to London, Oxford, Cambridge. In Roman eyes the Scots were the most uncouth of all Britons. But times have changed. The Scots are among the best-educated of all Britons, and among the most hospitable. Nevertheless, the rôle of their early schools ought not to be over-rated. More than a century after the passing of the Act of 1633 many Scottish parishes had no school at all. In Fife at the same period only one man in three could sign his own name; of the women, only one in twelve. In Galloway the majority of people could not read.

While resting beside the river, I noticed a sight that had come to seem unnatural . . . a father and his adolescent son who, having fished all day and caught much, marched homeward happily, each with an arm about the other's shoulder. Rome would have approved despite and also because of her stern *paterfamilias*. If pressed to define the noblest Roman trait with one word, I would answer 'discipline'. And were I required to cite an outstanding example of that trait, I would name a general, Aulus Postumius, who, in a battle against the Volsci and Aequi, ordered his own son, a subordinate commander, to restrain his men until they could best advance. The boy refused, led his troops into action, and won a resounding victory. After the battle the father ordered his son to be executed for having disobeyed orders in the face of the enemy. It has become fashionable to say that such discipline begat centuries of neurosis and therefore centuries of bloodshed. As a layman I refrain from comment, except to remark that I find the Roman malady less debilitating than the English disease.

The beginning of my journey's end was greeted by the Eildon Hills, humped on the skyline; splendid, but not Highland. Like the badger, the spirit of Scotland each year retreats into deeper country, away from television and tourism. Thus, in 1971 the number of Roxburghshire folk who speak Gaelic was less than one per cent; yet up in Ross and Cromarty the number was forty per cent, with two per cent who spoke no English. Those figures would have amazed Edward Burt, chief surveyor to General Wade's road-building campaign through the Highlands after the Jacobite risings. Burt's *Letters from a Gentleman in the North of Scotland* stated that the people of Inverness did not regard themselves as true Highlanders 'because they speak English . . . Yet although they speak English there are scarce any who do not understand the Irish tongue [Gaelic]; and it is necessary they should do so, to carry on their dealings with the neighbouring country people; for within less than a mile of the town there are few who speak English at all.' Burt, of course, was referring only to the peasants and farmers. In 1776 a young Englishman, Captain Edward Topham, noted that at Edinburgh 'the politer sort of people and Professors of the College . . . strive to shake off the Scotch pronounciation as much as possible'. Two centuries ago Dr. Johnson declared: 'the girls of the Highlands are all gentlewomen'. But he was compelled to add: 'They are now losing their distinction, and hastening to mingle with the general community.'

There is one aspect of modern Scotland which the Romans would have recognized, for today the chiefs of the clans exert a mystique or moral influence nowhere to be found among the English, Welsh, or Irish. The title of a Highland chief sometimes differs from that by which he is known south of the Border. In Gaelic, for example, the Duke of Argyll, chief of clan Campbell, is MacCailein Mor, Son of Great Colin. Some chiefs bear the name of their territory; thus, Cameron of Lochiel is known to Highlanders as Lochiel. To speak of 'The Macleod' or 'The Lochiel' is with one exception wrong; the exception being the chief of clan Chisholm. There is a saying: 'Only three persons have the right to the definite article before their name . . . the Pope, the Devil, and the Chisholm.'

The last three or four miles of Dere Street were vague. Parts of them seemed to concur with the road to Melrose, a town of dignity and quietness, with a ruined Abbey worthy of Newtown St. Boswells. The Law Courts at such towns still bear a Roman imprint. During the fifteenth century the so-called Reception of Roman Law into Scotland was fostered by jurists who had studied it in Italy and France. Many of the medieval Scottish lawyers were churchmen, steeped in canon law. While English jurists were amassing precedents, difficult to collect and study, Scottish jurists chose rather to rely on principles, as the Romans did. Three centuries later an English poet poked gentle fun at the Justice Shallows who sat

> Mastering the lawless science of our law,
> That codeless myriad of precedent.

The differences between English and Scottish law are numerous. About the year 1800 the Lord Chancellor of England, himself a Scot, confessed: 'I know something of the law, but of Scotch law I am as ignorant as a native of Mexico.' Scottish and Roman law allow the same court—in Scotland, the Court of Session—to administer both equity and law. Scottish juries sometimes return a verdict of Not Proven, which enables the accused to leave the court with a stain on his character. A Writer to the Signet is peculiar to Scottish law. Originally he was a clerk in the Secretary of State's office who drew up writs for the royal signet. Today the Writers conduct cases before the Court of Session, and hold the exclusive right to prepare charters and Crown writs. For many years two Scottish Lords of Appeal have by custom sat in London, to ensure that their own law is interpreted aright.

Scottish music, on the other hand, bore little resemblance to Roman, of which we know nothing except that it was chiefly 'background music' composed *ad hoc* or for a specific purpose. Insofar as the Romans chose to overeat and overdrink to music, the strains may be called 'the food of food'. The Greeks applied the word 'music' to any of the arts of the Nine Muses. Their drama was melodrama, a play with music. Aeschylus, indeed, composed the music for his own plays. The early notation, in Greek letters, was a system of *neumae* which reminded a singer of the approximate difference in the pitch of tunes he had already memorized. Western European music was created by the medieval Church, the French *troubadours* and *trouvères*, the German *Minne-sänger* and *Meistersänger*. One of Shakespeare's characters complained that bagpipes affected his bladder. True, the pipes always

were favoured more by the Highlands than by the Lowlands.
Every Highland chief had his piper, his poet, his harper. Yet the
Piobaireached may still be heard in the Lowlands as a salute, march,
or lament. The harp is seldom heard in Scotland. The last of the
harpers, Murdo MacDonald, harper to Maclean of Coll until 1734,
learned his art from the MacLeods' harper, Roderick Morison
alias *Ruaraidh Dall* or Blind Rory. The last of the great English
harpers—Richard More alias 'blynde Dick'—was described in
1520 as 'minstrel of our Lord King, the man who is blind and the
principal harper in England'.

The Scottish dance has fared more fortunately than the harp,
though nowadays debased by jazz rhythms. The Lowlands still
shared an enthusiasm which Captain Topham noticed in 1776
when he remarked on 'the perseverance which the Scotch ladies
discover in their Reels. . . . They will sit totally unmoved at the
most sprightly airs of an English Country Dance; but the moment
one of these tunes is played, up they start, animated with new life,
and you would imagine they had received an electric shock. . . .'

At last, by mixing tracks with trespass, I came to Newstead
and the site of *Trimontium*, the fort near three hills (*tres montes*), the
largest in the Lowlands, covering fifty acres, yielding a harvest of
weapons, helmets, harness, coins. Agricola built it; his successors
enlarged and thereafter held it until the Legions withdrew from
Britain. Now only a few green mounds remained. Little, then, to
be seen: or, to put it another way, only the Eildon Hills and
their miles of fertile farmland, almost within sight of Sir Walter
Scott's home at Abbotsford, which I first saw by moonlight
through the snow, when it resembled the vision of his Lady of
the Lake:

> So wondrous wild, the whole might seem
> The scenery of a fairy dream.

Beyond those hills the Street continued for a few more miles, until
it joined another road, leading to the Antonine Wall, the northern
limit of the Roman Empire in Britain.

So ended my journey from *Eboracum* to *Trimontium*, through
the largest tract of the wildest country in England, and some of

the bonniest in Scotland, along a road worthy of the men who made it:

> Men from Italy, Africa, Gaul,
> Resolute soldiers, strong and tall,
> Rome the mother of one and all. . . .

Peddars Way

PEDDARS WAY

LEGEND

.... Roman Roads

———— Main Roads

〜〜〜 Rivers

BRANCASTER

● Branodunum

Holme-next-
the-Sea

A149

● RINGSTEAD

● Burnham Thorpe

A1067

● Fring

SANDRINGHAM ●

A148

● LITTLE MASSINGHAM
● GREAT MASSINGHAM
Field Barn Plantation

Castle Acre ●

River Nar

A47(T)

A1122

SWAFFHAM ●

● North Pickenham

● Ashill

PEDDARS WAY

● SAHAM TONEY
● WATTON

A1065

● Thompson

A134

East
Wretham ●

A11(T)

THETFORD ●

A1066

Little Ouse

A143

Ixworth ●

A1088

© Cassell&Co. Ltd. 1971

8 Peddars Way: Ixworth to Castle Acre

THE windmill seemed to have achieved a miracle which men had sought in vain, the miracle of perpetual motion, wrought without haste, without stress, without sound. Whiter than the clouds above them, each sail rose and fell serenely. A farmhand told me that only twenty-seven windmills were still earning their daily bread in Britain. He may have been right, because in 1957 there were only thirty. I could neither recall nor discover any reference to Roman windmills; but there was a tradition that during the first century B.C. Hero of Alexandria had devised such mills, and that others were at work three centuries earlier in India. When Queen Victoria ascended the throne, windmills were so common that no one remarked on them unless a John Constable or a George Eliot set them in the limelight.

The mill itself stood beside a farm near Ixworth at the start of the pedlars' or Peddars Way in Suffolk, the land of the folk who dwelt south of the Norfolk. Never having seen Ixworth before, I was agreeably surprised to find a medieval village, enhanced by buildings from the sixteenth to the eighteenth centuries; oversailing houses, pargetting, Georgian bow windows; but nothing of the Roman fort. The question 'Why did the Romans build Peddars Way?' becomes more meaningful and therefore more answerable if it is rephrased as 'What was the role of Peddars Way?' Briefly, the Way linked the south with the north of Britain; to the south, it joined a road for Colchester (*Camulodunum*); to the north, it probably connected with a ferry across the Wash from Holme-Next-The-Sea to Burgh-le-Marsh in Lincolnshire. The Way seems to have followed the line of Ixworth High Street as far as Kiln Wood, where a lane led eastward into Bardwell (the place on the *brerd* or bank of Black Bourn), a pleasant village, marred by modern houses, with a Tudor Hall and a church whose porch

bore the arms of Sir William Bardwell (1367–1434). On my first
arrival, during April, the villagers were preparing for their annual
May Day Fair. Beyond Bardwell the Way disappeared—or at any
rate I could not find it—but a clue occurred near Barningham,
where a straight hedgerow marked a parish boundary (many such
boundaries followed a Roman road). After Barningham the Way
again became elusive. Books had indeed assured me that segments
of an *agger* were visible; but one *agger* looks much like another,
so I sat in a field, quite undismayed, for this was Gainsborough's
country as well as Constable's. In his generous praise of Gainsborough's subjects, Constable himself described the places and
people around me: 'The lonely haunts of solitary shepherds—the
rustic with his bill and bundle of wood—the darksome lane or
dell . . .' Already since Ixworth I had passed a farm whence certain
gobbling sounds confirmed that Daniel Defoe was still in many
ways a reliable fellow-traveller: 'this county of Suffolk', he wrote,
'is particularly famous for furnishing the city of London and all
the counties round, with turkeys; and that 'tis thought, there are
more turkeys bred in this county, and the part of Norfolk that
adjoins to it, than in all the rest of England. . . .' Nor were turkeys
the only old inhabitants who seemed as young as ever, for near
Bury St. Edmunds I had lately admired two Suffolk Punches,
scions of a breed which William Camden mentioned in 1583. Even
a layman can tell the difference between a Suffolk and a Clydesdale
or a Shire because the Suffolk has short legs without 'feathers'. A
pure Suffolk is always a chestnut, light or dark. The resemblance
to Mr. Punch is caused by the animal's ribbed-up appearance.
Unlike the Suffolk Punch, which was a rich man's rarity, the
Suffolk small black pig still prospered as 'a commercial proposition'. So also did the descendants of the Suffolk sheep—short-
woolled, black-faced, hornless—a breed that was first recognized
in 1810 as a cross between Southdown rams and horned Norfolk
ewes.

I rejoined the Way three miles further north, on the edge of
Boundary Plantation alongside the River Thet, the frontier
between Suffolk and Norfolk. There the *agger* was conspicuous,
heading slightly west of north, past the site of a Romano-British

settlement. When archaeologists excavated part of the Way near the river, they found that its course was sixteen feet wide, made of flints and gravel. Most Roman roads were raised on an embankment, about five feet high and up to fifty feet wide, flanked by a ditch on either side. The top of the road was metalled with gravel or chalk or flint, according to the soil. The surveyors used a *groma*, or swivelling wood cross, from whose four ends a metal weight was suspended on a cord; these weights could be aligned to check the direction given by smoke signals. When the Romans reached the River Thet they slung a timber bridge across boats anchored in the stream; had the river been wider, the bridge would have been supported by stakes.

Frontiers: many people nowadays fly across them without noticing. To me, on the other hand, even a county border is haunted by nuances that are the sum of architecture, accent, contours, crafts, industries, clothes, creeds, all of which are conditioned by the terrain. Geology is more than a study of rocks; it is an explanation of many aspects of human life. Certainly the geology changed at the frontier between Suffolk and Norfolk. Hill and pasture impinged on heath or breckland beyond Thetford, a town that has been overloaded with factories and cars. It would be interesting to know the name of the person who first proposed the statue to Tom Paine, who was born there in 1737, son of a Quaker farmer. Having failed as a sailor, stay-maker, school-usher, tobacconist, and exciseman, Thomas Paine achieved a sixth failure by rejoining the Excise Service and by again being dismissed (this time for persistent absenteeism). From a seventh failure (as inventor) he obtained a meeting with Benjamin Franklin, who gave him an introduction to Philadelphia, at a time when the colonists were losing patience with the arrogant ineptitude of English politicians. Edmund Burke appealed for reason on both sides: 'violent addresses', he warned the colonists, 'have been procured . . . by wicked and designing men, purporting to be the genuine voice of the whole of England'. Burke, as usual, was right, for the *émigré* Paine had circulated 120,000 copies of a stupid pamphlet entitled *Commonsense*, inciting the colonists to kill their magistrates, soldiers, and government officials. When the colonists followed his advice, and set up an illegal or unilateral Republic, Paine became secretary of its Committee of Foreign Affairs. By way of reward, he accepted a large sum of money and the estates of a colonist who had remained loyal. Having fouled his nest in England, and feathered it in America, Paine sold himself to the French Revolutionaries, again inciting Englishmen to bear arms against their own country. Yet even Paine's malice was found wanting, for at the height of the Terror, when today's extremists became tomorrow's reactionaries, he was sent to the guillotine by Robespierre. When the tumbril arrived, however, Paine was too ill to be chucked into it. Soon he was joined in prison by Danton, that blood-stained maniac, who had been condemned to death by even bloodier madmen. In fluent English Danton told Paine: 'If reason doesn't very soon return to this unhappy country, the massacres which you're witnessing now will seem like a bed of roses when compared with what must follow.' Danton was so correct that he did not live to see Robespierre condemned to death by fellow-egalitarians. Paine meanwhile managed to escape with his life and a full purse.

His best-known tracts are *The Age of Reason* and *The Rights of Man*. The former attacked Christianity in general and church-going in particular. In Paine's day, as in ours, not a few Christians disliked certain aspects both of the ritual and of the interpretation of their religion; but instead of stating his case charitably, Paine embellished it with ignorant arrogance. *The Rights of Man* revealed the same ill-nature. Having stated a case for pensions—'It is painful to see old age working itself to death'—the tract abused every form of government other than a People's Government of tyrants. Paine himself compared the French Revolution with the rising of Bonnie Prince Charlie, and then declared that the English were more bloodthirsty than the man who had condemned him to death for not being sufficiently vindictive and bloodthirsty. Paine died in America, taking to the bottle because the Americans would have nothing more to do with his spleen. It would indeed be interesting to know the name of the person who first proposed the statue to Thetford's renegade Englishman.

On Roudham Heath, meanwhile, the Way became a track

through the woods. Having emerged, it passed a flint church and a ruined windmill at East Wretham, where I discovered a link between three counties, beginning at Camborne in Cornwall, birthplace of Richard Trevithick who on Christmas Eve 1800 hitched his Puffing Billy to the first load of passengers ever hauled by steam. Trevithick had been apprenticed to John Hall's engineering works at Dartford in Kent. When he died—impoverished despite his inventions—his former workmates subscribed to rescue him from a pauper's grave. The last sentence ever written by Trevithick was as follows: 'However much I may be straitened in pecuniary circumstances, the honour of being useful, which to me far exceeds riches, can never be taken from me.' In East Wretham churchyard they buried Sir John Dewrance, another and more fortunate engineer, who married Trevithick's granddaughter, and became chairman of the company which first exploited the Kentish coalfields.

Suddenly the track gave a sharp left-right turn to join two miles of lane through Brickiln Coyert and thence to Galley Hill, at which point I halted because the lane was bearing westward off course. I therefore sat down to consult the map, and was struck by two facts: first, the multitude of meres in the district (Mickle Mere, West Mere, Fowl Mere, Ring Mere, The Mere); second, the multitude of farms (too many to be litanized). The earliest Roman citizens were farmer-soldiers, defending the land which they tilled. Their crops varied with the situation. Wheat, barley, millet, and chick-pea were common; oats were rare. Most farms supplied beans, lettuce, cabbages, nuts; apples and pears were plentiful; figs and vines, ubiquitous. Olives came later via the Greeks. The leaves of trees were used as fodder and litter. The farmhouse was a simple dwelling, flanked by stables and barns, according to the size of the estate. Every farmer kept a cow, a goat, and poultry. Even the smallest holder possessed a cart and a plough. For mowing he used a sickle; for digging, a spade; and several sorts of pick and hoe. It was a hard and often harsh life; and only a simpleton would share Rousseau's belief that it was golden. Yet it possessed a certain dignity and independence which were lost when the peasant was supplanted by property-developers. Gradually the farm came to be managed by a steward on behalf of a non-residential landlord. The spread of vast estates increased the demand for slaves, and diminished the demand for free labourers except when they joined as gangers at seasonal work, gathering olives as the Cockneys still pick hops beside Watling Street. The earliest Romans, like the French peasant today, loved the soil fiercely. In their eyes the highest 'status' belonged to a landowner, great or small. Nor did that trait wholly die, for the dream of every Legionary was to serve his time and then to cultivate his own plot in a *colonia* of ex-soldiers. Vergil wrote a long poem, *Georgica*, partly as a textbook of husbandry, partly as a challenge to his fellow-countrymen, that they might turn from the money-making cities, and renew the *colonia* of old times, for the sake of their own bodies and souls and for the well-being of the Empire:

flumina amem silvasque inglorius . . .

'let me be in love with rivers and woods, and forego fame. . . .'

The Way itself re-entered the woods—Blackrabbit Warren on the left, the woods of Breckley Heath on the right—and presently approached Thompson Water, a mile south-west of Thompson, one of the few villages that bear a modern man's name. Beware the Ides of etymology. My own village, for example, was called Charles, yet no man ever gave his name to it; Charles was a compound of two Celtic words, *carn lis*, meaning 'the bright palace' (of a chieftain who lorded it on an Exmoor hilltop in Devon). As for Thompson, that had indeed been named after a man, though not after the son of Thomas; it was originally *Tomestuna*, the *tun* or settlement belonging to *Tumi*, an old Danish name.

Merton Park, seat of the Greys, was scarcely above fifteen minutes' walk from Thompson; so I went there and admired the seventeenth-century house and Merton church with a brass to Sir William de Grey (1520) and his two wives and ten children. There, also, they laid Edward FitzGerald, a Suffolk man, who died while staying at Merton Rectory as the guest of George Crabbe's grandson. FitzGerald was a *dilettante* (a word so debased that it now means a dabbler or amateur). J. A. Froude used the word *dilettante* in its rightful sense when he said: 'The Romans cared for art as *dilettanti*.' With ample leisure and a sufficient income, Edward FitzGerald wrote among other things a translation of a poem in sixteen quatrains, the *Rubáiyát* by Omar Khayyam (*c.* 1123), a Persian mathematician, steeped in fatalism. The Persian's quest after Truth led him to coin a phrase that now reads, 'This is where we came in'.

> Myself when young did eagerly frequent
> Doctor and Saint, and heard great argument
> About it and about: but evermore
> Came out by the same Door wherein I went.

FitzGerald's translation is familiar to many people. The weary aesthetes of Victoria's *fin de siècle* lapped it as the milk-and-water of wisdom. Yet the translation fell flat when it first appeared. The publisher, Quaritch, could not sell two hundred copies. Several years later, however, Rossetti happened to find a second-hand copy in the fourpenny box outside Quaritch's bookshop. Impressed, he shared his pleasure with the literary world, and from that time onward many a young Epicurean—comfortably seated in the wilds of Richmond Park, looking forward to a six-course dinner—murmured to himself or maybe to Another:

> A Book of Verses underneath the Bough,
> A Jug of Wine, a Loaf of Bread—and Thou
> Beside me singing in the Wilderness . . .

'How many miles to Babylon?' our fathers asked. 'And can we get there by candlelight?' When I first got to Merton, several years ago, the sun was still high; and when I next returned, after several months, the snow was still deep; yet neither by snowlight nor sunlight could I find the Peddars Way. All was arable, as it had been in Defoe's day: 'This part of England is also remarkable for being the first where the feeding and fattening of cattle, both sheep as well as black cattle with turnips, was first practis'd in England . . .' Confronted by other men's crops, I followed the lane to Watton, a peaceful place, having an eighteenth-century clock tower astride the street; an octagonal belfry on the fourteenth-century tower of a Norman church; and at Griston Hall (so they say) the home of that wicked Uncle who caused the Babes to be taken to Wayland Wood, known locally as Wailing Wood.

About a mile east of Watton I met two ghosts. The first was the site of a Romano-British settlement beside a stream and some woods. No trace of the settlement was visible; none therefore of its predecessor, which had sunk deeper than the soil, into the Shades. The second ghost was Sir Thomas Browne, who delighted in such antiquities, and was moreover a classical scholar *primus inter pares* among Norfolk men. In 1623 he went up from Winchester College to Broadgate Hall (now Pembroke College), Oxford. Having graduated there, he studied medicine at the universities of Montpellier, Padua, and Leiden. Twelve years later, while staying at Shipden Hall, Halifax, he wrote *Religio Medici* or The Religion of a Doctor. In 1643 he set up as physician at Norwich, living and working there until he died, nearly forty years later. A loyal subject of the King, Browne disowned the Cromwellians, and went quietly about his business. In 1658 he published *Hydriotaphia, Urne Buriall: or, a Discourse of the Sepulchrall Urnes lately found in Norfolk*. In that book you hear the organ of English prose, the stateliest range of its antiphon and diapason, played by a master descanting on the eternal verities: 'Who knows the fates of his bones, or how often he is to be buried? who hath the Oracle of his ashes, or whither they are to be interred? The Reliques of many lie like the ruines of Pompeys, in all parts of the earth. . . .' King Charles II visited Browne at Norwich and there knighted him, in one of the halls of the great Dominican church which Sir Thomas Erpingham had lately rebuilt.

Browne died on his seventy-seventh birthday; a happy husband, a proud father, a spoiling grandfather, a beloved physician. Fortyseven years earlier he had raised his own monument, *Religio Medici*, a remarkable feat for a man who was still in his twenties: 'I have not seen one revolution of Saturn,' he admitted, 'nor hath my pulse beat thirty years.' Two centuries before the birth of Freud, the Norfolk doctor discovered his own id, ego, and superego: 'there is in our Soul a kind of Triumvirate, or triple Government of three Competitors, which distract the Peace of this our Commonwealth. . . .' Instead of 'expressing' himself by becoming a free-for-all battlefield, Browne achieved a better *modus vivendi*: 'a moderate and peaceable discretion may so state and order the matter, that they may be all Kings, and yet make one Monarchy, every one exercising his Soveraignty and Prerogative in due time and place, according to the restraint and limit of circumstance.' Always he probed to the heart of the matter, and, like a surgeon, dissected each side of the question. On the one hand he was a patrician ('that great enemy of Reason, Virtue and Religion . . . the Multitude'); on the other hand he was never a snob ('there is a Nobility without Heraldry, a natural dignity, whereby one man is ranked with another, another filed before him, according to the quality of Desert and preheminence of his good parts'). Being a scientist, he was something of a sceptic ('The whole Creation is a mystery, and particularly that of Man'); being an Anglican, he had faith in life ('This is the dormative I take to bedward; I need no other Laudanum than this to make me sleep; after which I close my eyes in security, content to take my leave of the Sun, and sleep unto the Resurrection').

Like most others of his kind and generation, Browne did not intend to publish his book. He would be content if the manuscript were read and approved by friends. One of those friends—either deliberately or negligently, we do not know—allowed a London printer to issue a garbled version of the manuscript; which so vexed the author that he supplied the pirate with a more accurate draft. By so slight a chance did so great a work win so wide a public. Browne's *Religio Medici* is a classic of eloquent wisdom. His knowledge of anatomy neither appalled nor persuaded him: 'Nor can I think I have the true Theory of death, when I contemplate a skull, or behold a Skeleton, with those vulgar imaginations it casts upon us. . . .' Wherefore, he said: 'I cannot go to cure the body of my patient, but I forget my profession, and call unto God for his soul.' *De profundis* he challenged agony itself: 'where life is more terrible than death, it is then the truest valour to dare to live.' There spoke the Christian Stoic, a man holding strong opinions gently: 'I cannot conceive why a difference in Opinion should divide an affection; for Controversies, Disputes, and Argumentations, both in Philosophy and in Divinity, if they meet with discreet and peaceable natures, do not infringe the Laws of Charity.' Lucretius would have admired Sir Thomas Browne's scientific attitude; Cicero would have admired his eloquence; Cato, his integrity; Vergil, his rusticity; and Livy, his urns.

Browne's memorable music accompanied me along the lane to Saham Toney, where it was exorcized by a place-name as puzzling as that which had caused William Camden to cry: 'what the origin of the name should be, as God shall help me, I dare not guess. . . .' Etymology, however, has advanced since Camden wrote his *Suffolk*. We now know that Saham Toney was the *ham* or settlement beside the *sae* or lake (it covers thirteen acres) which in 1199 was held by Roger de Toni whose forebears came from Tosyny in Normandy. Still without a trace of the Way, I sat by a stream in Page's Place, wondering who Page had been. From Page I fell once more to thoughts of Sir Thomas Browne, and the fact that in his time the Latin tongue was already becoming self-conscious, even as French was to become self-conscious to the Russian *noblesse* who spoke little else. The Renaissance and the Reformation undermined the rôle of Latin as the Esperanto among educated men. True, when Milton became Cromwell's secretary he wrote some of his despatches in Latin; true also that Latin still took precedence before French as the ultimate *lingua franca* of European diplomacy. Nevertheless, Latin no longer served as a passport throughout Christendom, the common tongue of medieval Swedish monks when they entertained six friars from France, two palmers from Hungary, and a knight apiece from Bohemia, Spain, and the Isle of Wight. Moreover, although the Church had rediscovered and transcribed the classical texts of Greece and Rome, many of her Fathers frowned on pagan literature, so that it was not until the Renaissance that a Christian could read Catullus with an easy conscience. Consider the Latinisms which were first minted during that period: 'Latinism' itself (1570), 'Latinist' (1538), 'Latinize' (1589), 'Latinity' (1619). The word 'latimer' (a corruption of the Old French *latinier*) had been used since 1480 as a synonym for 'interpreter'.

By this time I was at Ashill where a youth told me certain things which I accepted with a pinch of salt; such as, for example, that any villager might pasture his geese on Goose Common if his rent were less than £5 yearly, and that a Roman camp had been discovered on a ridge nearby. (I fancy he was trying to sell me Grounds Farm, two miles north-east, where the site of a small Roman building had indeed been identified.) One of Ashill's rectors, Bartholomew Edwards, served there for seventy-six years, from 1813 until 1899; failing by only a few months to beat the record for Anglican longevity in harness. I found, too, a monument to John Cotton (1696), ancestor of Sir Robert Cotton, the Huntingdonshire antiquary, whose collection of books and manuscripts went to the British Museum in 1753.

Somewhere between Ashill and North Pickenham lay Peddars Way, but since everyone assured me that nothing was to be seen of it, I kept to the lanes, having already followed more than enough vague parish boundaries. At North Pickenham I found the true Way, just beside a railway line, whence it emerged as a wide green road, full of skylarks and blackbirds and wild roses. Here without doubt the Romans had marched; sometimes in small parties under a centurion; at other times regimentally in full battle order, following their standards. The British Empire in decline demoralized the British Army by depriving it of many cherished loyalties and associations. The Roman Empire was wiser, for it understood the rôle of standard-bearer. Every Legion had an eagle or *aquila*, which was entrusted always to the first cohort. Every smaller unit had its own standard, topped by a hand outstretched in comradely salute. Below that hand came various devices. Thus, a Legion which had distinguished itself during a siege, might set a crown of walls on its standard; another, famous for its prowess during a landing assault, might show a ship. The standard-bearers wore animal skins over their helmets, as did the trumpeter who marched with them. Whenever camp was pitched, the men's first act was to strike their standards on the appropriate site. To lose a standard during battle was a disgrace which no unit could ever wholly outlive. Julius Caesar once despatched an army to recapture a standard that had been seized by the enemy. On most of the rare occasions when the barbarians did capture an *aquila*, they found it standing alone, fixed firmly into the ground, a memorial to the men who had died defending it.

Meanwhile the straight green road was bearing north-north-west toward Swaffham, through a countryside so evidently English and so conspicuously *sui generis* that I marvelled again at this kingdom's infinite variety. Norfolk itself ranks next in size after Yorkshire, Lincolnshire, Devonshire. Its coastline is nearly one hundred miles long. To the Romans it was simply a part of Britain; but when the Angles or *Engle* supplanted the Romans, the region was renamed as East Anglia, a part of Engle-land. Peddars Way touches every aspect of a changing scene, from the level farmland near Thetford and the heathy plantations near Swaffham, to the hillscapes above Ringstead and the sand dunes by the sea. Wherever flint is found, the typical Norfolk house uses it, as do the houses in the Chiltern Hills of Oxfordshire and Buckinghamshire. Nowhere else in Britain will you find a comparable range of domestic architecture. Through that countryside the Peddars Way marched on, green and lonely as the Icknield Way which Robert Plot described in 1677: 'it passes through no town or village in the County . . . nor does it (as I hear) scarce any where else. . . .' Plot's next words no longer apply: 'for which reason 'tis much used by stealers of Cattle . . .'

After a mile of such pleasantry the green road merged into a metalled lane. After another mile the lane swerved westward while the course of the Way met a railway line, emerged briefly as a track, and then disappeared among barley. I therefore turned aside into Swaffham, which I may justly call an old flame of mine because I never visit the place without the sun shining, even in December under snow. Swaffham was the home of the *Swaefas* or Swabians, some of the earliest settlers in Britain. Today it is marked chiefly by traffic lights and four main roads. At breakfast-time between September and May the traffic subsides somewhat, allowing you to admire the wide street and market-place with a pillared and domed Market Cross, crowned by Ceres, the goddess of Plenty, whom Vergil worshipped:

Nec requies, quin aut pomis exuberet annus
Aut fetu pecorum aut Cerealis mergite culmi . . .
Unfailingly the year lavishes fruit,
Or lambs, or a sheaf of corn . . .

Despite the traffic, Swaffham is still a farmer's town though no longer a spinner's. Said Celia Fiennes: 'The ordinary people both in Suffolk and Norfolk knitt much and spin, some with the rock [distaff] as the French does, others of their wheels out in the streets and lane as one passes . . . a man can weave 13 yards (of damask) in a day. . . .' Shaded by limes, the flint church contains the tomb of Catherine Steward, whose daughter, the widowed Elizabeth, married Robert Cromwell and begat a dictator. Elizabeth's brother, Sir Thomas Steward, was a Huntingdonshire landowner who bequeathed part of his wealth to Oliver Cromwell. While trying to imagine Miss Fiennes's distaff 'out in the streets and lane as one passes', I noticed a red van and on it a placard announcing that the average Englishman spent at least four hours a day staring at his television screen; a form of myopia which recalled Addison's comment on the man who had spent a lifetime learning to juggle with four eggs: 'I could not but reflect with my self, that the same Assiduity and Attention, had they been rightly applied, might have made him a greater Mathematician than Archimedes.' But Swaffham is too pleasant to leave a sour taste in the mouth. Even its acidity smiles, like the farmer whom I overheard sharing with another their mutual and immemorial discontent: 'I Gor-danged the last bloody government, and now damn me I'm Gor-danging the new 'un.'

About three miles north of Swaffham, on the Fakenham road, a lane crossed the River Nar *en route* for Castle Acre. Somewhere to the right of that lane, hidden beneath grassland and corn, lay Peddars Way. It must have passed close to Little Palgrave Hall, then over Hungry Hill, and thence into what is now Castle Acre, the *aecer* or field with a castle. Here indeed I found the history of England, written in stone, brick, hedgerow, voice, and one loud aircraft moaning like a drunken vagrant who has mistaken the wedding for a funeral. Although I have visited the village half a dozen times, I still find it hard to define Castle Acre, except by saying that with each revisitation the place reminds me of Emily Brontë's reply to those who remarked on her indifference to fine clothes: 'I would', she said, 'be as God made me.' Castle Acre has remained much as wise men made it, which is to say peaceful (except in high summer), compact, companionable, and harmonious with its environment among fields. You enter via a steep lane between old houses and an appropriate shop or two, crowned by the arched gateway of a castle that was built by William de Warenne, son-in-law to William the Conqueror. Passing under that arch, you find a village green shaded among trees, and lined by venerable cottages confronting their contemporaries across the grass. The largest building is the Victoria and Albert Inn, not wholly harmonious, yet so hospitable that when I called there, on a hot afternoon in May, the echo of my knock was answered by a hostess who without ado ushered me into the bar, and, almost before I had time to unlace my boots, reappeared with a tea tray. So, amid friendly semi-solitude, I sat in a shaft of the sun while bees among limes heightened the pervasive stillness. The taste of the tea, the quality of the bread and butter, turned back my scrapbook to 1920. Outside the window three children played on the green. I hoped that in years to come they would give thanks for having been sown, not on stony ground beside an industrial estate, but on loam as rich as Wordsworth's:

> Ye lowly cottages wherein we dwelt,
> A ministration of your own was yours;
> Can I forget you, being as you were
> So beautiful among the pleasant fields
> In which ye stood?

Beyond the village green a few hundred yards of lane led to Castle Acre Priory, passing the site of a Roman camp, a medieval church, and the hilltop husk of a Norman castle; all dominating the relics of a priory in a combe beside the Nar. The façade of the west front of Castle Acre Priory is etched like a wafer; behind it, in vivid turf, the base of broken pillars and the shell of fallen walls carve *Ichabod* on the sky. Yet neither the extent of the relics nor the degree of their ruin is immediately perceptible, because the eye is half-deceived by the stone veneer of that west front and by the Prior's House adjoining it, a late medieval building, enlarged during the seventeenth century. A man informed me that he had known the Prior's House when it was leased to a family of farm-hands and their donkey. In 1970 a member of that family, the last occupant of the Prior's House, was living in the village itself.

The nobility of the architecture, and the beauty of its setting, form a fitting introit to a more general chapter of history, for it was William de Warenne, first Earl of Surrey, who introduced the Cluniac Order into England. In 1072 he and his wife, Grundada, set out as pilgrims for Rome, but finding themselves endangered by war between French and Papal forces, they sought shelter at the Abbey of Cluny in Burgundy, receiving there a hospitality in keeping with the Abbey's fame. The Earl, indeed, was so impressed by the piety of the monks that, after much persuasion, he prevailed on the Abbot to allow him to found a Cluniac house, the Priory of St. Pancras, near his castle at Lewes in Sussex. The Order spread fast and far. Houses were founded at Much Wenlock, Northampton, Daventry, Bermondsey, Pontefract, Thetford. Castle Acre Priory, a branch of Lewes, itself had three cells or dependent houses in Norfolk, and one in Suffolk. Lewes Priory took precedence over all other houses within the English province, not by right but of honour.

The Cluniacs were not simply another batch of monks. They were the *élite* of monasticism. While the Cistercians marooned themselves as sheep farmers, and the friars wandered as 'worker priests', the monks of Cluny dedicated their days to the *opus Dei* or worship of God. By the number of their prayers, the perfection of their chanting, the precision of their ceremonies, the holiness of their lives . . . by these the Cluniac monks endued their corporate worship with a beauty and dignity never before attempted. So renowned was their austerity, so evident their piety, that William the Conqueror begged the Abbot of Cluny to send twelve monks whom he might set as bishops and abbots over his Saxon subjects. In return, he offered to pay a large sum of money. The Abbot declined without thanks: 'The monks of Cluny', he said, 'are not for sale.' The Abbot of Cluny acknowledged no ecclesiastical

10

superior except the Pope; all Cluniac houses were exempt
from episcopal jurisdiction; all were supervised by their priors,
subject only to the Abbot himself and *in extremis* to the Pope.
Once a year every prior attended the Chapter at Cluny. After 1301
the English priors were allowed, if they so wished, to attend every
second year; a concession to the pains of travel in general and of
seasickness in particular.

The lot of the English Cluniacs was not always a happy one.
Bedevilled by Anglo-French wars, they were classed as alien
priories, and burdened therefore by heavy fines. In 1307 the Abbot
of Cluny was deprived of his dues from the English houses. In
1351 Lewes Priory and Convent were recognized by Letters Patent
as 'denizens and not aliens'. In 1373 Castle Acre and all other
daughter-houses of Lewes received a similar status. The rest of
the houses were allowed to buy their own dispensation. The
monks themselves were not without sin. In 1351, for example,
the King ordered his Serjeant-at-Arms to arrest certain Castle
Acre brethren who had 'spurned the habit of their order and were
vagabonds in England in secular habit'. The Prior showed no
delight when his lost lambs were restored to the fold; he had them
whipped. In 1537 the King's iconoclast, Thomas Cromwell,
seized Lewes Priory for himself, having imported from Italy a
gang of skilled workmen to strip the priory of its valuables, to
demolish its church, and to 'develop' the other buildings as a
private residence. Within two months the new owner moved in,
accompanied by his wife, who found the place 'so commodious
that she thinketh herself to be here right well settled'. Castle Acre
Priory was formally dissolved in 1537, when the prior, Thomas
Malling, and ten of his monks signed a deed surrendering their
house to Henry VIII, who presented it to Thomas Howard, Duke
of Norfolk, from whom it passed via Queen Elizabeth to Thomas
Gresham; and from him to Thomas Cecil, sometime Earl of
Exeter, whose son sold it to Sir Edward Coke, ancestor of that
Earl of Leicester who in 1929 handed guardianship of the site to
the Ministry of Works.

The Romans neither saw nor foresaw the Priory of Castle Acre.
They saw only another hill to be climbed, and more trees to be

felled, and new sightings to be taken. All those things they did as part of the day's work. And having done them, they prepared to do the same again as part of the next day's work, for the unmade Way had miles to go before it reached the sea. Of the Romans' name for Castle Acre we know nothing. They may not have troubled to name it. There may not have been a place for them to name. Yet the proof that they marched through is visible and tangible, being a straight lane leading north-north-west from the Earl of Surrey's gate.

9 Peddars Way:
Castle Acre to Holme-Next-The-Sea

THE lane kept straight for three miles, steady as a landlocked compass. If you plotted your course by placing a ruler on the map, the bow wave ran parallel with its wake, and only a few hundred yards west of it, simply because the Romans deviated in order to ford two rivers, the Nar at Castle Acre and the Wissey at North Pickenham. But something swifter than bodily motion was achieved by such directness. On certain summits along their roads the Romans erected timber watch-towers whose upper storey was flanked on all sides by an open gallery. The steep-pitched roof served as an umbrella. Manned day and night, the towers collected and transmitted all kinds of news. The most effective transmission was by means of torches and a system of semaphore. That Rome could build, all the world knows; that she created new and beautiful designs is less widely understood. Granted, her architecture was moulded by Greece, yet it never became mere imitation. If Greece created the Doric column, then Rome recreated the arch, using it as a principle of construction. What we call a Norman arch is basically Roman. It was Rome, not Greece, which Celts and Saxons acknowledged as the inspiration of their own architecture. Bede, for example, states that Nechtan, Christian King of the Picts, wrote to the Abbot of Wearmouth in Northumberland, 'asking that architects be sent to him so that he might build for his people a stone church in the Roman style . . .' The men who designed the amphitheatre at Rome were no mean architects.

But to return to the Way: Edward Gibbon's *Journal* for 23 October 1762 contains the following lesson of experience: 'our most important actions have often been determined by chance, caprice, or some very inadequate motive.' Myself, I never was able to define 'chance' because I never was able to dissect the ultimate dynamics of events. Nevertheless, I continue to say that I discovered Great Massingham quite by chance. The ordering of that event was as follows: several years ago, when I neither needed nor especially wished to explore Peddars Way, I found myself at Castle Acre *en route* for Holt. Noticing *Roman Road* on the map, I decided to spend a couple of hours walking along it, before resuming my journey. So, I savoured those three miles of lane, downdale and uphillock among corn and coppice and cabbage. It was September, a season of pastel skies, of stubble and stook, and guns barking, and dogs pointing, and at twilight a shimmer of frost. I became so merged with the season that, instead of looking where the Way went (which was straight on), I looked only where the lane went (which was sharp right). Presently I found myself at Great Massingham, the most beautiful of all Wayside villages.

On my last revisitation the sun shone so thirstily that I made at once for the inn (one of several) and thence for the green (one of several) where I sat within sight of a pond (one of several). Great Massingham, in short, is a numerous place. Imagine, therefore, that you have reached a cross-roads on the edge of a village. Beside the white signpost are a pond and a common; ahead, the lane leads to more ponds, other commons, brick-and-flint cottages, thatched roofs, and a church among trees. Soon the lane grows wider, and on the left of it are yet more ponds and commons, sunshaded by trees. Such, in black and white, is many-coloured Massingham, the *ham* of *Maessa*'s people, concerning whom we know nothing except their descendants and the village which they built as a bridge across the centuries, spanning life's *lachrymae rerum* and *sursum corda*.

The place at which I had wandered off course was called Shepherds Bush. Our Old English *sceaphirde* has almost disappeared from England, except on Exmoor, the Lakeland fells, Yorkshire Dales, Cheviot Hills; and even there his status seems blurred. Yet W. H. Hudson, who lived until 1922, remembered an autumnal encounter with real shepherds: 'One day, in September, when sauntering over Mere Down, one of the most extensive and

loneliest-looking sheep-walks in South Wilts . . . I passed three
flocks of sheep, all with many bells, and noticed that each flock
produced a distinctly different sound. . . .' Presently he met the
shepherd with his dogs. 'When the shepherd had got up to them
[the dogs] he stood and began uttering a curious call, a somewhat
musical cry in two notes, and instantly the sheep, now at a considerable distance, stopped feeding and turned, then all together
began running towards him, and when within thirty yards stood
still, massed together, and all gazing at him. He then uttered a
different call, and turning walked away, the dogs keeping with
him and the sheep closely following. It was late in the day, and he
was going to fold them at the foot of the slope in some fields
half-a-mile away.' There are shepherds still alive who in their
'prentice years lived alone in a hut at lambing time, neither seeing
nor hearing a human being for several days. At other times they
lived more leisurely though not much more sociably. Such men
kept their eyes so widely open that the dictionary still contains
their name: shepherd's calendar (scarlet pimpernel), shepherd's
club (common mullein), shepherd's needle (crane's bill), shepherd's purse (a common weed). Even the shepherd's diet and
dress have entered the language: shepherd's pie (minced meat and
mashed potatoes), shepherd's plaid (black-and-white tweed check).
When winter walks this Way, you will see what John Clare saw
in Northamptonshire two centuries ago:

> The shepherd too in great coat wrapt
> And straw bands round his stockings lapt
> Wi' plodding dog that sheltering steals
> To shun the wind behind his heels
> Takes rough and smooth the winter weather
> And paces thro' the snow together. . . .

The Roman shepherds or *pastores* were the *élite* among farmfolk.
Whether freemen or slaves, they became the hardiest of men,
braced by fresh air and hard exercise throughout the year. When
the old order changed, and businessmen exploited the land as a
capital investment, the tenants were supplanted by slaves. Only
in the mountains did the free shepherd and stockman survive, the
salt of Italy and the heirs of Romulus.

At Field Barn Plantation the Way falls apart, like a ribbon to the scissors. Then, after perhaps two hundred yards, it reappears, still following the previous alignment, but this time a shade to the west, having curved toward the Plantation. Within less than two miles it crosses three lanes, the second of them a cul-de-sac leading east into Great Massingham. It seems worthwhile to follow that second lane because it passes the site of a priory, some fragments of which can be seen in the house and barns at Abbey Farm. Great Massingham—I welcome any excuse to return thither—is or ought to be famous for what Charles Lamb called 'the sweet food of academic institutions'. Thus, Sir Robert Walpole attended a private school in the village, whence by devious routes—which included imprisonment in the Tower of London—he became the first minister whom we now call prime. Before that, in 1676, another Norfolk man, Charles Calthorpe, founded a free school which for many years was housed in a room above the church porch. But the chief academician was Sir Stephen Perse, a native of the village, who became a famous physician at Cambridge, where he endowed (1617) a school which perpetuates his name. One of the school's headmasters, George Griffith, bequeathed the then considerable sum of £100 to the Master and four senior Fellows of Caius College 'to be by them employed to the best advantage for a supplement to the revenue of Dr Stephen Perse's Free School in Cambridge. . . .'

Little Massingham is Great's near neighbour, scarcely a quarter-hour's walk down the lane; smaller yet in its way not less attractive. Just north of Little Massingham lies a derelict railway line whose stationmaster's house is now frequented by hens free-ranging where once an iron horse champed. Do you remember the Great Eastern Railway which served these parts? Is your memory blazoned with the locomotive's dark blue livery, trimmed in red and black, bright with copper and brass, scarlet coupling rods, white-roofed cab? What a way that was, to see the heart of England and to hear it also, beating steadily when a signalman and an engine-driver passed the time of day ('Just right for my runner beans'), the hour of night ('Is it snowing at Burnham Market?'), the plight of England ('Twasn't like Sutcliffe to score

a duck), and the end of the world ('They say the price o' beer's
going up').

A footpath from Little Massingham rejoins the Way, passing a
wood and, to the north of it, Little Massingham Manor, islanded
among trees. The Way then crosses the derelict railway and skirts
the tip of Houghton Hall, Norfolk's largest country house, in a
deer park at the end of a mile-long avenue. The Walpoles were at
Houghton during the reign of King Stephen, nearly nine centuries
ago. The most famous member of the family—commonly known
as Sir Robert Walpole—was the King's first minister for twenty-
one years, a record unlikely to be broken. Walpole symbolized the
heyday of the Whig oligarchy, when a minority of peers united
with a majority of merchants to increase their own power by
decreasing the Sovereign's. Walpole clung to office until his
majority had dwindled to two, whereupon he consented to be
moved to another place, as first Earl of Orford. Houghton Hall
was his own doing. Work began in 1723 and ended thirteen years
later. There is a story that Walpole demolished a number of houses
near the church, thereby provoking Oliver Goldsmith to compose
The Deserted Village:

> Sweet Auburn! loveliest village of the plain
> Where health and plenty cheered the labouring swain . . .

A judiciously dishonest use of statistics can be made either to
prove or to disprove that proposition, as it can be made either to
prove or to disprove a second proposition:

> Amidst thy bowers the tyrant's hand is seen,
> And desolation saddens all thy green . . .

As the agnostic remarked when they asked him whether God
existed or did not: 'The truth lies somewhere between the two.'
Goldsmith himself achieved an antithesis: 'In regretting the de-
population of the country,' he told Sir Joshua Reynolds, 'I inveigh
against the increase of our luxuries.'

Luxury certainly lined the Way as it ambled north-west toward
the sea. There was bird-song enough to vie with Vergil's 'copses
that resound with the music of birds'. There was fruit to vie with
Horace's 'Autumn raising his head over the fields, adorned with

mellow apples'. There was sunlight to vie with the Sirmio landscape of Catullus and its 'brightness from the glowing light'. There
was corn to vie with the fields that Statius admired when he
exclaimed, 'What a fertile soil!'

All this time the Way goes on, sometimes marked only with an
agger, but for the most part a well-defined route, used by farmfolk
to and from their fields. Yet nowhere does it enter a village nor
pass within hailing distance. It does, however, pass within sight of
the Sandringham estate near Anmer or *aened mere* (the duck pond),
a royal village indeed, linked to Sandringham House by three
miles of King's Avenue, straight as a Roman road.

In 1861, for the sum of £220,000, the Prince of Wales bought
the Sandringham estate, covering 7,000 acres, from the Hon.
Charles Spencer Cowper. The property had become derelict, and
its house was too small for the needs of a gregarious entourage.
The Prince therefore built the present House, transforming the
land into one of the finest farming and sporting estates in Britain.
Like Osborne and Balmoral, Sandringham was a private establishment, a place where, when he became King, the new owner could
set aside what one of his ancestors, Henry VIII, called 'London
business'. Not everyone approved every aspect of life at Sandringham. The Hon. Miss Sturt, for instance, was dismayed when she
discovered the Prince at baccarat. To her fiancé she wrote: 'I think
it is a shocking affair for the Royal Family to play an illegal game
every night.' Perhaps because of those late nights the Princess
was persistently unpunctual, so that the Prince devised S.T. or
Sandringham Time, all clocks ticking half an hour ahead of those
at Greenwich. A keen sportsman, the Prince sometimes expected
his neighbours to sacrifice their crops to his own guns. One such
neighbour, a Mrs. Creswell, published an anonymous account of
her *contretemps* with Sandringham, and then retired to Texas, a
pheasantless republican state. But Edward VII was not easily
daunted. He once summoned his dentist to Sandringham, to
extract a painful molar. When Lord Crewe enquired whether an
anaesthetic had been given, the elderly King replied: 'Oh dear no!
I can bear pain.' Assuredly he did not bear malice, because the
dentist afterwards dined with his victim, and spent the night under

the same roof. In the end, however, Sandringham did kill the King. Despite a bitter east wind, he had insisted on inspecting the home farm and pedigree stock rather than disappoint the servants who had taken such trouble to prepare them. Next morning the King awoke with a heavy cold. Resolved as ever to fulfil his duties, he returned to Buckingham Palace. Two days later he made the last entry in a diary which he had kept since childhood: 'The King dines alone.' Having dined once more, he died.

George V was even fonder of Sandringham than his father had been: 'Dear old Sandringham,' he called it, 'the place I love better than anywhere else in the world.' He, too, was a keen sportsman— among the best shots in his kingdom—and at Sandringham he spent his honeymoon. There his second son was born and baptized, one day to reign as George VI. The father wrote in his diary: 'A little boy was born weighing nearly 8lbs. at 3.40 a.m. S.T.' The child's grandmother, Queen Victoria, received the news G.M.T. At Sandringham, as he would have wished, the King died. During his last hours he received from the Lord President of the Council a proclamation of a Council of State, which he must sign. His doctor, Lord Dawson, tried to guide the feeble hand. After several attempts the King made his mark and then, glancing at the assembled Councillors, said: 'Gentlemen, I am sorry for keeping you waiting like this.' Next day the diary which he had kept in his own hand for fifty years, showed an unfamiliar writing: 'My dearest husband, King George V, was much distressed at the bad writing above and begged me to write his diary for him next day.' The King's life had moved peacefully to its close.

The next King, Edward VIII, disliked Sandringham. He abolished S.T., and asked the Duke of York to suggest ways of partly dismantling the estate. The Duke obeyed, hiding his own affection for the place. With Lord Radnor, an expert surveyor and forester, he spent two weeks at Sandringham, preparing to write a report. But the incident pained and surprised him; and when he learned that Balmoral, too, had been half-banished, without any conference with other members of the Royal Family, his diary remarked: 'David only told me what he had done when it was over . . . He arranged it all with the official people up there.'

Under George VI the estate returned to life, and repaid that compliment by comforting the King's own life when the surgeons had done their best. After a happy day with a party of guns he died in his sleep.

Her present Majesty, Queen Elizabeth II, graciously opens the grounds of Sandringham so that her subjects can see the beautiful grounds where the Sovereign may forget awhile the cares of 'London business'.

Anmer is less than six miles from the sea beyond Wolferton. The early classical world feared the sea, not without cause. Shipping in the Mediterranean ceased during the stormy months. *Mare clausum*, said the Romans (the sea is closed). Like the Greeks, the Romans were much concerned with the hazards of seafaring. Roman ships lacked a magnetic compass, which was not invented until the twelfth century. A rough-and-ready pilot's book was used for certain seaboard routes. Thus, the *Periplous of Scylax of Caryanda* reported: 'From Leuce Acte to the harbour of Taodmantium is a half-day's sail. . . . The parts beyond the Isle of Cerne are no longer navigable, because of shoals, mud, and seaweed. The traders here are Phoenicians.'

During their wars against Carthage the Romans had been compelled to study the construction, sailing, and fighting of ships. In the year 67 B.C. the Mediterranean was so plagued by pirates that Pompey led a campaign against them, comprising 500 galleys, 5,000 cavalry, and 12,000 infantrymen. The success of his fleet gave a lasting impetus to Roman seapower. Unlike the English, whose ancestors were born with brine in their veins, the Romans taught themselves to become seamen late in life. At its zenith the Imperial Navy maintained squadrons throughout the Empire, from the Norfolk coast to the Danube, and from Ravenna to the Rhine. Again unlike the English, Rome never granted precedence to the Navy. Her Army was the Senior Service. Only freedmen and the poorest freemen served at sea. The naval recruiting officers were part-time tax-collectors living in Italian towns. Roman warships were triremes or sailing ships with three tiers of oarsmen; their patrol craft were lighter, having only two tiers of oarsmen. Transport vessels sailed under escort. The naval ratings were of

three sorts: oarsmen, seamen and marines. Admirals were styled
praefecti classibus. Such were the men who served as 'a security for
such as pass on the seas upon their lawful occasions,' sweeping a
course for Masefield's

> Quinquireme of Nineveh from distant Ophir
> Rowing home to haven in sunny Palestine,
> With a cargo of ivory,
> And apes and peacocks,
> Sandalwood, cedarwood, and sweet white wine.

Fring must be one of the smallest places in the world. You sight
its hilltop church long before you arrive, having crossed three
lanes within a mile or so. There is a Hall at Fring (set in a park)
and a farm (Church Farm, near a bridge across the River
Heacham). The church contains traces of a mural St. Christopher,
well-suiting a hamlet so close to Little Walsingham which once
ranked next after Canterbury as a shrine for pilgrims. At Fring the
Way wavers, probably because the Romans were seeking the best
ford across the river. Thereafter it dwindles to a footpath, but
is a lane when it crosses the Norwich road at Littleport. It was
here that I experienced a *déjà non vu* because the Way had reached
a lane which, I would have sworn, was not marked on the map. I
checked memory with map, finding that each verified the other.
No lane appeared on the map. What did appear was a railway line.
Examining the lane again, I saw that it had indeed been a railway,
though now it resembled the approach to a rich man's farm. As if
to end the matter, I found a railway signboard half-hidden in a
hollow.

So I went on, the contours climbing again, as they often do
when the sea lies below. It was a beautiful land, hip-high with
corn, except where it was white with sheep, or green with
vegetables, or shaded by woods. I had already complimented
myself on hours of serene wayfaring when a lane loomed up, and
beyond it no sign of Peddars Way. 'Corn!' I exclaimed. 'The
wretched farmer has ploughed and sown.' And I was right, though
wrong to blame the present farmer, because the damage had been
done long ago. Yet the fact remained—I proved it on later jour-

neys—that the Way had disappeared. If you approach from the north, you cannot even find traces of an *agger*. All you do find are crops and a pair of hedgerows, neither of which lies along the undoubted alignment. Yet the Way is there, under the soil; and after a few hundred yards it reappears as a green road over sandy hills. Sweeping that houseless horizon, a landsman would set himself at the heart of England. But a sailor perceives the sea before it is visible. Sometimes he hears it, sometimes he smells it, and sometimes he detects it with that sixth sense which is an amalgamation whereby five transcend the sum of their parts. Along this green road the smugglers came, bearing brandy for the parson. We have the parson's word for it, written in his own hand two centuries ago, in *The Diary of a Country Parson* by James Woodforde, rector of Weston Longeville in the County of Norfolk. Woodforde was a Somerset man, born near the Foss Way, where we shall be more formally introduced to him. Here it will do to quote his Norfolk revelation: 'Dec.29.1786 . . . Had another Tub of Gin and another of the best Coniac Brandy brought to me this evening abt. 9. We heard a thump at the Front Door about that time, but did not know what it was, till I went out and found the 2 Tubs—but nobody there.' The rector was such a good man, as men go, that it seems only just to observe that in his day a smuggler's cargo was rated no more villainous than was a pound of butter or a slice of bacon bought in 1940 from a neighbour's farm. Thomas Crabbe, another East Anglian parson, depicted a type of smuggler who suited his own sombre temperament:

> Where now are these? . . . Beneath yon cliff they stand,
> To show the freighted pinnace where to land;
> To load the ready steed with guilty haste,
> To fly in terror o'er the pathless waste . . .

Norfolk smugglers may have fled indeed, but their terror must have been considerably reduced by the path which the Romans had made, leading straight from the sea to whatever safety the brandy-boys had prepared for themselves in the woods above Fring.

A derelict windmill marks the last lap of Peddars Way. It stands on a hill above Ringstead, overlooking the green road that descends between high hedges. The windmill's early prototype contained a sieve, or temse, which reciprocated on a wooden frame that became hot with friction, and sometimes caught alight; whence the saying 'To set the Thames (or temse) on fire'.

At Ringstead an official Peddars Way sign serves as *alpha* and *omega*, for at that point the green road becomes a metalled lane, slightly off the original course, yet running closely parallel until it comes within sound of the sea. At that sound, whenever I pass this way, I make two short detours to a pair of famous shrines.

The first shrine is Brancaster, the site of *Branodunum*, a few hundred yards seaward of the coast road. Once garrisoned by Dalmatian cavalry, *Branodunum* served as a fort of the Saxon Shore, ready to repel invaders or to destroy them when they had landed. The Saxon Shore was the creation of Carausius, Admiral of the British Fleet and Count of the Saxon Shore. Sir John Rhys believed that Carausius came from Wexford, where he was known as *Cu-roi* or Hound of the Plain. Hound he certainly was, and not of the nicest, because he turned pirate himself, or at any rate shared the swag which he allowed the pirates to collect. Rather than face trial at Rome, Carausius seized power in Britain and the Low Countries, and contrived to gain official recognition until, six years later, he was assassinated by his own treasurer, a man named Allectus. Even today the ruins of some of the forts which Carausius built may be seen along the south-east coast. The rôle of his warships resembled that of the frigates which Nelson described as 'the eyes of the Fleet'. Their task was to detect and report the approach of pirates. The ships were called *pictae*, a devious derivation from the Pictish currachs. The hull and rigging of each ship were painted sea-green; sea-green also, the uniform of their twenty oarsmen. For sixty years the ships and troops of the Saxon Shore kept the pirates at bay. In A.D. 387, unable any longer to suffer such frustration, a large force of Scots, Picts and Saxons launched an assault in which the Count of the Saxon Shore was killed. Of the fort at *Brandodunum* only a green mound remains. Richard Jefferies visited a similar site in the west country: 'Fifteen centuries before', he mused, 'there had been a Roman station at the spot. . . . There the centurions rested their troops after their weary march across the downs, for the lane, now bramble-grown and full of ruts, was then a Roman road. There were villas, and baths, and fortifications; these things you may read about in books. They are lost now in the hedges, under the flowering grass, in the ash copses, all forgotten. . . .'

The second detour leads inland a few miles to the birthplace of Horatio, Vice-Admiral Viscount Nelson, Duke of Brontë, sixth of the twelve children of the Reverend Edmund Nelson, rector of Burnham Thorpe. The village church contains some Nelson keep-sakes; the inn is called the Lord Nelson; the shop-cum-post office is called Trafalgar Stores; but Nelson's home, the old rectory, which stood about a mile from the church, was demolished (the site is marked by a signpost alongside a stream).

Horatio Nelson had the sea in his veins, and Norfolk in his bones. On his mother's side he was descended from that Sir John Suckling to whose coat-of-arms Queen Elizabeth added a sprig of honeysuckle in token of his loyalty when she made a progress through Norfolk. In Nelson's boyhood the twenty-first of October was observed as a festival because, on that day, in the year 1759, His Majesty's ship *Dreadnought* (Captain Maurice Suckling) had with two other ships engaged a superior French force in the West Indies; upon which occasion Captain Suckling, of Woodton Hall, Norfolk, used the sword of his great-uncle, Captain Galfridus Walpole.

Nelson's mother died when he was nine years old. During a Christmas holiday the boy chanced to read, in a local newspaper, that his uncle, Captain Maurice Suckling, had been given com-mand of the *Raisonnable*, of sixty-four guns. Horatio at once sent a message to his father, who was then at Bath: 'I should like to go with my uncle Maurice to sea.' The request was passed on, and in due time the Captain made the following signal: 'What has poor Horace done, who is so weak, that he above all the rest should be sent to rough it out at sea. But let him come; and the first time we go into action, a cannon-ball may knock off his head, and provide for him at once.' Had it done so, Napoleon would very probably have invaded England. In the event, Horatio Nelson was appointed to the *Raisonnable*, rated as a midshipman from 1 January 1771. He was twelve years old.

Thirty-four years later, at dawn on 21 October 1805, Nelson appeared on the quarter-deck of H.M.S. *Victory*, which was cruising with a strong force off Cape Trafalgar. Time and the enemy had marked him, for he had lost an arm and an eye. Despite his courage and genius, the highest rewards were still withheld from him. He remained a subordinate officer. His devotion to his mistress and their child had not received the understanding which it deserved. The quirks of Nelson's temperament are of great interest, but an analysis of them ought to be left to those who are qualified to undertake that task. Meanwhile, only one thing mattered. The French warships were in sight. If Nelson could defeat them, he would restore peace to Europe, and liberate some of the nations which Bonaparte had conquered. If Nelson could not defeat them, Bonaparte would invade England. Nelson knew that he was about to die. Probably he wished to die. When one of his Captains went over the side, to rejoin his own ship before the battle, Nelson was heard to say: 'God bless you, Blackwood. I shall never speak to you again.'

As the enemy drew within range, Nelson turned to his Signal Officer, Lieutenant Pasco, saying that he wished to make a signal to the Fleet. After brief consultation, one word of the signal was changed—'confides' became 'expects' . . . 'England expects that every man will do his duty.' When the immortal standfast was sighted, it was greeted with three cheers by every ship in the Fleet. Captain Blackwood, a man not given to word-painting, said that the effect was 'truly sublime'. A second signal followed, warning the Fleet to be ready to anchor after the battle, for Nelson had quizzed the sky, and saw that the weather might break. He was right. A storm did sink many of the survivors. Four minutes after that warning, he ordered Number 16, the signal for close action, which remained at the *Victory*'s top-gallant masthead until it was shot away. At 4.30 that afternoon Nelson died of his wounds. On receiving the news, the government bestowed on his brother, a country parson, the earldom which it had withheld from the deceased.

Twelve years after the Battle of Trafalgar somebody thought it would be a good idea to give Nelson a monument; but so many other Britons thought otherwise that the monument was not finished until Queen Victoria's reign. While others assemble at his feet—protesting, striking, kicking—'the saviour of Europe' stands foursquare to the winds of change,

> riding the sky
> With one arm and one eye.

The last few hundred yards of Peddars Way enter the edge of Holme-Next-The-Sea, and pass through it to the shore. Even in summer the dunes seem bleak, the sea distant, the marshland melancholy. Yet here, or somewhere close by, the Romans emptied the last load of rubble, set the final paving stone, and sighted the first ship that should carry passengers over the Wash to Lincolnshire and thence perhaps to *Eboracum* and *Bremenium* and *Trimontium*.

Foss Way

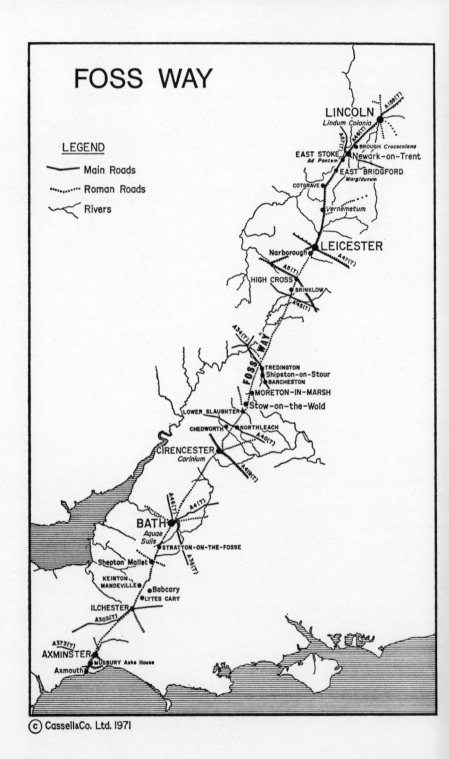

FOSS WAY

LEGEND

⎯⎯⎯ Main Roads

···········Roman Roads

⋎⋏⋎ Rivers

LINCOLN
Lindum Colonia
A158(T)
A46(T)
BROUGH *Crococolana*
EAST STOKE Newark-on-Trent
Ad Pontem
EAST BRIDGFORD
Margidunum
COTGRAVE
Vernemetum
LEICESTER
Narborough A47(T)
A5(T)
HIGH CROSS
BRINKLOW
A45(T)

FOSS WAY

A34(T)

TREDINGTON
Shipston-on-Stour
BARCHESTON
MORETON-IN-MARSH
Stow-on-the-Wold
LOWER SLAUGHTER
CHEDWORTH NORTHLEACH
A40(T)
CIRENCESTER
Corinium
A419(T)

A46(T) A4(T)
BATH
Aquae Sulis
STRATTON-ON-THE-FOSSE
A36(T)
Shepton Mallet
KEINTON MANDEVILLE
Babcary
LYTES CARY
ILCHESTER
A303(T)
A373(T)
AXMINSTER
MUSBURY *Ashe House*
Axmouth

© Cassell & Co. Ltd. 1971

10 Foss Way: Lincoln to High Cross

LINCOLN is dominated by Rome; not imperial Rome but papal Rome, enshrined in a hilltop cathedral whose stones were consecrated in 1092, four days after the death of its founder, Bishop Remigius. Having been enlarged, the cathedral was shattered by an earthquake. The surveyor reported succinctly: *Scissa est*. Then, within a twelvemonth, came a new bishop, St. Hugh of Avalon, formerly Treasurer of the *Grande Chartreuse*, who forthwith ordered Geoffrey de Noiers to rebuild the ruin, which others after him adorned; not least among them being the eighteenth-century carpenter who made the mahogany pulpit in the north-east transept. When Defoe saw Lincoln Cathedral he exclaimed: 'Its situation indeed is infinitely more to advantage than any cathedral in England . . . It stands upon an exceeding high hill, and is seen into five or six counties.'

The city's earliest name, Lindon, is identical with the Welsh *lleyn* or lake, a reference to the River Witham in the valley. The first Roman fort (A.D. 47) was protected by ditches and a timber rampart reinforced with rubble and clay. From it the Ninth Legion deterred the *Iceni* to the east and the *Brigantes* to the north. Within twenty-five years the fort became a *colonia*, a community of retired legionaries, covering forty acres on top of the hill, defended by a ditch that can be seen in the garden of Fosse House in Church Lane. *Lindum Colonia* had four gates, four main streets, and a public bath. Because the veterans received a gratuity and grants of land, their town expanded and soon reached the plain, where excavation has uncovered the sites of luxurious houses. One imperial relic survives, the Newport Arch, the oldest city gateway still in use in Britain, through which the Ninth Legion marched and counter-marched, chanting its songs, dreaming its dreams, and sometimes carrying its dead.

Lincoln reached the peak of its career during the Middle Ages, when the diocese became the largest in England, stretching as far south as Oxfordshire. Within the small Roman site alone stood sixteen churches. Another thirteen were strung along the line of the present High Street. G. G. Coulton was near the mark when he reckoned that medieval England possessed one church for every hundred families. Robin Hood's doublet of Lincoln green confirmed the city's status in the wool trade. In 1794 Thomas Stone found the cottage crafts flourishing: 'This County has been remarkable for its manufacture of stuffs for ladies apparel, the spinning of which has been chiefly performed by their fair hands. . . .' Another Augustan admired 'the prodigious numbers of large sheep'. Today even the Lincolnshire Wolds have been transformed from a sheep-walk to a granary and vegetable garden. Lincoln's identity as a country town was destroyed by railways and the Industrial Revolution. The contemporary Civic Centre could not and does not blend with the fifteenth-century Guildhall and an endearing Friends Meeting House (1689).

The escape from Lincoln is slow, sordid, steep; and I know it well because I once rode a horse along the entire Foss Way. That was nearly twenty years ago. I still remember the relief with which, after four miles of traffic, I trotted down a lane to Thorpe-on-the-Hill, to visit a redbrick chapel that was built (1909) in memory of a local ploughman, John Hunt, who taught himself to read good books. After studying at a Wesleyan College in Hoxton, he served for ten years as a missionary among the Fijians, translating the Bible into their language, and dying among them at the age of thirty-six. Hunt's influence in Fiji remains strong. Most of the islanders are Wesleyans, and their late Queen was crowned by a Wesleyan minister.

I doubt that anyone would follow this tract of the Way for pleasure. The country is flat, the road narrow, the speed scorching. Like Watling Street, this Roman road reveals *longueurs*. Unlike Watling Street, it soon overtakes them and is seldom re-overtaken. Even so, the northernmost sector of Foss Way makes a disappointing introduction to Lincolnshire, England's second largest county and the foremost among farming shires. From north to south it is seventy-five miles long; from east to west, forty-five miles. Two facts confute the legend that Lincolnshire is flat. The first fact is the Lincolnshire Wolds and the little towns and villages, from Caistor to Ashby Puerorum; the second fact is a railway tunnel under Bassingthorpe Hill near Grantham, which stands 370 feet above the sea and is the highest point on the line between King's Cross and Edinburgh. But such ruminations scarcely sustained me among the speedsters. I suffered them for six miles and then took the next lane on the left, which led to sanity and a barn in which I relaxed awhile, reading Sir Thomas Browne, who approved a brief respite from contemporary life: 'It is better', he said, 'to sit down in modest ignorance, and rest contented with the natural blessing of our own reasons, than buy the uncertain knowledge of this life with sweat and vexation. . . .' Twenty minutes later I rejoined the traffic. A tedious tract lay ahead, so I beguiled myself by listening to Roman music: 'Not without cause therefore some both Italian and Spanish Poets of prime note have rejected Rime both in longer and shorter Works, as have also long since our best English Tragedies, as a thing of it self, to all judicious ears, triveal and of no true musical delight; which consists only in apt Numbers, for quantity of Syllables, and the sense variously drawn out from one Verse to another, not in the jingling sound of like endings, a fault avoyded by the learned Ancients both in Poetry and all good Oratory.' Although written in English, Milton's sour dismissal of rhyme was sheer Latin. Since it is lunacy to suppose that Milton's taste fell short of the best in his own time, it follows that he and his readers enjoyed more leisure than we do, and were able therefore to savour the architecture of his syntax. Two centuries after Milton's death, Thomas de Quincey was still maintaining a Roman resonance: 'O burden of solitude, that cleavest to man through every stage of his being! In his birth, which has been, in his life, which is, in his death, which shall be—mighty and essential solitude that wast, and art, and art to be, thou broodest, like the spirit of God moving upon the surface of the deeps, over every heart that sleeps in the nurseries of Christendom.' No man would now choose to write like that. The style has fallen behind the times, with snuff and knee breeches. Our own notion of excellence tends to overpraise brevity, forgetful that a sentence which looks very long in print, or echoes too ornately on the untutored ear, may, when it is spoken by a good speaker, sound neither excessively long nor unduly ornate.

About three miles short of Newark the Way enters Brough, whose Old English name (*burgh*) usually signifies a Roman settlement. At Brough the settlement was called *Crococolana*. Another mile or so leads past Langford Hall near the Fleet Stream, whence the 'long ford'. Here the main road runs parallel with a grassy tract of the Foss, thirty feet wide, foretasting the pleasures that lie ahead. Excavation revealed two roads on this sector, more or less side by side. The older course was ten feet narrower than the newer.

I like Newark-on-Trent despite the traffic. In 1832 the electors chose Gladstone as Tory Member of Parliament. Two years later the premier, Sir Robert Peel, appointed him a Junior Lord of the Treasury. Since Gladstone was still in his twenties, and had not revealed any great talent, the Whigs complained that he had been promoted because he was related to Sir Robert, with whom he shared the distinction of achieving a Double First at Christ Church (Peel himself was the first man ever to take those two dark blue ribands). Defoe, also, liked Newark: 'a very handsome well-built town.' Miss Fiennes admired it for a different reason: 'here I met with the strongest and best Nottingham ale. . . .' However, she did approve the splendid church: 'there remains the holes in the Church walls that the bullets made which were shott into the town in the Siege laid to it by the Parliament Army in the Civil Warre.' Prince Rupert's relief of Newark Castle was the best thing he ever did. Lord Clarendon, who knew the Prince well, described his sortie as a 'great feat of arms'. It began at Bingham, a few miles south of the town, where scouts had reported that Meldrum, the rebel general, was withdrawing his besieging forces from the castle walls. In fact, he was simply moving his guns and some infantry to the Spittal, a fortified ruin on the edge of the town. Rupert, at all events, advanced on Newark by moonlight, keeping well to the south of the castle. At nine o'clock next morning he attacked the Spittal. The rebel cavalry broke and fled, leaving the infantry to its fate. Seeing the flight, the loyalist garrison sallied from the castle and helped the Prince to mop up.

In 1646 the King surrendered to his fellow-Scots, trusting that they would extend more courtesy than he had received from the English. The Scots accepted his surrender, and promptly sold him to the English for cash. The formal deed was signed near Newark, at *The King's Arms* (now called *The Saracen's Head*) in Southwell, and was witnessed by a renegade Scot, Alexander Leslie, whom the King had lately created Earl of Leven. The rebels required the King to order the Newark garrison to surrender. The governor of the castle, Lord Bellasis, obeyed: 'the Castle', wrote Celia Fiennes, 'was then demolished so that only the ruinated walls remaine. . . .' They stand well, on a mound overlooking the main road.

In 1783 the Trent Navigation Company drew up plans for a canal; in 1915 the projected improvements were still unfinished. At Sleaford, away to the north-east, a contemporary of the Trent Canal went bankrupt within a few years. In 1970 a printer's shop in that town still bore an inscription, 'Navigation Office, 1792'. The Romans suffered no such reverses. On the contrary, they linked *Lindum Colonia* to the sea via rivers and canals, of which the foremost, Car Dykes, was nearly eighty miles long. Even in Stukeley's day it was still possible to ship merchandise from the Fens to York. The canals were built during the reign of Nero, when Rome's northern frontier was at *Lindum Colonia*. In or about A.D. 71, having advanced that frontier to *Eboracum*, the Romans built a Fossdyke Canal to the River Trent. Slave labour was available because the *Iceni* had lately rebelled and were chastened by being drafted in gangs as 'navvies' or makers of shipways (*navis*, a ship). Moreover, the Romans used the canals as drains, trapping the overflow from higher ground. They inherited their skill from the marsh-dwelling Etruscans who had drained the swamps near Ansidonia. The outstanding example of such expertise is the *Cloaca Maxima* or chief drain, a work of the early Republic, which drained the valley of the *Forum Romanum* into the River Tiber. Augustus enlarged and raised the *Cloaca Maxima*; it still serves as a modern sewer.

Beyond Newark the Way continues (in Defoe's phrase) 'as

straight as a line can mark it out', passing the site of a Roman settlement, *Ad Pontem*, near East Stoke, where Lambert Simnel came to grief. Simnel, a lad of obscure origin, was set up as the successor to Richard III whom Henry VII had recently extinguished at Bosworth Field. Not even the Pretender could feel certain of his alleged identity. At one time he was described as the son of Edward IV; at another, as the son of the Duke of Clarence. The power behind the plot was John de la Pole, Earl of Lincoln, whom Richard III had named as his heir to the throne. De la Pole supported Simnel, knowing that, if the lad ever did gain the throne, he could easily be made to lose it. Simnel meanwhile secured the support of many of the Irish. Amid great pomp he was crowned in Christchurch Cathedral at Dublin, in the presence of the Earl of Kildare, Deputy Governor of Ireland, together with the Lord Chancellor and many of the Irish nobility, judges, and bishops. With a troop of German mercenaries the new 'king' landed in England and was soon defeated after a skirmish near East Stoke (many textbooks give the site of that skirmish as Stoke-on-Trent). From East Stoke the bloodstained fugitives were chased to Fiskerton Ferry, along a track that is still called Red Gutter. Many of their dead were buried in what is still called Dead Man's Field. The 'king' himself fared more fortunately. Instead of hanging him, Henry VII employed him as a scullion in the royal kitchens. Having washed up obediently for several years, Simnel ended his days at Barton Bendish, only a few miles from Peddars Way, where the King had sent him, as falconer to Sir Thomas Lovell.

The site of *Margidunum* lies a mile south of East Bridgford. An elderly man assured me that his grandfather had seen the stone ramparts; but all I ever found was a grassy mound. Archaeologists believe that *Margidunum* was a very early fort, which the Romans soon abandoned, thereafter re-aligning the Foss via a knoll, known locally as The Hump.

At Cotgrave the Foss forsakes its south-westerly direction, dropping due south, past another settlement, *Vernemetum*, in the parish of Willoughby-on-the-Wolds near the Leicestershire border. Willoughby is an interesting village with several old houses marred by several new ones. About the year 1240 a Nottingham merchant, Ralph Bugge, bought an estate here. His grandson, Richard Bugge, received a knighthood—such was the flexibility of medieval English society—whereupon he changed his name to Willoughby, as though anticipating the words which Matthew Arnold wrote in 1865: 'has anyone reflected what a touch of grossness in our race, what an original shortcoming in the more delicate spiritual perceptions, is shown by the natural growth among us of such hideous names, as Higginbottom, Stiggins, Bugg?' Bugge himself was not the only creature who evolved from a chrysalis stage by deed poll. The Welsh Sitsyllts, for example, became the English Cecils; Writhe changed his name to Wriothesley; and Dr. Keys, founder of a Cambridge College, was so zealous a classic that he Latinized himself as Caius. At the far end of the village I found parts of the Bugges' medieval manor house, a beautiful building, more than worthy to be restored and re-occupied. On a later visit, in 1970, I found a typewritten notice on the wall of the house, announcing that it would shortly be demolished together with several handsome cottages. Architecture must evolve. Yet it does seem strange that old buildings should be demolished simply because they *are* old.

The Foss meanwhile has become a dual carriageway, obliterating all sense of history, all remembrance of repose, every inclination to stop and stare at a famous scene, the Belvoir country, happy hunting ground of the Dukes of Rutland, of whom the fifth employed James Wyatt to build (1801) the present Belvoir Castle. When the Earl of Rutland entertained James I at a Norman castle on the site, the canny King was so impressed by the vista of Manners' acres that he whispered to a friend: 'My God, what a traitor the man would make!' Formerly called the Duke of Rutland's Hounds, the Belvoir Hunt was started in 1730. Hunting has become more popular than ever before. *Baily's Hunting Directory* names more than two hundred British packs, about half being foxhounds, and the rest beagles, otterhounds, staghounds and harriers. Many and magnificent are the stories of English hunting characters. My own favourite concerns a member of the Cecil family, the Dowager Marchioness Mary Amelia, a Regency hind, who died when Victoria was Queen. Having established the blue-and-silver habit of the Hertfordshire Hunt, her ladyship continued to follow it when she was blind and very old. Emerging from the stables of Hatfield House, accompanied by a groom, she would proceed to her place at the head of the field; and whenever she approached a jump, the groom forestalled her inability to see it by shouting: 'Damn you, my Lady, jump!' The Roman Britons bred three types of hunting dog—Irish wolfhound, bulldog, retriever—which were exported to trans-Channel huntsmen.

Hunting, however, seems out of place on the Way that enters Leicester, which the Romans called *Ratae Coritanorum*, after a local tribe, the *Coritani*, whose territory included Lincoln and Doncaster. The sites of the forum and basilica are known; the present Jewry Wall was probably part of the latter. Hadrian ordered the *Coritani* to set milestones along the Foss. This we know because in 1771 a labourer unearthed one of the stones. The road overseers wished to use it as rubble, but somebody noticed that the stone bore a Latin inscription, marking the fourth year of Hadrian's reign, and giving a distance, *a Ratis III*, which confirmed the city's Roman forename. The milestone was therefore mounted on an obelisk, to serve as a memorial of times past. Now it adorns the Leicester Museum.

Roman Leicester probably had a theatre, a colonnaded square, and several temples; it certainly possessed a bath, but I wondered whether it had been much frequented, because the builders miscalculated the course of their aqueduct, leaving the citizens to fill a municipal cistern by carrying buckets of water from the river. It seems unlikely, however, that *Ratae Coritanorum* in the first century A.D. was so insalubrious as Leicester in the eighteenth century A.D., when a *Report on the Sanitary Conditions of the Labouring Population* was sent to the Home Secretary, by order of the House of Lords, the number of deaths from fever that year being twice the number of deaths at the Battle of Waterloo.

Hidden among the shops and factories of Leicester you will find several jewels: parts of a Roman wall which were used as the narthex or vestibule in a Saxon church (the wall became known as Jewry Wall, perhaps because it belonged to the Jurats or medieval aldermen); Wyggeston's Chantry House (*c.* 1511) and Skeffington House (*c.* 1600); the Norman church of St. Mary de Castro; fifteenth-century gateways to the castle; old Free Grammar School (1573); medieval timber-framed Guildhall. Celia Fiennes noted the town's nonconformity: 'Here are a great many Descenters in the town.' Defoe noted its weavers: 'They have a considerable manufacture carry'd on here, and in several of the market towns round for weaving of stockings by frames. . . .' Between 1801 and 1841 the population increased threefold from 16,000 to 51,000. In an effort to earn a different kind of livelihood, the city aspired to become 'the Cheltenham of Leicestershire'. Two mineral baths were flourishing during the early twentieth century, serving and served by the Bath Hotel (when the British Association stayed there in 1907 they paid top price or 4s. 8d. for a bedroom and three meals). Not a great way from Leicester, at the village of Staunton Harold, the curious traveller will find the only surviving English church that was built during the only English republic. An inscription states: 'When all things sacred were throughout ye nation Either demollisht or profaned Sir Richard Shirley Barronet founded this church whose singular praise it is to have done ye best things in ye worst times And hoped them in the most callamitous. . . .' Sir Robert Shirley died in the Tower of London, a prisoner of the rebels. His church was completed ten years later, in 1665.

For several miles the main road through Leicester threads an un-Roman way among traffic lights, dual carriageways, and what Edward Thomas called 'jerry-built cages' of appalling mediocrity.

Seekers after the green Foss are teased indeed between Leicester and High Cross. Near Narborough, however, a number of place-names serve as hopeful signposts; Foss House, Foss Bridge, Foss Garage. The Way becomes a straight road and then a country lane into the parish of Sapcote (*sceapcot* or sheep shelter) which John Frewen Turner tried to exploit as the Spa of the Golden Well. In 1806 he built a bath-house over the well. Bath Street remains, but the well was harnessed to a pump, and Turner's bath-house became a stable.

Soon the lane ends at a T-junction, leaving the Way to continue as a green road between trees. For the first time since Lincoln a wayfarer shares the delight which Wordsworth felt when he reached England from France, and went striding through a valley near Dover, exclaiming that at last he was free:

> 'tis joy enough and pride
> For one hour's perfect bliss, to tread the grass
> Of England once again.

Sometimes the Way grows narrow; sometimes only its shadow survives, an *agger* beside hedgerows; but the air is fresh, the birds are gay, the grass is green. There are times when the grass turns brown, as it did in 1776, to the dismay of William Stukeley: 'I travelled by Narborough,' he remembered, 'on the west side of the river and a sorry wet journey under foot for one that was resolved to keep upon the road; sometimes I rode half a mile to the horse's belly in water upon the Roman pavement.' Near Claybrooke Lodge Farm you can follow the hoofprints of Stukeley's horse, but nothing remains of 'the true old road at the length of a pasture' which led him to High Cross.

On our journey along Watling Street, you may remember, we shivered and shouted when we, too, reached High Cross. Having taken the plunge, Foss Way relaxes and looks back, complacent as a man who has snatched his heel from the brink of oblivion. Such complacency is justified because the Foss is about to recover its senses. Michael Drayton, a Warwickshire man, hailed the entry of the Foss into his own county. In the Sixteenth Song of his verse travelogue, *Polyolbion*, which was published in 1616, he described High Cross as the meeting place of two of four roads which, he said, had been especially honoured by an ancient King:

> Appointing first our course, this privilege he gave,
> That no man might arrest, or debtors' goods might seize
> In any of us four his military ways.

Drayton's medieval predecessors bestowed an even greater honour on the Foss, for Henry of Huntingdon and Robert Gloucester stated that Foss Way began at Totnes in Devon and ended somewhere short of John o' Groats in Caithness. Probably they had cribbed the news from Geoffrey of Monmouth, whose *Historia Regum Britanniae* or *History of British Kings* foreshadowed the decimation of Britain itself: 'The king, therefore, called together all the workmen of the whole island, and commanded a highway to be builded of stone and mortar that should cut through the entire length of the island from the Cornish sea to the coast of Caithness, and should run in a straight line from one city unto another the whole of the way along.'

If the cattle at High Cross could speak, and were able moreover to read, they might quote the wisdom of Edmund Burke when he reflected on the loud minority of Britons who applauded the sound of the guillotine as it crossed the English Channel: 'Because half a dozen grasshoppers under a fern make the field ring with their importunate clink, whilst thousands of great cattle, reposed beneath the shadow of the British oak, chew the cud and are silent, pray do not imagine that those who make the noise are the only inhabitants of the field. . . .'

11 Foss Way: High Cross to Bath

Having taken the plunge, Foss Way continues in peace as a country lane through Warwickshire, the homeland of George Eliot, who praised it alike in prose and in the greater harmony of verse:

> The bunched cowslip's pale transparency
> Carries that sunshine of sweet memories,
> And wild-rose branches take their finest scent
> From those blest hours of infantine content.

For six miles the lane ambles among rolling contours to Brinklow, a village of venerable houses, some of them thatched and white-washed, others of beaming brick. In the year 1486 William Caxton, England's pioneer printer, published a book, *Morte d'Arthur* or the Death of Arthur, which (as he put it) had been 'reduced into Englyshe by Sir Thomas Malory Knight'. No other information was given. There were at that time several families named Malory, each of whom begat one or more Thomas, including Sir Thomas Malory of Newbold Revel near Brinklow. For centuries the authorship of an English classic remained unknown. During the 1930s, however, a manuscript of the book was discovered—very likely it had been copied for Caxton's use—and in it a paragraph which he omitted from the published version: 'And this booke endyth where as Sir Launcelot and Sir Tristrams com to courte. Who that woll make any more lette him seke other bookis of King Arthure or of Sir Launcelot or Sir Tristrams. For this was drawyn by a knight presoner Sir Thomas Malleore that Gode sende hym good recover. Amen.' We know from other sources that Sir Thomas Malory of Brinklow was indeed imprisoned at the Grey Friars in London, for his part in the Wars of the Roses.

Morte d'Arthur is the most beautiful prose work of the Middle

Ages, an embroidery of the Arthurian Cycle. Poised midway between Chaucer and Spenser, Malory devised a style that is lyrical and flowing. When Sir Ecton beholds the corpse of Sir Launcelot, his elegy distils the attar of medieval chivalry: 'thou were the courtliest knight that ever bare shield; and thou were the truest friend to thy lover that ever bestrode horse; and thou were the goodliest person ever came among press of knights; and thou were the meekest man and the gentlest that ever ate in hall among ladies; and thou were the sternest knight to thy mortal foe that ever put spear in the rest.' Chivalry was not a practice of the Romans. Courage they knew, and stamina and integrity; but their captives were paraded in triumph through the street, and thereafter either killed or enslaved. Individual Romans practised chivalry, the conduct becoming a *chevalerie* or gentle man; but chivalry as a code of international conduct was a Christian flower. Few men practised it always; no nation refrained from violating it often; yet it flourished throughout the later Middle Ages, and was able somewhat to curb the weeds that surrounded it. Chivalry never was a synonym for cheek-turning. It was Spenser's 'brave poursuit of chevalrous emprize'. The *trouvères* and the *troubadours* preached it as part of their gospel of romantic love. Among those who practised it, a brave knight's surrender was no longer a death sentence; the soldiers received quarter; a lady and her maid became as a knight's mother or his sister. Edmund Burke cried: 'The age of chivalry is gone. That of sophists, economists, and calculators has succeeded; and the glory of Europe is extinguished forever.' One understands what Burke meant, and agrees with it; but the lament remains a rare example of his own idealism vanquishing his common sense. Despite the misconduct of sophisticated savages, international behaviour continues to improve, whereas the subtler shades of *chevalerie* are being obliterated among individuals. Cardinal Newman's definition of a gentleman sounds out of date: 'he is tender towards the bashful, gentle towards the distant, merciful towards the absurd . . . He never speaks of himself except when compelled, never defends himself by a mere retort, he has no ears for slander or gossip . . . If he engages in controversy of any kind his disciplined intellect preserves him from the blundering discourtesy of better, perhaps, but less educated minds . . .'

Brinklow itself is the place beside a *brinc* or steep hill at the east end of the village, once crowned by a Mowbray castle, from which you can see Edge Hill. The Romans took a bearing on that *brinc*, but the modern road deviates, swerving south-east and then south-west before resuming a straight course for two miles, whereafter it again wavers and again recovers, having meanwhile crossed the River Avon, which here becomes something of a Rubicon or frontier. Ever since High Cross the Way has traversed a Warwickshire whose familiar sights, said George Eliot,

> Were but my growing self, are part of me,
> My present Past, my root of piety.

South of the Avon the Way enters another Warwickshire; and although the differences may seem merely a mirage of subjective nuances, they can be analysed as a series of tangible minutiae. For example, brick houses give way to stone, or rather they are joined by stone. Here and there a drystone wall appears, like an outrider from the Cotswolds. The country talk takes on a different timbre, difficult to detect, yet loud and clear for those that have ears to hear.

Through this new landscape the Way travels for more than twelve miles, veering slightly when it approaches Eathorpe, where it runs between an avenue of oaks in the grounds of Eathorpe Hall before rejoining the road *en route* for the Cotswolds, a vague name for an ill-defined region of stone houses and prime sheep: 'the famous Cotswold Downs,' wrote Defoe, 'so eminent for the best of sheep, and finest wool in England . . .' Defoe believed that the Cotswold breed had been exported by King Richard I to Spain, 'which now produces so fine a wool, that we are oblig'd to fetch it from thence, for the making of our finest broad clothes; and which we buy at so great a price.' But it seems unlikely that the sheep were as old as Defoe supposed. Modern researchers cannot trace them beyond the early fourteenth century. More than any other native product (except perhaps the long bow), sheep raised England to a greatness that is symbolized by the Lord

Chancellor's cushion or Woolsack. Victorian stockmen improved the Cotswold breed by crossing it with the Leicesters which the Culley brothers took to Northumberland in 1767, whence they spread to the Scottish Lowlands, and in 1869 became known as Border Leicesters. The breed is easily identified by a tuft of wool on its forehead, which flops over the eyes, as on an Old English sheepdog.

Whenever I come this way I am thankful that so few people use it on their journeys to Devon and Cornwall. Mile after mile the country road keeps to itself, pausing only when it crosses other roads. Two miles beyond Foss Hill, at Halford, the Way is used by the Birmingham traffic. At Tredington the Romans swerved in order to avoid a steep hill. Modern Tredington, strung along the main road, is a huddle of modern bungalows vibrant with the tread of innumerable tyres. Old Tredington stands back from the traffic. At early morning, or late at night, Shakespeare would recognize the hamlet's tapestry of timber and stone and brick, arranged along a lane whose curves carve a quadrangle or quasi-collegiate precinct, topped by the tall-spired church with Saxon masonry and a massive door, scarred by Civil War bullets. I first knew Tredington when it echoed R. G. T. Coventry's nocturne:

> Here, while still evening falls,
> And the grey light grows less,
> Peace builds the shadowy walls
> With ancient quietness.

At Tredington my horse once cast a shoe, so I rode two miles down a green lane to Shipston-on-Stour, anciently *scepestun* or the place with a sheep dip. The farrier was impressed when I told him that the Roman Farriers' Guild had built a temple to Neptune and Minerva at *Noviomagus* (Chichester). The best of Shipston lies away from the main road. The market square is flanked by eighteenth-century brick houses. Sheep Street's stone homes were made to measure for merchants, attorneys, retired yeomen, younger sons. A cul-de-sac from the main road leads to a small Nonconformist chapel, fringed with a little lawn. Shipston-on-Stour was the birthplace (1860) of Francis Haverfield who excavated a section of Akeman Street near Blenheim, revealing a surface seventeen feet wide, made of six inches of gravel on ten inches of larger stones. He noticed, too, that in many widely-scattered Roman villas it was impossible to find coins later than those of A.D. 360, a time of violent invasions.

Shipston is the hub of a land of sequestered villages from Tredington to Brailes, from Honington to Barcheston. Honington was *Hunig-tun* or the place where honey is made; a honey of a place indeed; no pub, no shop, not even a Post Office nowadays (what a dream cottage it was, wideawake with talk of seed time and harvest and that woman who's carrying on with the carter's cousin). Gone, then, the thatched Post Office; but not yet the tree-lined lane of medieval stone, Tudor timber, Queen Anne brick. The Wren-like church stands apart, within a few yards of Honington Hall, Augustan seat of the Wiggin family.

Barcheston you *must* see. Follow the Banbury road from Shipston for half a mile, taking the first turn on the right. No doubt it is sheer fantasy, but whenever I visit Barcheston the place seems to have become smaller. Since it contains less than five buildings, I sometimes wonder for how much longer it can continue to diminish. The church tower, they say, is a Cotswold Pisa, leaning one foot in fifty. Barcheston has two claims to fame; first, it was the place where William Sheldon launched the sixteenth-century craft of tapestry weaving. He had married the daughter of the squire of Barcheston, thereby inheriting both the mill and the manor. Noticing that the best tapestries came from the Low Countries, he sent a Barcheston man, William Hickes, to study Flemish weaving and to import Flemish weavers into Barcheston, where his looms produced 'tapestry, arras, plonkets . . . and sarges'.

Barcheston's second fame shows no signs of ageing. Shakespeare knew Barcheston. Like a true Warwickshire man he called it Barson. In *Henry IV*, you remember, Justice Shallow is conducting Sir John Falstaff and Master Silence around his orchard in 'Glostershire'. Suddenly Pistol arrives, post-haste and saddle-sore, having galloped from London with news that Sir John's crony, Prince Hal, is now King Henry. Turning to Sir John, Pistol exclaims: 'Sweet knight, thou art now one of the greatest men in the realm!' Master Silence, however, disagrees because Pistol has has not yet explained *why* Sir John may expect preferment at Court. Therefore Silence continues to rate Falstaff no higher than a Barson householder: 'By'r lady,' he cries, 'I think a' be, but goodman Puff of Barson.' Alas, Falstaff and his friends are soon to become less than Puff, for the playboy Prince has grown up overnight, and when his erstwhile cronies ride to greet him, he confounds Falstaff's euphoric promise that Master Shallow shall shortly 'choose whatever office thou wilt in the land'. Rushing forward to greet the new King, Falstaff is rebuffed:

> I know thee not, old man: fall to thy prayers;
> How ill white hairs become a fool and jester!

The royal procession moves on, leaving Falstaff and his friends alone on the stage; and there for some moments they stand, silent until genius speaking through the lips of Falstaff cries: 'Master Shallow, I owe you a thousand pound.'

Meanwhile the Foss has followed five rollicking miles to Moreton-in-Marsh and Gloucestershire, a proud place-name, partly Celtic, partly Saxon, being compounded of the Old Welsh *gloew* (a bright or glowing place) and the Old English *ceaster* (Roman fort). Moreton, in fact, is a frontier post. About a mile and a half east of the town, on the Chipping Norton road, a Four Shire Stone marks the meeting of Gloucestershire, Warwickshire, Worcestershire, Oxfordshire. The Stone was old when Celia Fiennes passed it: 'thence to Broughton in Oxfordshire, passing 4 Shire Stone'. Despite its marshy name, Moreton is not a damp town, but it does stand near a boundary, so that Marsh is most likely a corruption of *march* or frontier. The manor of Moreton belonged to Westminster Abbey from the reign of Edward the Confessor until 1830, when it was bought by Lord Redesdale, who restored the ancient Market House. The main street is Foss Way, much widened, green-verged, lined with trees that are trimmed by the householders nearest them. In 1826 William James built Moreton Station as a terminus for his Stratford and Moreton Tramway, a horse-drawn venture, which in 1836 sent a branch to

Shipston. The branch subsequently became a railway for steam locomotives, and remained in use until the 1930s. In the yard at Moreton Station you can see the cottages which James built for his tramway employees. One would like to have travelled in those trams. In 1864 a magazine, called *London Society*, described the adventure: 'The journey was performed outside an ordinary railway carriage which had been adapted to the necessities of horse traction. Attached to the carriage in front was a platform, on which the sagacious horse mounted when it had drawn our carriage to the top of an incline, thus escaping being tripped up as we descended at a rattling good speed . . . When the carriage came to a stand, the horse dismounted and drew us along as before . . .' Rome, one feels, ought to have invented a Hadrian's Tramway.

From Moreton the Foss proceeds to Donnington through a high Cotswold country of stone walls, wide skies, green pastures, plump sheep and loud larks. Within sight of Stow-on-the-Wold it passes the scene of a battle of the Civil War, where Lord Astley, marching from Worcester to Oxford, was intercepted by a strong force of rebels. Astley was skilful as well as courageous. Clarendon named him as one of the seven 'with whom he [the King] only consulted his martial affairs, and how to carry on the war . . .' Four years previously, as Sir Jacob Astley, he had uttered a famous prayer before leading his men into battle at Edgehill: 'O Lord, thou knowest how busy I must be this day. If I forget thee, do not thou forget me. March on, lads!' Astley, at all events, encamped on a hill above Stow; and there, half an hour before dawn, on 21 March 1646, the rebels attacked his band of raw Welsh recruits, many of whom surrendered with their arms and ammunition. Unhorsed during a charge, and surrounded by the enemy, Lord Astley gave up his sword, saying: 'You have done your work, boys. You may go play, unless you fall out among yourselves.' And fall they did, squabbling for power.

Now the Way climbs to its highest town,

Stow-on-the-Wold
Where the wind blows cold.

As at Shipston and Tredington, the best parts lie off the main road, around a market square. Maugersbury, a hamlet of Stow, recalls the town's Saxon name, which became Edwardstone and, in 1330, *Stowe Sancti Edwardi*, a reference to the church of St. Edward, which belonged to the Abbots of Evesham, who received licence (1107) to hold a weekly market at Stow. Founded *c*. 870, the parish church was rebuilt by medieval wool merchants. Nearby are a Masonic Hall (formerly the Tudor Grammar School) and St. Edward's House (formerly a church house). The Town Hall contains several Roman relics and an array of weapons, portraits, and documents of the Civil War, collected by Captain Christie Crawford.

The Way leaves Stow as a high-banked avenue of trees, abandoning its south-westerly course and turning south-east for a mile, as though to reach Burford. Suddenly it swerves south-west again, over the River Dickler, past Lower Slaughter, in Saxon times a *sloghtre* or muddy place, but nowadays an idyll of Cotswold houses beside the River Eye. To go there in summer is a waste of time, unless you wish to join the other cars vainly seeking to park. It is wiser to follow Andrew Lang, who arrived in springtime, finding

> A land of waters green and clear,
> Of willows and of poplars tall,
> And in the Spring-time of the year
> The white May breaking over all . . .

'The road', said Hilaire Belloc, 'is an instrument to facilitate the movement of man between two points on the earth's surface.' Edward Thomas entered a *caveat*: 'The straight road . . . can only be made by those in whom extreme haste and forethought have destroyed the power of joy, either at the end or at any part of its course.' Between Stow and Northleach the Foss Way achieves ten invigorating miles of straight joy. It travels high, it travels wide. All around, the hills are studded with cattle, sheep, corn. One of those ten miles wisely passes Bourton-on-the-Water without entering. Of all villages beside the Foss, Bourton is the most commercialized. It recalls Martial's remark about Rome:

For men, my friends, who there would seek a space
To sleep or think, this one affords no place.

Between Bourton and Northleach, the Foss makes two deviations in order to avoid a marsh at Broadwater Bottom. Near
Northleach it forsakes the modern road and becomes an *agger*
alongside a drystone wall. The road itself is halted by traffic lights
opposite Northleach police station, formerly an eighteenth-
century prison, built by George Onispherous Paul, a cloth merchant of Huguenot descent, who set up as a country landowner.
John Howard introduced him to an architect, William Blackburn,
with whom he designed four other prisons. In those years the
philanthropists favoured shock therapy, so long as the voltage
was applied humanely: 'Bread, water, and air, as the means of
healthful existence, should be denied to no prisoner.'

Mammon has not marred the beauty of Northleach, but it has
grievously breached the peace. Traffic from Gloucester roars
within a few feet of a steep market place overlooked by ancient
houses, country shops, and the old forge (in 1970 it was for sale,
together with the anvil). The church of SS. Peter and Paul stands
behind the market place, and is therefore less harried. Wool merchants built it nearly six centuries ago. The brasses in Northleach
church are justly famous, not for their *noblesse* nor feats of arms,
but as memorials to the yeomen of England—Bushe, Fortey,
Midwinter—men, as one brass testifies, 'upright, true, and kind'.
Here lie the backbones of our prosperity from the fifteenth to the
eighteenth centuries; shepherds of sheep, weavers of wool, reno-
vators of roads, builders and rebuilders of churches. When that
prosperity declined, William Dutton built six almshouses, and
bequeathed his own home and a sum of money, hoping that they
would be used to revive the wool trade or 'any other such trade
as may keep the people from idleness'.

Red, amber, green; away the Foss goes, not so narrow as at
High Cross, yet once more in peace, indelibly Roman in its directness 'between two points on the earth's surface'. After about a
mile, a lane on the right leads via Yanworth to Chedworth and the
remains of a Roman country house or villa, prototype of those

which the Comte de Montalembert described in eighteenth-century England: 'Scarcely any persons who hold a leading place in the circles of their society live in London. They have *houses* in London, in which they stay while Parliament sits, and occasionally visit at other seasons; but their *homes* are in the country.' The lane to Chedworth is a delight, twining for three miles into the hamlet of Yanworth, whose Norman church and Cotswold cottages are unmarred by any kind of blemish. By modern standards, life was unjust and unhygienic when those cottages were built; yet sometimes the cottagers confirmed John Drinkwater's vision:

> I see the little cottages that keep
> Their beauty still where since Plantagenet
> Have come the shepherds happily to sleep,
> Finding their loaves and cups of cider set.

Beyond Yanworth the lane loiters among hills until it reaches a summit overlooking a wooded valley at Chedworth. There is no hamlet here. Instinctively you say: 'What a wonderful site for a house.' Now the lane descends, and at last the villa appears; not indeed as the Romans saw it, nor even as a gamekeeper saw it when, in 1864, he uncovered a fragment of Roman mosaic pavement while digging out a lost ferret for Mr. James Farrer, uncle of the Earl of Eldon who owned the estate. Lord Eldon agreed that the site should be excavated. Within a short while Mr. Farrer disclosed one of the best-preserved Roman villas in Britain. Protective sheds were built about the pavements; walls were roofed against rain; a public museum was built to contain many kinds of relics. In 1924 the National Trust acquired the site, with six and a half acres of surrounding woodland.

Chedworth villa is a green oasis divided by stone walls and, on rising ground, a series of buildings adroitly restored and maintained. It is not enough to stand and stare from the outside. You must go indoors, even though the roof has vanished, and the walls are low, and no slave comes out to give you welcome. Nor is it enough to suppose that the Romans invented domestic comfort. A thousand years before Caesar invaded Britain, the Sumerians were building bathrooms and latrines inside their houses, and brick-lined drains through the streets. Nevertheless, Rome first of all enshrined the hearth. A Roman home was literally sacred. Exile from Roman soil seemed a bereavement more grievous than death. A Roman Senator would have shuddered when Richard II banished the Duke of Norfolk:

> The hopeless word of 'never to return'
> Breathe I against thee, upon pain of life.

Every true Roman felt the call of home. Ovid rejoiced to have been born in Sulmo: *Sulmo mihi patria est*. When he was banished to a remote island, for his part in a Court scandal, he boasted that he would find peace anywhere: 'My mind to me a kingdom is.' But he did not find peace, and the failure killed him. Vergil set the whole of Italy to song, its farmers and its soldiers. They say that eleven Latin words were carved on his tomb, narrating the full biography: 'Mantua gave me life; Calabria death; Naples, a tomb . . . the poet of herdsmen, farmers, heroes.'

Chedworth villa was built and enlarged between A.D. 180 and 350. It follows the typical Roman courtyard pattern, with buildings on three sides of its square. At the west end of the north wing was a large bath-house. Behind it the Romans built a water shrine with a tank to hold fifteen hundred gallons, fed by a spring that still flows from its bed of Fuller's earth. A small stone cross was found, which suggests either that one of the owners of the villa was a Christian or that a Christian Saxon occupied the villa while it was still habitable. A silver spoon, now lost, bore an inscription, *Censorime gaudeas* (May you live happily, Censorimus). One feels that the wish was fulfilled. Even during adversity Censorimus must have found strength in the sweep of the hills; consolation in the song of the birds; and from the farm and its game a repletion which succours serenity.

Home: the word deserves repetition because a Roman's love of home was more than aesthetic or patriotic. 'At home', said Cicero, 'a Roman has his altars, his hearth, his household gods, his private worship, his rites and his ceremonies.' Rome would have understood at least the title of Beethoven's *The Consecration of the House*. Throughout the Empire the sanctity of a Roman hearth was symbolized by a flame which, until a Christian Emperor extinguished it, was tended by consecrated virgins in the temple of Venus. Hardly less venerated were the cults of *Penates* (divine guardians of the household larder) and of *Lares* (the spirits of a man's ancestors). A similar piety had been observed by the earliest Athenians, who decreed that no man might hold any of the chief magistracies if he failed to tend the graves of his own family. All this was summarized when Cicero's enemies destroyed his home, and were themselves confounded by his question: 'Is there anything more hallowed, is there anything more closely hedged about with every kind of sanctity, than the home of each individual citizen?' Chedworth villa has its own epitaph, composed by a Roman in loving memory of all such places. Unlike many English poets, Horace was not starved into silence. A patron, Maecenas, presented him with a small farm on the Sabine Hills. In return, Horace gave to the world a gift which it might otherwise not have received; and he wrapped that gift in a rural song: 'This', he confessed, 'was one of my dreams . . . a little bit of land with a garden; near the house, a spring of living water, and beside it a small wood. Heaven has fulfilled that dream, more richly than I had ever hoped.'

The occupants of Chedworth had only a short distance to travel before they reached Foss Way, nearly six hundred feet up. Past Foss Bridge it goes, past the lonely Hare and Hounds Inn, past Foss Cross and Hollow Foss; all the while a country road through summer cornfields, autumn furrows, permanent pastures, seasonable woods. Away to the left lie the four Ampneys—St. Peter, St. Mary, Crucis, Down—homeland of Ralph Vaughan Williams who with Sir Edward Elgar put English music on the map of the world. Son of the vicar of Down Ampney, Vaughan Williams was a master alike of words and music. Of Beethoven's Ninth he wrote: 'It seems sometimes to have come straight from the eternal source of Truth without human intervention.' His Englishry displeased the cosmopolites: 'The Bohemian is not a natural growth in England. Our Café Royals, our Chelsea Arts Balls, our all-night clubs are shams; importations from Paris which have suffered a good deal on the voyage.' His artistic credo defied the clique:

'The composer must not shut himself up and think about art; he must live with his fellows and make his art an expression of the life of the whole community.' How strange, that while poetry and architecture lit the classical world, music itself lagged so far behind that nearly two thousand years passed, before St. Cecilia set the light to comparable music.

At Ampney Downs the Way bends south-west via Ragged Hedge Covert, then drops due south, and then resumes a south-westerly course towards Cirencester, the second largest city in Roman Britain, served by another Roman road, running from south-east to north-west, and by the port of Cricklade-on-Thames, a waterway from Gaul. Ptolemy called the city *Korinion*; the Romans spelt it *Corinium*; a few countryfolk pronounce it Sissiter; most people say Siren.

Corinium was the capital of the Cotswolds, which is to say of the wool trade. The sites of a dozen villas have been found within ten miles of the town. During the third century A.D. its earthen ramparts were strengthened with stone facings. When Diocletian divided Britain into four parts, *Corinium* became the capital of *Britannia Prima*. Three centuries later the Legions departed, the Saxons arrived, the city crumbled. All that remains of it is contained in the museum. There you may see weapons, jewellery, tools, cosmetics, pottery, and mosaic pavements admirably renovated and reassembled. There, too, is a famous acrostic or crossword puzzle, scratched on a fragment of tile:

ROTAS
OPERA
TENET
AREPO
SATOR

which can be translated as 'Arepo the sower guides the wheels'. As at many other places *en route*, Rome's most enduring monument is the church, noble as a cathedral. Its tower is 134 feet high, the porch is twenty-four feet wide. The tomb of Robert Pagge, who rests with his feet on a woolpack, tells of Cirencester's heydays: 'A beloved merchant, he was pleasant to his neighbours. With full hands he helped those in need. He adorned both churches and highways.' It was not of Robert Pagge and his kind that Milton said,

The hungry sheep look up, and are not fed.

What we now call the statistics of Pagge's prosperity make nostalgic reading. Thus, at Cirencester market in June 1577 a Warwickshire farmer sold eighty stones of wool within seven days; two Leicestershire farmers sold sixty stones apiece; Northamptonshire farmers sent forty packs of wool each week. Two centuries later Defoe could still rub his hands when he visited Cirencester: 'Wool', he declared, 'is sold here in quantities so great, that it almost exceeds belief . . . They talk of 5000 packs a year.'

The next few miles of the Foss are endangered by motorists racing to steal the middle of a narrow road with blind summits and sharp bends. At Thames Head Inn a public footpath leads across fields to the source of Britain's premier river, a pilgrimage that every Briton ought to make. The source lies in a wooded dell, marked by a statue of Father Thames. The Sahara itself could not seem more parched, for the stream flows underground until it crosses the Foss. Only after prolonged rainfall do the waters rise and shine. Many a citizen must have walked from *Corinium* to the source of *Tamesis*, the river which linked them with *Londinium*. Since I cannot improve them, I take leave to quote some words which I wrote in *Portrait of the Thames*: 'No traffic disturbs Thames Head, no road; only the hills, a cottage hidden in a copse, and that harmony of breeze, bird-song, and sheep which we call silence. The Thames, in short, is born at home, with the birds and the cattle and the farmfolk all about. At this remote place the beginning is also an end . . . for here began and hither returns the mainstream of English history. From these skies, in this dell, were distilled the waters which Caesar crossed; which saw the rise and watched the fall of castles and abbeys and dynasties; which slapped De Ruyter when with a masthead broom he led his Dutchmen up the Thames, and shivered Parliament with salvos; which carried a goodly part of the commerce of the world's richest merchant; which quenched the flames unleashed by Hitler; which nourished both the substance and the spirit of innumerable men and women, unknown in their own day, and to this age less than nameless.'

Ever since Cirencester the Way has gone straight, and at Jackaments Bottom it continues to go straight, but the modern road swerves sharply off course, leaving the Foss so much at peace that it becomes a green road through fields. Ahead, if you take it leisurely, lies a whole day's march, most of it along the green road, flanked by hedges and trees. If you did not know otherwise, you might suppose that the road had been made to measure for Hazlitt, the man who said: 'Give me the clear blue sky over my head, and the green turf beneath my feet.' Given those things—and a three hours' march to dinner—Hazlitt loved the world at his feet: 'I laugh,' he declared, 'I run, I leap, I sing for joy.' It is important to remember, of course, that Hazlitt was by way of being a poet; nothing at all to do with the computer business. Having ridden and walked this green road several times, I allowed my last journey to overlook the present and to examine the past. When did the Roman Empire fall? The answer to that question will vary with the definition of 'Roman Empire'. As an international régime, governing the civilized world, the Roman Empire fell during the Dark Ages; as a powerful European bloc, renamed the Holy Roman Empire, it was revived by Charles the Great at the dawn of the Middle Ages, and existed thereafter for nearly a thousand years, growing steadily less influential. When Goethe was a child he entered the Roman Hall of Frankfurt, where the walls were covered with portraits of so many Emperors that space remained for only one more, that of Francis II, who ruled until 1806. On his death even the ghost of the Roman Empire died. Some people claim to have seen the ghost of that ghost, stalking through a Germany which Bismarck united under King William I, whom he persuaded to adopt the style of Emperor. When the last of the German Emperors died in exile in 1941, there was neither a ghost to haunt nor anyone to be haunted.

True to type, the Foss avoids all human settlements, though some have sprung up within a mile or so. At Easton Grey the green road is in Wiltshire, the county whose capital was Wilton, the place in a *wilde* or wasteland, long since cultivated as the land of Siegfried Sassoon, Maurice Hewlett, Richard Jeffries, and Sir Christopher Wren. Near Easton Grey the Way passes the site of a Romano-British settlement.

At Lady's Wood the Way crosses a lane and for three miles becomes one itself, passing Fosse Cottage, entering a coppice, and emerging as a track while the lane meanders into Yatton Keynell, named after its medieval lord, Henry Caynel, who was named after his birthplace at Cahagnes in Normandy. John Aubrey, raconteur and historian of Wiltshire, said of himself that he had 'entered his grammar in the school at Yatton Keynell, in the church, where the curate taught the oldest boys Virgil, Ovid, and Cicero'.

At Fosse Gate the green road once more becomes a lane and remains so for five miles. Crossing a stream, it bears southward to Batheaston in Somerset, land of *Somortun-saete* or the folk who dwelt in and around Somerton. Here at last the westerly lilt of Cirencester becomes the full-throated voice of the west; soft as the climate itself; to all West Country men a singing signpost. Following that piper, the Foss bears south-west and is lost under the traffic of *Aquae Sulis* (or place of mineral springs, dedicated to *Sulis Minerva*), now called Bath. The Roman town was small, covering about twenty-two acres. The Roman Baths, the largest in Britain, contained three pools, of which the chief, now called the Great Bath, was at first roofless; later a roof was added, pierced at each end with air vents. The colonnades are intricately carved. The water itself rises from a spring, at a temperature of 100° Fahrenheit. Physicians still prescribe it as a palliative for rheumatism.

Walking among the stately pillars, even an historian tends to forget the squalor which surrounded such splendour, both in Britain and throughout the Empire; gladiators hacking one another to death while a mob howled for more; foetid tenements and the fortunes that were squandered on a single banquet; roads flanked by crucified criminals; a greedy rich and an idle poor. As the Empire declined, so its citizens became more and more obsessed by bodily hygiene, as though water could wash away their malaise. Baths had begun as the necessity of farmer-soldiers when they returned from their labours in the fields, but the farmer's *aqua pumpagnis* degenerated into scented water. Seneca denounced the habit of bathing solely for pleasure. In 33 B.C. Agrippa approved the habit by building free public baths and an adjoining *vomitorium* where gluttons might make themselves sick before returning to refill their stomachs. The arch-priest of public baths was the Emperor Caracalla, son of a Syrian mother and an African father. His name—a Celtic word—meant a sleeveless cloak, the garment which supplanted the native *toga*. Having killed 20,000 opponents (among them his own brother), Caracalla debased Roman citizenship by granting it to almost anyone who happened to be living within the Roman Empire. That done, he built enormous baths, in which the people could enjoy what he called 'the attractions of civilization'. The sexes bathed together, publicly and nakedly stewing themselves. The medieval English word 'stew' meant a brothel.

The public behaviour of some Caroline visitors to Bath was so immature that the city council uttered a warning: 'No persons shall presume to throw or cast any dog, bitch, or other live beast into any of the said Baths under penalty of three shillings and fourpence. . . .' Samuel Pepys felt similar misgivings: 'Methinks it cannot be clean to go so many bodies together in the same water. . . .' However, he dutifully 'sweated for an hour' and was agreeably surprised when he discovered that the price included a *divertimento*: 'by and by comes musick to play to me, extraordinarily good as ever I heard at London almost, or anywhere.'

Less than a century after his death, the Bath which Pepys had known was superseded by a new city, created chiefly by two men, Ralph Allen and Beau Nash. The former was baptized (1693) at St. Columb Major in Cornwall. When the child was eleven years old his paternal grandfather became St. Columb Major's first postmaster. Profiting from experience, Allen himself joined the postal service, and at the age of nineteen became deputy postmaster at Bath. Seven years later he was controlling the postal services of a large part of England and South Wales, which in those years were farmed out to private enterprises. Allen did not regard his venture solely as a source of personal profit. Instead of trying to become a millionaire, he created order from disorder, and laid thereon the foundation of our modern postal system. So, after more than fifteen hundred years, England recovered something of the efficiency which she lost when the Legions departed. The Roman Imperial Post had been a miracle of organized stamina, achieved at public expense for the use of civil and military authorities. In the third century A.D. the Antonine Itinerary showed every postal route throughout the Empire. Britain possessed sixteen such routes, radiating from London to the chief cities and military headquarters. Each route had posting-stations every twelve miles, where horses could be changed and where couriers could eat and sleep. In large cities the station contained baths. Each district was required to equip and maintain its own posting-stations. Roman Emperors would have been horrified by the slowness with which the news of Queen Victoria's accession reached Perth.

Postage, however, was only one of Allen's claims on our gratitude. Having established himself as a leading citizen of Bath, he developed the quarries at Hampton Down. Assisted by two architects, the Woods, he built many of the city's finest streets, squares, and terraces. He died as he had lived, moderately rich, universally respected, loved by all who knew him. A poet, Alexander Pope, and a novelist, Samuel Richardson, were proud to be his friends. Another novelist, Henry Fielding, portrayed him as Squire Allworthy in *Tom Jones*: 'Neither Mr Allworthy's House, nor his Heart, were shut against any Part of Mankind, but they were both more particularly open to Men of Merit. . . .' Unlike many of his kind, Allen did not look back in anger on his humble origins: 'For though he had missed the Advantage of a learned Education, yet being blest with vast natural Abilities, he had so well profited by a vigorous though late Application to Letters, and by much Conversation with Men of Eminence in this Way, that he was himself a very competent Judge in most kinds of Literature.'

Richard Nash came of a different breed. He was a snob; that is, one who worships birth and rank, without caring whether they have bestowed the superiority which they are supposed to possess.

13

Nash was born at Swansea in 1674, son of a Welshman who sold
hair restorer: 'My mother', he claimed, 'was niece to Colonel
Poyer who was murdered by Oliver [Cromwell]. . . .' Nash
omitted to mention that Poyer was a Cromwellian 'colonel' who
had gone over to the other side, but was captured by the rebels,
and shot as a traitor. Nash managed to get himself to Jesus
College, Oxford, whence he departed prematurely, leaving behind
his debts and his hopes of a degree, but carrying away a violin, a
tobacco pipe, a pair of boots, and two unactable plays. After some
desultory time-wasting, the young dandy obtained a post as
assistant to the entertainments officer at Bath, a situation well-
suited to a temperament that was at ease among card-sharpers,
bullies, prostitutes, and the various other types who are themselves at ease in fashionable resorts. Accused of cheating at cards,
the entertainments officer fought a duel and was killed. Nash
thereupon succeeded him. Though he never ceased to glance at
the mirror before entering, Beau Nash acquitted himself better
than anyone had expected, and far too well for some. He persuaded
Parliament to allow the city to arrest and, if necessary, to expel any
person whose misconduct might otherwise have escaped the law.
He raised a large sum of money for improving the roads. He compelled hoteliers to observe an official tariff and to maintain an
efficient service. He prosecuted profiteering shopkeepers. He
persuaded the Abbey to greet wealthy visitors with a peal of bells
(and then sent a bill to them). Augustan Bath symbolizes England's
closest approach to the best years of the Roman Empire. Judged
by foreign standards, the poor and the sick fared relatively well.
Among educated people the manners of social intercourse combined dignity and ease, to a degree never before nor after equalled.
Curbed by a waning royal prerogative, the government was an
oligarchy of landowners, many of whom were industrialists also.
In the England of Elizabeth I or of Elizabeth II, a Roman gentleman would have felt uncomfortable; but among the great houses
of the Augustan aristocracy he would have found much to remind
him of his villa at Sulmo or of his house near the Capitol.

Quot homines, tot sententiae: one or two visitors are impressed less
by the Baths than by the Abbey. Although hemmed in by shops,

and encircled by a commercial skyline, Bath Abbey prevails. 'The Lantern of England' men called it, so many and so airy are its windows. The oldest feature is an arch of 1122, in which year the Abbey was rebuilt. Four centuries later they added Prior Byrde's Chantry. After another three centuries Sir Gilbert Scott spent ten years matching a new nave with the old chancel roof. The work was overdue. Sir John Harington had long ago informed Queen Elizabeth's Chancellor: 'The fair church her Highness gave orders should be re-edificed stands at a stay; and their common sewer, which stood before in an ill place, stands now in no place, for they have not any at all.'

12 Foss Way: Bath to Axmouth

FOSS Way leaves Bath as a main road which climbs Odd Down and then becomes elusive. I tracked it by delving into Combe Hay, a village of stone houses, set partly on the slope and partly in the depth of a wooded valley. The lawns of its eighteenth-century vicarage decline to a lake; a notice on the church door bears the names of the vicar, warden, organist and verger. Marked by an *agger* twenty feet wide and tall as a man, the Foss crosses a lane from Combe Hay about three hundred yards south of Fosse Farm. Here indeed the Way explains its name, *fossa* or a ditch. This steeply overgrown sector continues for perhaps a mile and a half before rejoining the main road north of Cam Brook, whence it proceeds into Radstock, a colliery town, where a tract of the Way was found to be imprinted by chariot wheels.

The next four miles are pleasant, but sufficiently unexciting to cause the traveller to turn his thoughts away from them and on to a question: why did the Roman Empire decline and fall? Gibbon's *Decline and Fall* failed to answer the question. 'I do not remember', said Coleridge, 'a single philosophical attempt made throughout the work to fathom the ultimate causes of the decline or fall of that Empire.' Coleridge then supplied the want, which he described as 'the *imperial* character overlaying, and finally destroying, the *national* character.' Rome under Trajan was indeed an Empire without a nation. African money-lenders, British acrobats, Spanish pimps, Egyptian coin-clippers . . . all were welcomed if they stayed awhile and paid their taxes. Society was riddled with men and women whom an early republican would have chased from his fields. Rome itself became a cosmopolitan Babel. Juvenal found the alien influence intolerable: 'I cannot bear', he cried, 'to see Rome becoming a city of Greeks.' But Greeks were not the only evil: 'At Rome', he added, 'live the scum of the earth.' Yet there were some who maintained the glory that really was Rome; her *gravitas, simplicitas, pietas*. Away in Britain, wrapped in the cold mist of a ruined Wall, officers and men carried on, as their fore-fathers had done. Amid the chaos of black profiteers, brown saboteurs, and white drug-pedlars, somewhere a Roman official drew no more than his lawful salary, and scorned to accept bribes, and governed according to the book. The Roman Empire did not fall because of the price of the corn, nor the problems of communication, nor the rise of virile nations. Neither is there any need to cry 'Materialism'. Most men always have been 'material-ists'. The catastrophe occurs when too many of them become too much so. 'At Rome', said Sallust, 'even a man's soul is for sale.' The fall of the Roman Empire was caused by the fall of the Roman people. The farmer-soldiers proved insufficient to maintain a rising standard of greed; *imperium* passed from Rome to the provinces, and from Roman-born provincials to non-Roman-born provincials. It was as though in 1914 the British Empire had been ruled by a French King with the assistance of a Dutch premier, a German foreign minister, two Zulu slaves, and a commander-in-chief whose Persian origins predisposed him to opium. Rome fell because the Roman people drowned themselves among those whom they had conquered. Coleridge, then, diagnosed the symp-toms, but not 'the ultimate causes'. Greed, laziness, cowardice, indiscipline, pleasure-seeking, atheism, religious eccentricity . . . the tributaries of decadence are too numerous to be counted, and their source too deep to be fathomed. It is as though Nature had set a limit to the span of every nation. No matter how judiciously a breed seeks new vigour by crossing itself with others, the old stock either dies or is diluted beyond recognition.

The four uneventful miles enter Stratton-on-the-Fosse, near the Abbey and School of St. Gregory at Downside. The school has an adventurous history. It was founded at Douai in France, about the year 1609 (records were lost during the French Revolution) by Benedictine monks, for the sons of British Roman Catholics, who at that time suffered civil disabilities. The school was so well esteemed that Queen Anne ordered the Duke of Marlborough to spare it when he stormed Douai in 1710. Describing his pupilage there in 1721, Gilbert Langley wrote: 'At first entrance we are divested of our secular Robes, and cloath'd with a Cassock and Gown. . . .' Cricket was played so earnestly that in 1775 a treatise on the game became a set book. Although the French revolutionaries plundered the school, they allowed its monks and pupils to escape to England, where their plight was eased by Sir Edward Smyth, himself an Old Gregorian, who offered them hospitality at Acton Burnell in Shropshire. When Sir Edward died, his hospitality was withdrawn. After a long search for new premises, Prior Sharlock acquired Mount Pleasant Manor at Downside. Thither moved the school in 1811; and there three years later the monks laid the foundations of an abbey that was completed during the twentieth century.

Cato would have approved the school's Latin curriculum. At Easter, Michaelmas and Christmas, said Gilbert Langley, the boys were 'compelled at all Times and upon all Occasions, under a certain penalty, to speak the Latin Tongue'. Would Cato have approved of the Greek lessons? One doubts it. Beyond any doubt at all he would have disapproved of schools as we know them today. Roman children were educated at home. Rather than submit his own son to be taught by others, Cato turned schoolmaster. First on his agenda came self-discipline and loving-kindness, which the child perceived in his own parents. Then came manliness via riding, boxing, swimming, and the use of arms. History arrived by hearsay. Literature was either read aloud or written down by Cato himself, in large capital letters, so that his son might read the more easily. Cato taught well, for the boy begat a happy family, and at the battle of Pydna won fame as a soldier. Part of Cato's ideal became one of the statutes of All Souls College, Oxford: *Bene nati, bene vestiti, et mediocriter docti* (Well born, well dressed, and moderately learned). A century ago it was the ideal of Dr. Arnold of Rugby: 'First, religious and moral principles; secondly, gentlemanly conduct; thirdly, intellectual ability.'

Three miles beyond Downside, at a wood called Ashwick Grove, the main road sweeps westward through a long arc to Shepton Mallet. The Foss holds its straight course for another four miles, partly as a track, partly as a footpath, crossed by four lanes. At Beacon Hill, nearly a thousand feet high, the track enters a wood. From that summit the green hills of Somerset catch the eye, and will not let it go. Approaching Shepton Mallet, in a district known as Charlton, the Way becomes a farm track before rejoining the main road on the eastern edge of Shepton Mallet, a *sceap-tun* or sheep farm that was held by Robert Malet during the reign of Henry I. Defoe noted the pastures hereabouts: 'all a grazing, rich, feeding soil . . .' Shepton, he added, employed itself in the 'knitting of stockings, principally for the Spanish trade'. Shepton church tower is pinnacled, buttressed, gargoyled, and crowned by the base of a spire which the medieval masons did not finish. The roof contains three hundred and fifty oak panels, each with its own carved boss, each carving different. The pulpit is hewn from a single block of local stone, perched on a post with a flight of steps. The market cross was erected in 1500 by William and Agnes Buckland, who then invoked our prayers *in saecula saeculorum*. Nearby are some covered market stalls, the oldest timber shambles in Britain.

Now the Way runs straight for nearly five miles, thereafter edging further westward from Pye Hill. Having re-straightened itself, it ambles through a pleasantly unpretentious country. Halting by the way, I once talked with a farmer who had finished his sowing: 'I've done all I can,' he said. Then he glanced at the sky: 'Now it's up to Heaven.' Where Heaven lies, what it is like, whether indeed it exists . . . those questions continue to be debated. Nevertheless, the farmer's credo reminded me of the first stanza of Merchant Taylors' school song, which states that men plough and sow, but that the seed comes from Heaven:

> *Homo plantat, homo fodit,*
> *Prudens, irrigat, custodit;*
> *Sed, fovente Deo, prodit*
> *Incrementum.*

Tibullus would have shaken his head at such strange sounds, for classical Latin poetry differed greatly from its European heirs. It could be witty, it could be gay, but not even the blithest pagans attained the *joie de vivre* of

> *La vierge, la vivace, et le bel aujourd'hui* . . .

Utterly beyond them lay the crown of English poetry, its lyric lilt:

> I heard a linnet courting
> His lady in the spring:
> His mates were idly sporting,
> Nor stayed to hear him sing
> His song of love . . .

Great poets have ennobled English by rhyming it:

> So long as man can breathe, or eyes can see,
> So long lives this, and this gives life to thee.

Neither Vergil nor Lucretius can vie with that aspect of Shakespeare's supremacy. Rhythm, not rhyme, is the measure of Latin verse.

Medieval poets enlivened Latin with rhyme, but they did not improve it thereby; they made it something beautifully alien. Latin poetry perfected itself without rhyme. Propertius would not have been impressed by the thirteenth-century Bavarian who wrote:

> *Dum Diane vitrea*
> *sero lampas oritur*
> *et a fratris rosea*
> *luce dum succenditur* . . .

Even in their shorter lines the Latin poets avoided Milton's 'jingle of like endings'. When Horace hoped that *Romanitas* would prevail among savage Britons and bloodthirsty Basques, he wrote:

> *visam Britannos hospitibus feros*
> *et laetum equino sanguine Concarium*

The music lies in the scansion, the long vowels and the short; a taste not to be acquired without several years' hard labour among genders and gerunds. All music is untranslatable; and the music of the Latin poets echoes both the merits and the defects of the Latin language. Thus, *scripsi* may mean either 'I wrote' or 'I have written'. The Romans had no word for 'yes'. After several centuries the Gauls used either *ille* (that) or *hoc* (this). In northern France the *ille* became first *oil*, then *oui*: whence the two major dialects of France, *langue d'oil* and *langue d'oc*. Yet how subtly the Latin has seeped throughout Europe: *senor*, *signore*, *monsieur*, *sire* . . . all are the Latin *senior*, a Roman's respectful address to his elders. The word 'jewel' comes from the late Latin *jocale* or plaything. The word 'joke' comes from the classical Latin *jocus* or play. How long that influence lasted! In 1628 Sir William Harvey chose Latin as the language in which to publish his treatise on the circulation of the blood. In 1688, when Sir Isaac Newton 'discovered' gravity, he propounded his hypothesis in Latin, *Principia*. When two twentieth-century English philosophers, Russell and Whitehead, joined to confuse the laity and to amaze the mathematicians, they gave their book a Latin title, *Principia Mathematica*.

After crossing the River Brue, the Way passes within a short distance of Keinton Mandeville, a *cyning-tun* or King's Manor, which in 1243 was held by Geoffrey de Maundevill. The village is a bleak-looking regiment of plain houses confronting one another across an unimpressive street. One of those houses bears a time-stained plaque, stating that it was the birthplace (1838) of Brodribb, a man whose story is literally the most dramatic *en route*. John Henry Brodribb, son of a small shopkeeper, was sent as a child to live with his aunt, a Mrs. Penberthy, at Hasleton near St. Ives in Cornwall. 'Hasleton', he remembered, 'was a village nestling between sloping hills . . . a wild and weird place, fascinating in its own peculiar beauty, and taking a more definite shape in my youthful imagination by reason of the dances and legends of the people.' Some of those people spoke the Cornish language when they chose, and to all of them a Devonian was 'foreign'. From Cornwall the lad went to London, became a clerk, and in his spare time learned to dance, fence, declaim. At the age of eighteen he forsook security and followed his star, which led north to the Lyceum Theatre at Sunderland, where, on 29 September 1856, under the name of Henry Irving, he made his first public appearance, as the Duke of Orleans in Bulwer Lytton's *Richelieu*. For ten years he toured the provinces, studying those lessons which, although they can be learned, are beyond any man's power to teach. Then at last the star moved south to London, and stood above a greater Lyceum, where he played the lead in Leopold Lewis's translation of *The Bells*. As the first-night curtain came down, Irving knew that the years of endeavour had not been in vain. London laid its laurels at his feet.

In 1874 he played Hamlet two hundred times. In 1878, with Ellen Terry as leading lady, he became manager of the Lyceum. In 1895—having declined it twelve years earlier—he accepted a knighthood, the first that was ever offered to an actor, an acknowledgement that by his artistry and personal dignity he had raised his profession from its seat below the salt. Eight times he toured America. In 1905, when he was nearly seventy, he revived *Becket* at Drury Lane. 'He looked', wrote Ellen Terry, 'like some beautiful grey tree . . .' They say that Sir Henry Irving and Dame Ellen Terry one day went down to Hasleton, to visit an old lady who had taught John Henry Brodribb the three Rs in her cottage-school: to whom they presented a pair of spectacles in a silver case. But Hasleton and Keinton Mandeville had bequeathed something more than literacy. Irving himself attributed 'much of my endurance of fatigue, which is a necessary part of an actor's life, to the free and open healthy years I lived at Hasleton, and to the simple food and regular routine offered by my aunt'. That West Country legacy sustained him through more than sixty years of hard labour and intense emotion. On 1 October 1905, he performed *Becket* at the Theatre Royal, Bradford. An hour later he died, saying, 'Into thy hands, O Lord, into thy hands'. His ashes were laid in Westminster Abbey *non sanz droict*.

Beyond Keinton Mandeville the Way and the road keep a straight course for about two miles, not overburdened by traffic except during the summer. Suddenly and for no apparent reason the road swerves right and left while the Way runs into a wall of trees and undergrowth so dense that only a bonneted beekeeper could enter and emerge from there alive. Somewhere in that tangle lay the Foss. I walked through a meadow alongside it, trying to find an entry. After a couple of hundred yards I did find an entry, but the briars were so ruthless, the ground so swampy, that I soon withdrew. No doubt the main road had changed course in order to avoid the swamp.

Just before the impasse, a lane leads east into Babcary, the place on the River Cary (Welsh *caru* or endearing), which seems the correct name for a gentle stream and a village of thatched houses with a church embowered among lime trees. Here served James Woodforde, author of *The Diary of a Country Parson*, whom we met with his brandy on Peddars Way. Woodforde was the son of the rector of Castle Cary. In 1752 he took a scholarship to Winchester College; in 1761, a fellowship at New College, Oxford; in 1764, the curacy of Babcary. Woodforde began to keep a diary while he was still an undergraduate: 'A pair of curling Tongs 2s. 6d. Ester Oratorio 5s. 2 White Waistcoats 36s.' Thus did he blend the visible with the invisible signs of grace. On 12 January 1764, the entry was again well balanced: 'After breakfast I rode upon Cream to my curacy at Babcary about six miles hence, where I dined on a Sheep's heart that I carried in my pocket, at the Parsonage House, where I am to be when I go to Babcary on any occasions.' Three days later the wind stood fair: 'This is the first Sunday I ever officiated at Babcary Church, and I liked it very well.' His flock liked it too: 'I was rung into the Parish by Mr John Bowyer's order, who gave the ringers a pail of Cyder. . . .' A few weeks later the new curate was practising the Benedictine maxim that work is prayer, *laborare est orare*: 'I have been very busy all this day in planting my Peas and Beans and Radishes.' Charity began at home: 'I churched a poor woman at Babcary yesterday and she gave me sixpence, which I sent to her again.' Other women were less fortunate: 'The Parish of Cary made him marry her, and he came handbolted to Church for fear of running away. . . .' Like a good shepherd, the curate loved his flock: 'I got up this morning at two o'clock to get or make a sermon for Farmer Bertelet's funeral this afternoon.' In 1774, after a spell as Sub-Warden of New College, Woodforde was presented to the living of Weston Longeville in Norfolk, where he served until his death nearly thirty years later, still keeping the diary, the portrait of country life. Parish pride, national crises, smuggling, illegitimacy, the price of ale, a fickle climate, the daily backsliding and the stint of kindness; all leap alive from Parson Woodforde's pages. Sometimes he is sad, sometimes he falls ill, once or twice he loses his temper; always he asks forgiveness when he has lapsed from his quiet and kindly ways. There is no straining after effect, no eye on posterity. He writes simply and sincerely, as when the grown man records his mother's funeral: 'Papa gave me this afternoon my moneybox that poor Mama kept for me from a Boy in which were half a guinea, two half crown pieces, a sixpence, two small silver coins and ½d.' Roman literature had some notable letter-writers, but nothing like Woodforde's *Diary of a Country Parson*.

Four more straight miles follow, flat and fertile, without entering a village, though passing within sight of Lytes Cary, a National Trust house, built four centuries ago by John Lyte whose son, Henry, was both a linguist and a botanist. His *Niewe Herball or Historie of Plants* was a translation, from the French, of a book by the Dutch botanist, Rembert Dodoens. Lyte's own field-work led him to study the distribution of hyacinths 'especially about Wincaunton, Storton, and Mier in ye West partes of Englande'.

At last the Way does enter a human habitation, the little town of Ilchester, formerly *Givelstre*, the *castra* or Roman camp on the River Gifl (latterly Yeo). To the Romans the town was *Lendiniae*, co-capital (with *Durnovaria* or Dorchester) of the *Durotriges*, a predominantly Dorset tribe, so warlike that Vespasian needed to storm twenty of their hill forts. Once the chief town of Somerset, Ilchester today murmurs *Ichabod*. Gone are the five paved roads that met within its Roman walls, the Saxon mint, the medieval friary and nunnery. All save one of its six churches are gone. But the head of a thirteenth-century borough mace (inscribed 'Do not forget me') has outlived the town's lost boroughship. Of Rome nothing survives except some bricks that were used to build the church tower. Ilchester was the birthplace (*c.* 1210) of Friar Roger Bacon, author of an encyclopaedia in sixteen Latin volumes, most of which he compiled from his study on Folly Bridge in Oxford: 'Chariots shall move', he prophesied, 'with an unspeakable force, without any living creature to stir them' . . . 'An instrument may be made to fly' . . . 'By art also an instrument may be made, where with men may walk in the bottom of the sea or rivers'. We have lived to see the fruits of Bacon's foresight.

The best parts of Ilchester lie away from the main road, along a lane to Limington, where a young and ambitious priest, Thomas Wolsey, served as vicar, having obtained the living from the Marquis of Dorset, whose son he had met at Magdalen College, Oxford. The guidebooks tell a story about Wolsey and Limington, saying that he once got drunk after a fair at Lopen, a few miles away, and was set in the stocks by the High Sheriff of Somerset, Sir Amyas Paulet (the guidebooks call him Poulett). I find no proof that the story is true. It seems to have been started by Wolsey's biographer, Cavendish, to explain why, when he became Lord High Chancellor, Wolsey ordered Sir Amyas Paulet not to leave London without his permission. According to the story, Paulet, as Treasurer of the Inner Temple, set Wolsey's badge above the Temple Gateway, whereupon the mollified Chancellor allowed him to return home to Somerset.

At Ilchester the Foss makes a sudden and sharp turn westward to the edge of Stoke-sub-Hambdon. The Celts built a camp on Hambdon Hill, 462 feet above the sea, which the Romans used as a guard-post at a ford across the River Parrett. Two miles west of Hambdon Hill the Foss crosses the Parrett at Petherton Bridge, where the main road bears west for Ilminster. The Foss holds the course as a narrow lane into Over Stretton, the *ofer* or hill beside the *straet tun* or settlement on a straight (Roman) road. Here the lane ends. Maps mark the Foss as a footpath immediately opposite the lane end. I am not wholly convinced that I did find the Foss. However, a rough path appeared, and continued for about three hundred yards, more or less conforming with the maps. North of Lopen it becomes a tractor-trodden lane which grows wider and steeper, overlooking the site of a Roman villa near the foot of Easterdown Hill. At Dinnington the whole world seems either to have lost or to have found itself, according to how you interpret a land where men call their grand-daughter 'My little maid'.

Two more deep miles reach Windwhistle Hill—higher even than it sounds—where the Foss is joined by a main road sweeping westward, past a lane that delves among an avenue of trees and thence into a secluded valley called Cricket St. Thomas (*Cruchet* or hillock). There is no village here; only a small church and a large house, the home of Alexander Hood, first Viscount Bridport, son of a Devon parson, who served as one of Nelson's captains. His brother, Samuel, became another famous sailor, Viscount Hood. By marrying into Nelson's family, the Hoods inherited and still bear his title of 'Duke of Brontë' in Sicily.

The road goes more or less straight for eight miles into Axminster. Despite some sharp bends, there seems no reason to doubt that Foss Way lies underneath or within a few feet of the modern course. This is Devon at last, England's third largest county; a land of mountains, moors, and forests (one acre in twenty is woodland). Here, too, the Foss makes one of its rare entries into a town, Axminster, a bustling, bucolic place. The narrow streets and miniature market are alive-alive-o as cockles, for the sea lies over the hills, and Devon itself is a nursery of mariners: John Oxenham, John Davis, Stephen Borough, Sir Humphrey Gilbert, Sir John Hawkins, Sir Richard Grenville, Sir Walter Raleigh, Sir Francis Drake: no other British county can rival that roll-call. The Romans built a fort at Axminster; on its site the walls of a house named Weycroft contain some Roman tiles. The Abbey of Newnham—now reduced to a few stones— was founded eight centuries ago by a Norman, Reginald de Mohun. Makers of mosaics, the Romans would have admired Axminster carpets, a craft that came from Flanders at the end of the Middle Ages. Shakespeare mentions it in *Twelfth Night*:

> The spinsters and the knitters in the sun,
> And the free maids that weave their thread with bones . . .

According to one eighteenth-century observer, the first Axminster carpets were made in 1755 'by the pliant fingers of little children' at Court House near the parish church. One hopes that the children did not work more than ten hours a day. For nearly a century the carpets excelled all others in Britain. Then the fashion changed, and the machinery was moved to Wilton in Wiltshire. Carpets are still made at Axminster, but not as they used to be.

Only six more miles remain before journey's end, yet every one of them looks handsome. This is South Devon, soft Devon; in summer time a car-parked playground; at all seasons the home of fishermen and farmers; a sunny land of many-coloured cob: 'the poor cottager', wrote Carew, 'contenteth himself with Cob for his Walls.' Suddenly the road gives two sharp turns, and on the right of it, hidden among trees, stands Ashe House, birthplace of a man who fortified and enlarged the British Empire.

John Churchill, son of Sir Winston Churchill, came of a line of lesser gentry. He was born during Cromwell's republic, under what seemed an unlucky star, when the loyal Churchills had become so impoverished that several of them sought refuge at Ashe House, home of John's indomitable grandmother. When the monarchy was restored, the skies cleared, summoning John Churchill to climb the rungs of his genius. The way led first to Court, where his sister's beauty balanced the family's poverty and lack of worldly connections. After service at Tangier, Churchill was promoted to Captain. Six years later, as Colonel, he married Sarah Jennings, Maid of Honour to the Princess Anne, with whom he lived happily until he died forty years later. After a quarter of a century of marriage, in a society which took its mistresses for granted, he was so deeply in love with his wife that, when sailing to the wars from Kent, he wrote: 'I did for a great while have a perspective glass looking upon the cliffs in hopes I might have had one sight of you.' His wife had already assured him: 'Wherever you are whilst I have life my soul shall follow you, my ever dear Lord Marlborough, and wherever I am I shall only kill the time, and wish for night, that I may sleep, and hope next day to hear from you.'

In 1682 he was created Baron Churchill and soon afterwards Captain-General. William of Orange raised him to an earldom; Queen Anne, to the post of Master-General of the Ordnance. As a soldier he could advance no higher. Despite the intervention of Dutch political commissars, who set the status of their nation before the safety of Europe, Marlborough won four brilliant victories against the greater forces of the European dictator, Louis XIV. News of the victory at Blenheim reached the Queen via a note which he scribbled to his wife, on the back of an officer's wine bill: 'I have not time to say more, but beg you will give my duty to the Queen, and let her know that her army has had a glorious victory . . . The bearer, my aide-de-camp Colonel Packe, will give Her an account of what has passed.' The Queen created him Duke of Marlborough; Parliament endowed him with a palace and a pension; the nation hailed him as a liberator. It is now the fashion to depict every battle as a 'futile' waste of life. The horrors are fanfared, the just cause is denied. A second saviour of Europe, Marlborough's descendant, Sir Winston Churchill, did not follow that fashion: 'Modern opinion', he wrote, 'resents this uninspiring truth . . . great battles, won or lost, change the entire course of human history, create new standards of value, new moods, new atmospheres. . . .' Such are the facts of life as it is at present constituted throughout the world.

Marlborough's career ended prematurely when the widowed Queen, predeceased by her children, fell deeply into the clutches of politicians. At the very moment when England could have destroyed French aggression, she deserted her allies by withdrawing her army. Marlborough himself was dismissed from the service. His political enemies showed their gratitude by trying to arraign him on a charge of fraud. Baseness was met with dignity. Long after the Queen had died, one of the Duchess's last acts was to set her statue in the Long Gallery at Blenheim Palace, inscribed: 'To the memory of Queen Anne, under whose auspices John, Duke of Marlborough, conquered, and to whose munificence he and his posterity with gratitude owe the possession of Blenheim.' Marlborough never regained his rightful influence, but on the accession of George I, he was at last restored to honour. There he remains, secure in the biography by his descendant, which shows him as he was, an imperfect mortal and the greatest of all British soldiers. No man, they say, can long deceive his valet. How much more deeply, therefore, did Marlborough reveal himself to the wife with whom he lived for forty years; and when, as a widow, that wife received a proposal of marriage from the Duke of Somerset, she wrote her own biography of Marlborough, in one of the world's supreme love letters: 'If I were young and hand-

some as I was, instead of old and faded as I am, and you could lay
the empire of the world at my feet, you should never share the
heart and hand that once belonged to John, Duke of Marlborough.'

At Musbury, near a pleasant inn, the road wavers. Time has
meddled with the original course, even as the mice meddled with
the fort (the name Musbury means 'the old fort inhabited by
mice'). The last two or three miles lead into Axmouth, a holiday
resort on the estuary of the River Axe. I walked those few miles
as the Romans had done, at four to the hour; and while I walked I
gathered into one impression such facts as I knew and could
remember about the Latins, the farmer-soldiers of Latium, a
region near Rome; men who learned to govern themselves and
then to govern others, their neighbours, the Sabines and the
Etruscans; and after that to govern yet more people, first for self-
defence, then for prosperity, finally for vainglory. There are some
who believe that Rome ought never to have conquered anyone,
not even in self-defence. Her duty, they say, was to allow the
natives to stew in their own juice; and if any of the savages
popped an aunt or a grandmother into the pot, that was their
concern and no one else's. But the world at that time was not
ordered in that way. The matter can be stated as a question: did
the Britons at any time do or say anything which suggested that
they or their grandchildren would devise and enforce wise laws
justly, or write *De Rerum Natura*, or wash themselves daily in
warm water, or build the Foss Way that here runs to meet the sea,
doing business with the world's trade, to the benefit of all whom
it concerned? Had Rome not conquered Britain, for how many
centuries would this island have remained a lair of Nordic
pirates, of Pictish woadmen, and of Celts who, though they
carved beautiful bracelets, could neither read nor write?

Presently I halted, and followed a path through fields; and
there at last I saw it, as Bach had foretold; the great fugue and
toccata, the sea. Once again I remembered Caesar's praise of
British warships: 'Their prows', he wrote, 'were raised very high
and in like manner the sterns were adapted to the force of the
waves and storms.' The height of those ships, he added, protected

14

them against spears and arrows. But in Caesar's sight the high prow possessed more than a practical interest, for it was the Roman custom to remove the prow or *rostrum* from captured warships and to set it as a trophy on the orators' platform in the Forum, whence our own use of the word rostrum as a synonym for a thumped tub or a secular pulpit. The Roman fleet protected the slave trade; as also for centuries did the British fleet. Then came the first light of dawn. In 1772 a Negro slave escaped to England, where his status was made the subject of a lawsuit. The Lord Chancellor delivered a famous judgement. 'In England', he said, 'the claim of slavery never can be supported. The power claimed never was in use here or acknowledged by the Law.' He did not say that all Englishmen led an easy life, nor that all Negroes were in every respect the equals of men who had inherited centuries of self-government and the arts of civilization. But he did set the slave free from his chains. Twelve years later three great Tories—Pitt, Grenville, Wilberforce—were sitting together 'at the root of an old tree at Holwood, just above the steep descent into the vale of Keston'. Pitt, who was then Prime Minister, said to Wilberforce: 'Why don't you give notice of a motion on the Slave Trade?' Wilberforce gave notice, and for twenty years the vested interests defied it. Slavery, after all, was taken for granted by every nation on earth. Yet Wilberforce and his friends prevailed. On 2 March 1807, the King gave his assent to a Bill which outlawed slavery from the British Empire. Not many years later the Royal Navy was ordered to seek and destroy every slave-ship it could find throughout the world, even although the mission might cause an aggrieved Power to declare war.

I walked down the field until I could see the waves breaking on the shore; and there again I rested, encircled by larks and sheep. Beautiful lay the land and the sea beyond, like a necklace whose beads had been threaded by the centuries; here a Norman church, there a Victorian chapel; on one hill, a Tudor cottage; on the next, a Georgian mansion; and under my feet, or somewhere close by, a Roman road. But now a new bead had been added, unlike any that went before. It seemed impossible to believe that when I first began to study history, this kingdom was the richest and most powerful in the world; that its passport demanded and received a safeguard for every holder on his lawful occasions, a reminder of the words of Admiral Blake: 'I would have the whole world know that none but an Englishman shall chastise an Englishman.' How many law-abiding Englishmen felt safe, once they ventured seaward of Clacton pier? Yet I had been born into an era when old Froissart's writ still ran: 'Englishmen suffer indeed for a season, but in the end they repay so sternly that it may stand as a great warning. . . .' England in my schoolbook days remained as it was in Shakespeare's, 'the envy of less happier lands'. From that proud eminence I used to pity the fallen Romans, Spaniards, Dutchmen, Portuguese. Once down, no Empire has ever re-arisen. Nor would wisdom wish to resurrect the British Empire. Its mission has been fulfilled albeit imperfectly because concluded prematurely with indecent haste.

Glancing down at the waves, I saw that John of Gaunt lay beneath them, dead and buried, because they had ceased to serve

> in the office of a wall
> Or as a moat defensive to a house.

As though for the very first time, I became aware that I no longer lived at the hub of a worldwide Empire, guarded by grey ships stretching like an horizon across an horizon; shields which became swords only in self-defence and after the utmost provocation. On the contrary, I inhabited a small island which seemed hourly to grow smaller, eroded by too many natives, too many aliens, too many factories, too many cars. Just so, after his fashion, a Roman of the old school must have winced when he watched the wind of change bearing away the last Roman soldier from Britain. Did he discover that the future would one day turn away, ignorant and arrogant, when he tried to tell them of times past, the good and the bad, the ideal and the failure even to attempt it? Certainly he assumed that some new nation would conquer the world. Not for him our own hope that mankind may live long enough so to conquer itself that it no longer feels compelled to conquer others.

'For nearly three hundred years', said Sir Winston Churchill, 'Britain, reconciled to the Roman system, enjoyed in many respects the happiest, most comfortable, and most enlightened times its inhabitants have had.' A thousand years hence, if men still exist, and are able to tell the truth, they will pay a similar tribute to the finest hours of the British Empire.

Index

Index

Abbotsford, 116
Aber Bowlan, 58
Aeschylus, 115
Aldboro Moor, 176
Aldborough, 177
Alfred, King, 117
Allen, Ralph, 182-3
All Souls College, Oxford, 188
Anmer, 143
Anne, Queen, 187, 197-8
Aristotle, 18
Argyll, Duke of, 114
Arnold, Dr., 188
Ashe House, 187
Ashwick Grove, 188
Asquith, Lord, 182
Astley, Lord, 182
Atherstone, 44
Aubrey, John, 181
Augustus, Caesar, 5, 159
Avalon, Hugh of, 155
Axminster, 196
Axmouth, 199

Babcary, 193
Bacon, Sir Francis, 34-5, 65, 82
Bacon, Roger, 194
Baillie, John, 182
Barcheston, 169
Bardwell, 121
Bardwell, Sir William, 122
Barham Downs, 10
Barham, R. H., 10-11
Barningham, 122

Barton Bendish, 160
Bath, 181-5
Bavington Hall, 95
Beacon Hill, 184
Becket, Thomas, 15-17
Bedale, 79
Bede, Venerable, 14, 15, 107, 138
Beethoven, Ludwig von, 176
Bek, Bishop, 83, 85
Bellasis, Lord, 159
Belloc, Hilaire, 173
Bewclay, 92
Bewick, Thomas, 62, 83-5
Binchester, 84
Bingham, 158
Bishop Auckland, 83-4
Bishopsbourne, 11-13
Blackburn, William, 174
Blunden, Edmund, 43
Boroughbridge, 77
Borrow, George, 62
Boscobel, 45
Boundary Plantation, 122
Bourton-on-the-Water, 173
Bracton, Henry, 31
Braithwaite, Richard, 80
Brancaster, 148
Breakspear, Nicholas, 74
Brigantes, 74, 77
Brinklow, 166
British Transport Commission, 47
Brontë family, 134
Broomhaugh, 87
Brough, 158

Browne, Sir Thomas, 112, 128–130, 157
Brownhart Law, 108
Brusselton, 83
Buckland, William, 53
Bugge, Richard, 161
Burke, Edmund, 123, 165, 167

Caedmon, 107
Caio, 58–9
Calthorpe, Charles, 141
Calvin, John, 59, 63, 111–12
Camden, William, 41, 89, 90, 122, 130
Canons Park, 33
Canossa, 74
Canterbury, 14–18
Caracalla, Emperor, 182
Caractacus, 53
Carew, Thomas, 197–8
Carlyle, Thomas, 111
Carmichael, Sir John, 106
Carter Bar, 106
Cassivellaunus, King, 6
Castle Acre, 133–7
Cato, 188
Catterick, 80
Catullus, 143
Caxton, William, 166
Celso, 90
Cerialis, P., 89
Charles, 126
Charles I, 159
Charles II, 45–6, 74, 96, 128
Chaucer, Geoffrey, 18, 27
Chedworth, 195–7
Chew Green, 106
Chipping Norton, 171
Chisholm, The, 114
Chollerton, 92, 93

Churchill, John, Duke of Marlborough, 187, 197–8
Churchill, Sarah, Duchess of Marlborough, 198
Churchill, Sir Winston, 2, 197
Churchill, Sir Winston Spencer, 47, 198, 201–2
Cicero, 24, 30, 41, 176-7
Cilycwm, 55
Cirencester, 178–9
Clare, John, 140
Clarendon, Lord, 158
Claudius, Emperor, 107
Clifton-upon-Dunsmore, 143
Cluny, Abbot of, 135–6
Cobham, 25
Coke family, 136
Colchester, 8, 28
Coleridge, S. T., 79, 112, 186
Coll, Maclean of, 116
Combe Hay, 186
Conrad, Joseph, 9, 10–13
Constable, John, 121, 122
Constantine, Emperor, 14, 28, 74
Constantius, Emperor, 74
Coquet Head, 106
Corbridge, 87–8
Cotgrave, 160
Cotton family, 131
Coulson, C. G., 156
Coulson, William, 103
Coventry, R. G. T., 169
Crabbe, Thomas, 147
Crawford, Captain Christie, 173
Creswell, Mrs., 143
Cromwell, Oliver, 83, 133, 184
Cromwell, Thomas, 136
Cynewulf, 107

Danton, Georges-Jacques, 125

Darnley, Lord, 25
Dawson, Lord, 144
de Corbell, Archbishop, 22
de Gray, Archbishop, 73
de Grey, Sir William, 126
de Guérin, Maurice, 95
de la Pole, Richard, 160
de Montfort, Simon, 22
de Quincey, Thomas, 6, 157
de Warenne, William, 134, 135
Defoe, Daniel, 2, 8, 10, 19, 20, 21,
    44, 79, 89, 99, 100, 105, 122,
    127, 155, 159–60, 163, 168, 169
Denbigh Bridge, 48
Denbigh, Earl of, 44
Derwentwater, Countess of, 98
Derwentwater, Lord, 97–9
Dewrance, Sir John, 125
Dickens, Charles, 23–4, 25, 26
Dinnington, 195
Donnington, 172
Dover, 8–9
Down Ampney, 177
Downside, 187
Drayton, Michael, 43, 164
Drinkwater, John, 175
Druids, 66–7
Dunning, 109
Dunstable, 35–6

East Bridgford, 160
East Stoke, 160
East Wretham, 125
Easton Grey, 180
Eathorpe, 168
Ebchester, 86
Edge, John, 43
Edgware Road, 32
Edward I, 110
Edward II, 79

Edward IV, 160
Edward VII, 143–4
Edward VIII, 131
Eldon, Lord, 175
Eliot, George, 121, 166, 168
Elizabeth I, 136, 149, 185
Elizabeth II, 147
Erpingham, Sir Thomas, 128

Farmers, 63
Farrer, James, 175
Faversham, 20–1
Fawkes, Guy, 36, 37
Feather Wood, 105–6
Fenny Stratford, 37
Field Barn Plantation, 141
Fielding, Henry, 183
Fiennes, Celia, 10, 19, 20, 22, 25,
    44, 77, 78, 82, 133, 158, 171
Fiskerton Ferry, 160
FitzGerald, Edward, 126
Forster, Sir John, 106
Forster, John, 23
Forster, Thomas, 97
Froissart, 201
Frontius, 102
Froude, J. A., 126
Fuller, Thomas, 34

Gad's Hill Place, 23–4
Gailey, 45
Gainsborough, Thomas, 122
Galley Hill, 125
Gamels Path, 106
Gaveston, Piers, 77
George I, 98, 99, 198
George V, 144
George VI, 145
Gibbon, Edward, 30, 38, 40, 83,
    138–9, 186

Gladstone, W. E., 158
Gloucester, Robert, 164
Gort, Field-Marshal Viscount, V.C., 86
Graham, Cunninghame, 12
Great Massingham, 139
Green Hammerton, 76
Griffith, George, 141
Griston Hall, 128
Grounds Farm, 131

Hadrian, Emperor, 28, 32, 48, 74
Hadrian's Wall, 89–90
Hanwick, 84
Harbledown, 18
Harvey, Christopher, 43
Harvey, Sir William, 17
Haselrigg, Sir Arthur, 83
Hatfield House, 162
Haverfield, Francis, 169–70
Hazlitt, William, 180
Henry II, 16, 64, 69
Henry VII, 160
Henry VIII, 17, 55, 99, 106, 136
Hickes, William, 170
High Cross, 43–4, 164–5
Hill-Johnes, General Sir James, V.C., 61
Hodgson, John, 85, 99
Hogarth, Georgina, 23, 24
Holme-next-the-Sea, 151
Honington, 170
Hooker, Richard, 11
Horace, Q. F., 5, 29, 42, 63, 92, 142, 189
Horsley, J., 91
Houghton Hall, 142
Hudson, W. H., 139–40
Hunt, John, 156

Ilchester, 194
Irving, Sir Henry, 191–2

Jackaments Bottom, 180
James I, 110, 161
James II, 20, 96
James, William, 171–2
Jefferies, Richard, 148
Jonson, Ben, 34
Julius Caesar, 5–7, 21, 67, 81, 131, 199–200
Justinian, Emperor, 31
Juvenal, 186

Keinton Mandeville, 191
Kethe, William, 106–7
Keys, Dr., 161
Khayyam, Omar, 127
Kilburn High Road, 32
Kipling, Rudyard, 29, 102, 110
Kirkwhelpington, 99
Kitchener, Lord, 22

Lamb, Charles, 141
Lanchester, 85
Lang, Andrew, 175
Langford Hall, 158
Langland, William, 75
Langley, Gilbert, 188
Leadgate, 86
Leeds, 73
Leeming, 79
Leicester, 162–3
Lenborough, 38
Limington, 195
Lincoln, 155–6
Little Brickhill, 36
Little Massingham, 141
Little Walsingham, 146

Llandovery, 55
Llanfair Clydogau, 68–9
Lloyd-Johnes, H. T. C., 61
Lochiel, Cameron of, 114
London, 28–32
Lopen, 194, 195
Lord Leycester Hospital, 46
Lovell, Sir Thomas, 160
Lower Slaughter, 173
Lyte family, 194
Lyte, Cary, 194
Lytton, Lord, 104

Mabinogion, The, 54
Macadam, John Loudon, 81
Macaulay, Lord, 46
MacDonald, Murdo, 116
Macsen, King, 51
Malling, Thomas, 136
Malory, Sir Thomas, 166–7
Marcelinus, A., 109
Markyate, 35
Marlowe, Christopher, 18, 77
Martial, 26
Martin, Jonathan, 73
Marshall, William, 76
Masefield, John, 146
Maugham, Somerset, 18
Melrose, 114
Merchant Taylors' School, 189
Merton Park, 126
Milton, John, 130, 157
Ministry of Works, 136
Mithraism, 29
Monmouth, Geoffrey of, 165
Mons Graupius, 109
Montelambert, Comte de, 175
Monteviot House, 110
More, Richard, 116
Moreton-in-Marsh, 171–2

Morison, Roderick, 116
Musbury, 199

Nairn, 108
Narborough, 163
Nash, Richard, 183–4
National Trust, 55, 59, 61
Nelson, Vice-Admiral Viscount,
    148, 149–50
Newark-on-Trent, 158–9
Newbold Revel, 166
Newman, Cardinal, 167
Newstead, 116
Newton, Sir Isaac, 191
Newtown St. Boswells, 110
Northleach, 174
Norwich, 128
North Pickenham, 131

Oakengates, 46
Ogilvie, W. H., 100
Old Kent Road, 27
Otterburn, 100
Over Stretton, 195
Ovid, 176

Pagge, Robert, 178–9
Paine, Thomas, 123–4
Pasteur, Louis, 20
Pater, Walter, 17
Patrixbourne, 13
Paul, G. O., 174
Paulet, Sir Amyas, 195
Peel, Sir Robert, Bt., 132
Penberthy, Mrs., 191
Penderel family, 45–6
Pennine Way, 102
Pepys, Samuel, 182
Perse, Sir Stephen, 141
Piercebridge, 83

Pitt, William, 200
Plautius, Aulus, 27
Plautus, 33
Plot, Robert, 132
Pompey, 147
Portgate, 90
Porth-y-rhydd, 56
Postumius, Aulus, 113
Powell, George, 66
Pritchard, Rhys, 55
Propertius, 190
Prys-Jones, A. G., 66, 87, 104
Pumpsaint, 60–1

Quaritch, Bernard, 127
Quebec, 85
Quiller-Couch, Sir A. T., 12

Radnor, Lord, 144
Radstock, 186
Redbourn, 35
Redesdale, 99–100
Redesdale, Lord, 171
Remigius, Bishop, 155
Reynolds, Sir Joshua, 142
Rhys, Sir John, 54, 148
Richard I, 168
Richard II, 76
Richard III, 160
Richmond, 82
Riding Mill, 87
Rimini, 6
Ringstead, 148
Rochester, 103–4
Rookwood, Ambrose, 36
Rupert, Prince, 158
Rutland, Duke of, 161

Saham Toney, 130
St. Albans, 7, 33–5

St. Columb Major, 182
Sallust, 187
Sandringham, 143–5
Sapcote, 163
Scapula, Ostorius, 53
Scotch Corner, 82
Scott, Sir Walter, Bt., 116
Seneca, 182
Senecio, L. A., 88
Severus, Emperor, 74
Shafto, family, 94–5
Shakespeare, William, 2, 8, 10, 23,
    43, 115, 169, 170–1, 176, 201
Sheldon, William, 169
Shepherds Bush, 139
Shipston-on-Stour, 169
Shirley, Sir Robert, Bt., 163
Shooters Hill, 26
Simnel, Lambert, 160
Sittingbourne, 22
Smyth, Sir Edward, 188
Spenser, Edmund, 13
Staunton, Harold, 163
Stewart family, 133
Stoke-sub-Hambdon, 195
Stone, Thomas, 156
Stoney Stratford, 40–1
Stratton-on-the-Fosse, 187
Stuart, Hon. Miss, 143
Stuart, James Francis Edward, 97
Stukeley, William, 164
Surtees, R. S., 86
Swaffham, 132–3
Swift, Jonathan, 35
Swinburne, A. C., 18, 87
Swinburne family, 86

Tacitus, 14, 28, 33, 53, 67, 109
Telford, Thomas, 35, 48
Terence, 34, 92

Ternan, Ellen, 23
Terry, Dame Ellen, 192
Thames Head, 179
Theodora, Empress, 108
Thetford, 123
Thockrington, 93–4
Thomas, Edward, 61, 62, 173
Thomas, R. S., 69
Thompson, 126
Tibullus, 189
Topham, Captain Edward, 114, 116
Tredington, 169
Trevelyan, G. M., 87
Trevithick, Richard, 123
Tuke, John, 76
Turner, J. E., 163

Urbicus, Lollius, 103

Ver, River, 35
Vergil, 63, 126, 132, 142, 176
Vespasian, Emperor, 194
Victoria, Queen, 37, 46, 59, 121, 151, 183
Voltaire, F-M. A. de, 2

Waghorn, Lieutenant, 22
Wall, 45
Walpole, Captain Giraldus, R.N., 149
Walpole, Sir Robert, Bt., 141–2

Warwick, 46
Waterfalls, 95–6
Waters Upton, 46
Watton, 127–8
Webb, Mary, 45, 49
Wellington, 46
Wesley, John, 56
Weycroft, 196
Whittonstall, 87
Wiggin family, 169
Wilberforce, William, 200
William I, 134, 135
Williams, Ralph Vaughan, 176
Williams, William, 55
Willington, 85
Willis, Browne, 38
Willoughby-on-the-Wolds, 160
Wilton, 196
Windwhistle Hill, 195
Withington, 47
Wolsey, Cardinal, 195
Woodforde, James, 147, 193–4
Woods, Brothers, 183
Wordsworth, Dorothy, 8, 10
Wordsworth, William, 57, 95, 134, 164
Wren, Sir Christopher, 29
Wroxeter, 47–9

Yanworth, 175
Yatton Keynell, 181
York, 73–6

DATE DUE

MAY 17 2012	

GAYLORD   PRINTED IN U.S.A.